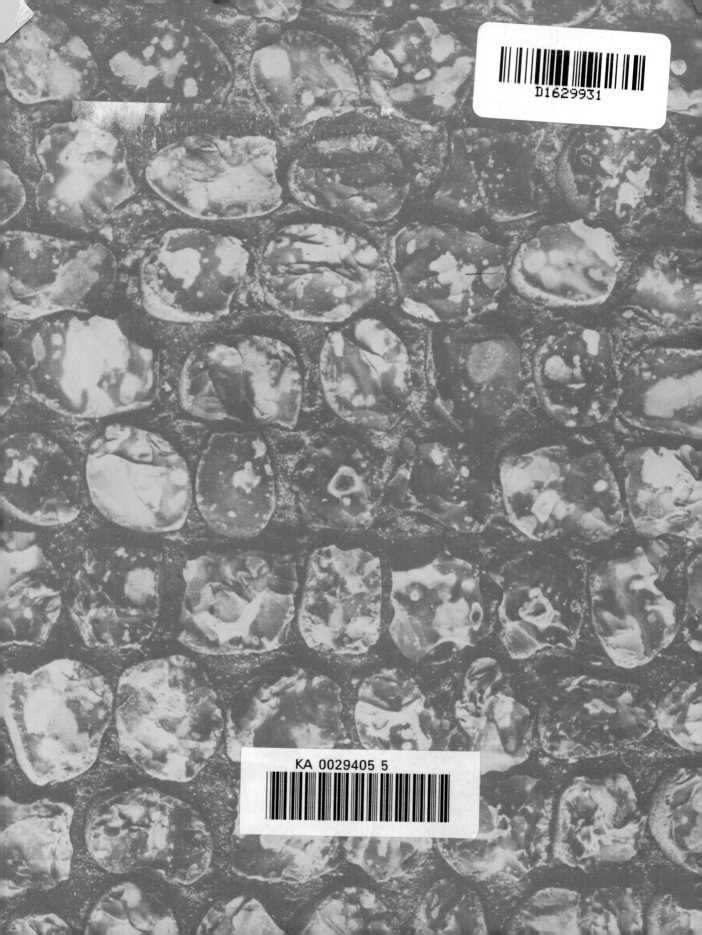

ENGLISH STONE BUILDING

ENGLISH STONE BUILDING

ALEC CLIFTON-TAYLOR
AND A.S. IRESON

LONDON
VICTOR GOLLANCZ LTD
in association with Peter Crawley
1983

British Library Cataloguing in Publication Data

Clifton–Taylor, Alec
    English stone building.
    1. Building, Stone
    I. Title   II. Ireson, A. S.
    691'.2   TH1201

    ISBN 0-575-03214-6

Designed by Leslie and Lorraine Gerry
Filmset and printed in Great Britain by
BAS Printers Limited, Over Wallop, Hampshire

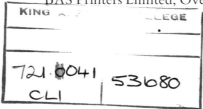

FOR
A LONG-CHERISHED FRIEND
PHILIP ROCKLEY BURKETT
OF KIMBOLTON
AND
A DEAR WIFE
ETHEL MARY IRESON
OF STAMFORD

CONTENTS

ACKNOWLEDGMENT

Since this is a book rooted above all in visual experience, combined in the case of one of us with a lifetime's familiarity with stone from the standpoint of those who procure, work and market it, there is little dependence here on other men's books, so no bibliography seemed to be called for.

Parts of the book, however, and especially the second chapter, are intimately linked with geology; as neither of us is a professional geologist, we count ourselves very fortunate that Mr. Ronald Roberts of the Geological Museum agreed to scrutinize the entire text. He made many invaluable criticisms, and we should like to place on record our warm gratitude to him.

From the aspect of presentation the book was read, twice, by Mr. Robert Storrar, who also offered an abundance of pertinent comments.

Among others who have been consulted here and there about specific points, one must be singled out. Miss Alison Kelly, who has devoted many years to the study of Coade stone in all its aspects, gave us most generous help with that section.

We are very grateful to Mr. David Green for having drawn the Geological map and for his beautiful illustrations of tools on pages 76 and 87–89.

Our cordial thanks are also due to Mrs. Stella Forward, who typed the entire book from a none too clearly written manuscript.

Finally we should like to say how much we owe to our publishers. Mr. Stephen Bray of Gollancz, who, fortunately for us, is a perfectionist, has gone to immense pains over the production of this book in all its aspects, including keeping down the cost. And in having the sponsorship of Mr. Peter Crawley we count ourselves greatly blessed. There will be more to say about him in the Prologue.

N.B. For our decision to adhere, throughout the book, to the historic, pre-1974 county boundaries, see page 275.

PROLOGUE

by Alec Clifton-Taylor

Some readers may like to have a short note about how this book came into being.

It was after the publication of *English Brickwork* in 1977 that Peter Crawley, who had been its midwife as well as its godfather (work that one out), announced to me that he now wanted me to undertake a book on English stone. This I was very reluctant to do, not only because I was already overworked, but because I felt that in *The Pattern of English Building*, the third (Faber) edition of which was entirely due to his sponsorship, I had already written most of what I felt I had to say about this subject.

However, Peter Crawley is not a man who takes No for an answer, and for him at least the subject was not closed. He also started tickling my palate by acquiring a new camera with which he was able to take architectural photographs of quite outstanding quality, especially, at my request, very close-up pictures to show some of the many different ways in which, through nearly a thousand years, English stone has been so resourcefully employed. He made the book look very tempting.

Then I had an inspiration. I was well aware that my old friend Arch Ireson, who had already given me most generous help with *The Pattern . . .*, had an immense knowledge of English stone, amassed not so much by reading as by looking, and often by first-hand contact with it, acquired over a period of more than sixty years as a member, and presently as the joint proprietor, of a building firm located in one of our most illustrious stone towns, Stamford. It was from here that in 1947, at the prompting of our mutual friend the late H. J. Massingham, he launched the Men of the Stones, of which he is happily still the very active Honorary Secretary.

'I am', he has written, 'about as close a surviving example of the mediaeval master mason as it is possible to find today. Our family vocation is documented back to the early days of the eighteenth century in an unbroken male line which has on a number of occasions married members of other stone families; and, although records have not been proved, we probably go back further than that. Related to the family, although not in the direct line, was Nathaniel Ireson of Wincanton (1686–1769), the Somerset master builder whose career and chief works are recorded in H. M. Colvin's *Biographical Dictionary of British Architects, 1600–1840*. In the middle of the nineteenth century there were, in the Nene Valley alone, over twenty Iresons who were stonemasons. I am a skilled architectural stone carver myself and have employed many fine craftsmen. I have worked on many famous buildings, including several cathedrals, churches and quite a number of large country houses. I have also erected new stone buildings and added new extensions to old ones.'

Here, then, was a massive store of largely untapped knowledge about stone, most of it differing considerably from what had been presented in *The Pattern* . . . Its possessor had no thought of putting it into a book; although a copious letter-writer, he has never had the time, nor really the inclination, to assemble into a book the fruits of a life-time of experience. Hitherto he had been content to place some of it, very unselfishly, at the service of others, such as the late Donovan Purcell and myself.

Peter Crawley agreed: Arch Ireson and I would do the book together. I drew up a detailed plan, and it was not long before he started covering the skeleton with flesh. The book has in fact been written by me, but without him it could not have been. There are very few sections for which he has not provided some nourishing provender: in the third chapter, which is one of the longest, he was the chef for almost the entire banquet. When I think of him I recall an old Chinese proverb: 'He who hears, forgets; he who sees, remembers; he who does, knows'.

To get the book into its final form has entailed much correspondence and days of highly concentrated discussion, often concerned with classification, for, while it is still hoped that this book will be of some value to the stone specialist, I was determined that it should also be absolutely clear to the interested layman. So the use of technical terms has been reduced to the minimum, and those that it has been essential to retain, as for example the names of some of the not generally familiar masons' tools, have all been carefully explained in the Glossary.

All the photographs are the work of Peter Crawley, and what the book owes to him as its illustrator will be quickly apparent to every reader: even, in fact, to those who never get to the point of actually reading it, and in these televisionary days such people are, I suspect, numerically on the increase. It is my belief that a book which has only one photographer throughout acquires a kind of visual unity which is of considerable value. Peter has not spared himself in driving to all parts of England at our behest, often returning with photographs so beautiful that, if cost were no object, almost every one would deserve to be printed to the size of a whole page. So valuable is his contribution that we felt it only right that his name, as illustrator, should appear upon the title-page. To this, with becoming modesty, he declined to agree. So, as usual, he had the last word.

1

OUR FIRST STONE BUILDERS

This book is about the building stone of England: how it was found, how it was worked, and what has emerged from the labours of an exceptionally dedicated body of men, the stonemasons. 'A brick or roughcast house is a home and quite satisfactory as such', wrote one of them over forty years ago, 'but a stone house, even if it is only a low stone cottage, has something of the monument about it. Who can maintain that the same effect would be produced if the piers of St.Paul's were made of nine-by-three-inch bricks, or the tower of Gloucester Cathedral were carried out in pebble-dashed cement rendering?'★

In the Middle Ages stonemasons were among the best paid and most highly regarded of all workers. Today these are, alas, no longer by any means the best paid, but they are still held in high respect. Why? Can it be because they devote their lives to handling a natural material which, in varying degrees, itself evokes feelings of reverence? There can be no one who is not the better for spending his days in the presence of stone. Whoever heard of stonemasons coming out on strike?

Our first builders in stone could not be described as masons: indeed, they were not craftsmen. They were hunters, shepherds and tillers of the soil who made simple shelters with whatever materials were most readily to hand, just as did other primitive peoples all over the world. In England those materials were usually earth and wood; but in a few areas, notably Cornwall, timber was in short supply. So that is where evidence of our earliest stone houses is to be found. Although later on we shall mention Stonehenge, we are not otherwise concerned here with stone circles, cromlechs, dolmens and the like. But at Chysauster, on a hilltop two or three miles north-east of Penzance, a group of eight dwellings survives from the Iron Age. Each group of now roofless huts was ranged around an

★Erick Benfield, *Purbeck Shop (Cambridge, 1940)*

oval court bounded on the inner face by a dry-stone wall about 5 ft. high. The settlement is at least two thousand years old. Near another Iron Age settlement on the Land's End peninsula, Carn Euny, some five miles west of Penzance, there was a wooded valley, which was a rarity there; so some of the round huts were of timber and turf. But there are remains of stone-built houses too, some of them also circular, which may go back to the first century B.C.

The arrival of the Romans was the signal for great advances in stone construction. It is unfortunate that, unlike a number of other countries, England does not preserve a single Roman building in anything like good condition; but, although always extensively restored, Roman masonry can still be seen in various parts of our island. It also turns up from time to time in archaeological excavations. Much the most impressive example of Roman stone building is the Great Wall constructed between 117 and 126 A.D.; it ran for a distance of $72\frac{1}{2}$ miles, from Wallsend-on-Tyne to the Solway Firth. The scale of the undertaking was prodigious: the wall was 10 ft. thick at the base and 15 ft. high, with forts at intervals. The core, left to gangs of supervised native labour, was of rubblestone mixed with puddled clay and capped with turf, but the facing, on both sides and throughout its whole length, was of squared stones, dressed and set in mortar. This masonry, which was of a far higher quality than any that England had seen hitherto, was the work of the legionaries themselves. There was fortunately plenty of excellent sandstone close at hand, and, for the middle section, dolerite. Long sections of the wall have long since disappeared; the surviving portions are about 8 ft. thick and nowhere more than 6 ft. high.

Even if their major undertakings in Britain should perhaps be described as works of engineering rather than of architecture, the Romans, as all the world knows, were wonderful builders. Some of their methods and practices were so sound that in the stone trade, even today, they still linger: the three-legged lewis, for example. This is a device used to help in the lifting of heavy blocks of stone, which will be described later. Among the most familiar mouldings or ornaments of architectural practice, Greek in origin, which were probably introduced into England by the Romans, we may cite the ovolo, cavetto, corona, scotia, torus, cyma recta, cyma reversa (the ogee), acanthus and anthemion (the palmette or honeysuckle).

Highly gifted artists as they were in some directions, the Anglo-Saxons are not generally credited with having shown much prowess in the field of architecture. Their principal buildings were churches, and most of them

1 **All Saints, Wittering, Soke of Peterborough (now Cambridgeshire)**

were timber-framed; of these there is now nothing above ground with the sole exception of the nave of the little church of St. Andrew at Greensted in Essex, built not later than 1013 with the half-trunks of oaks split vertically. Apart from this, all the Saxon architecture that does survive is stone. It includes no large building, but parts of a good many smaller ones, where stone was locally available. The most impressive surviving features are generally towers or chancel arches. Saxon masonry is somewhat crudely dressed, but has at best a simple beauty as at Wittering near Stamford, where the immensely massive chancel arch (**1**), built of Barnack ragstone, has a primitive spirituality that is both moving and impressive. At Barnack itself, $2\frac{1}{2}$ miles to the north-east, the two lower stages of the massive church tower, built of the local rubblestone, with ragstone dressings, survive from Saxon times (**4**). The limitations of these people as designers are very evident. And, builders in stone as they certainly were, it is unlikely that they were known as stonemasons.

The Conquest effected a revolution in English stone building. The Norman prelates wanted enormous churches, far larger than any that had been previously built in England with the exception of Edward the Confessor's Norman-inspired and just completed Abbey at Westminster. So, after a thousand years, history repeated itself: stonemasons arrived in England with their deep-rooted craftsmanship, which they were eager to transmit to those of the indigenous population willing to learn. New skills were developed in the handling of stone, of which the ruling Normans were quick to take advantage.

Some of our finest cathedrals and castles date from the Norman period. It was a tremendous age for building, which is all the more remarkable when it is realised that the total population of England at the Conquest was probably no more than $1\frac{1}{2}$ millions and at the end of the twelfth century did not much exceed two millions. For architectural work on such a scale, trained craftsmen were needed in numbers far in excess of what England already had. So it is not surprising that some of the masons whose names are known to us were obviously Norman French.

Some of the stonemasons' words introduced by the Normans are even now still in use. Banker, meaning a working bench, is an obvious example and mallet is another. And here are some of the many architectural terms which are of French (in some cases Old French) origin: voussoir, vault, tierceron, buttress, crocket, niche, oriel, garderobe, chevron, billet, trefoil, quatrefoil, cinquefoil, fillet, chamfer.

Norman influence is also evident in the standardization of the various building units: in the course heights, for example, and in the voussoirs and various mouldings. We suspect that many people will not have noticed that Norman mouldings and carvings – chevrons, billets, beak-heads and so on – were designed to fit the individual blocks of stone rather than to create a perfectly regular repetitive pattern.

Thus did the trade and the craft of the stonemason gradually become well established in England. Local and very English styles were developed step by step. Under the Normans the principal buildings, even in the non-stone areas, were all cathedrals, churches or castles. But wherever stone was abundant it came in the course of time to be accepted as the best material for manor houses and merchants' houses, for public buildings such as markets, and for bridges. The smaller town houses, farmhouses, barns, and eventually cottages followed later, usually a good deal later if both stone and wood were locally available, for wood was substantially cheaper. It did not matter, for there was now plenty of work for the stonemasons. Between 1200 and 1900 the art of architecture saw some radical changes, especially in ideas affecting design, but the stonemasons, as seven centuries of often glorious building attest, were equipped to meet every challenge.

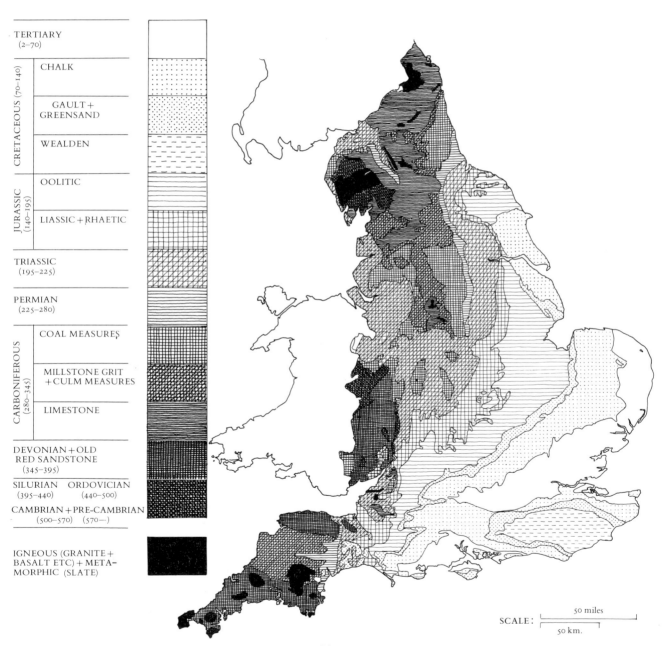

KEY TO DEPOSITS showing
approximate age of each in millions of
years

Geological sketchmap of England

TERTIARY (2–70)	
CRETACEOUS (70–140)	CHALK
	GAULT + GREENSAND
	WEALDEN
JURASSIC (140–195)	OOLITIC
	LIASSIC + RHAETIC
TRIASSIC (195–225)	
PERMIAN (225–280)	
CARBONIFEROUS (280–345)	COAL MEASURES
	MILLSTONE GRIT + CULM MEASURES
	LIMESTONE
DEVONIAN + OLD RED SANDSTONE (345–395)	
SILURIAN (395–440) ORDOVICIAN (440–500)	
CAMBRIAN + PRE-CAMBRIAN (500–570) (570—)	
IGNEOUS (GRANITE + BASALT ETC) + META- MORPHIC (SLATE)	

SCALE: 50 miles
50 km.

2

THE ENGLISH BUILDING STONES

It would seem right to begin by considering what varieties of stone were available to English builders. Happily there were a great many. It is indeed doubtful whether any other country as limited in area as England has been able to offer so wide a choice in the matter of building materials. It is not our intention in this chapter to offer more than a very general introduction to English building stones: the subject has been treated in much greater detail elsewhere.★ The ways in which many of them have been used is the principal subject of the rest of the book.

Only one building stone was imported from abroad in considerable quantities, and across many centuries: the light creamy-yellow limestone from Caen in Normandy. Wren, at Westminster Abbey, described it as 'more beautiful than durable', but this stone was still coming in during the 1830s, both for Canterbury Cathedral and Kingston Lacy in Dorset. Apart from the fact that the Norman kings had a vested interest in the quarries, Caen stone was very accessible to English builders in the South and East when all stone had to be transported by water. The quarries were located on the banks of the Orne, and the stone could be loaded straight into barges and shipped across the Channel. Not much English stone was as conveniently placed. Moreover, to the Norman French masons Caen stone was a familiar material, as the English stones were not; here was an established industry with its own momentum. So Caen stone travelled all over the South-East in the Middle Ages, and at least as far north as Norwich. Henry III's Westminster Abbey was largely built of it, and to several cathedrals, Old St. Paul's, Rochester, Canterbury, Chichester and Winchester, it made a major contribution. And although it has worn none too well externally, the elegance of this beautiful stone can still be enjoyed to the full inside the almost contemporary naves of Canterbury and

★See Alec Clifton-Taylor, *The Pattern of English Building* (3rd. edition, 1972), pp. 21–209

16

Winchester, and in Westminster Abbey too, since the cleaning.

The Caen quarries still exist; in 1944 they were used as a place of refuge by the citizens during the heavy fighting which destroyed so much of their town. But they have not been worked for a very long time. In recent years, however, other limestones have been imported from France: St. Maximin from the *département* of Oise, Courteraie from Meuse, Lépine from Vienne and Richemont from Charente are among the best known. These will be referred to in Chapter 10.

THE LIMESTONES

England has extensive deposits of limestone, particularly on what for convenience is known as the Jurassic limestone belt, which sweeps across the country from Dorset to the coast of Yorkshire. As in all natural things, there is great variety, for, although neighbouring quarries are likely to be similar, the stone from most of them has its own distinctive texture and character.

These are all sedimentary rocks, which implies that the matter of which they are composed, usually conveyed by water, sometimes by wind, was accumulated in layers. So these rocks are nearly always stratified. What matters to the builder and to the stonemason is that some of the strata are much thicker, and in other ways better, than others. In general it can be said that with limestone the top layers of the freestone quarries are often coarse-grained and difficult to work, the middle layers are close-grained and even textured, and therefore less hard and more amenable to the masons' chisels, while the bottom layers tend to be fine-grained and best suited to carving.

In the limestone country quarries at one time abounded; almost every town and village had its own. But although the good stone may go down as much as 25 ft. or even more, it is usually only rubblestone, which, because of its hardness, can only be hammer-dressed.

The other main group of limestones are the freestones, so called because they can be freely worked with hand tools in any direction. These may also occur near the surface, as for example at Leckhampton, but usually they lie deeper. Deposits are much less numerous; few of the hard rubble quarries yield freestone as well. But when they do, the two kinds of limestone have frequently been used together; the main facing for the walls will be coursed rubblestone, with the freestone confined to the 'dressings', as at Farleigh Hungerford Castle (3). The freestone may occur in much thicker strata, and,

as will be explained in some detail later, can be dressed and carved with relative ease when it is first quarried. So this was the kind of limestone employed for all the finest buildings in the limestone areas. In urban settings, freestone has nearly always been preferred, and rightly so, but in the heart of the country, as at Fotheringhay (**2**), it can also make a memorable impact. At Barnack church both types of limestone are easily recognized (**4**). Where, as here, the architecture is obviously of two dates, the rubblestone will almost always be the older. The lower part of Barnack's massive tower is, as already mentioned, Anglo-Saxon; the top stage and the spire are Early English. Both are of local stone; rubblestone below and the famous Barnack rag above, and for the dressings throughout. (The term 'rag' normally implies a stone of hard, coarse and shelly texture that cannot be ashlared, but Barnack rag was an exception: it could be dressed, often by using a jadd pick (**41**) rather than a chisel).

Although they have some redoubtable rivals, the oolitic limestones are generally regarded as being visually the finest of all the English stones. To mention only the cathedrals, it was they which furnished virtually all the stone for Lincoln, Peterborough, Ely, Oxford, Gloucester, Wells, Salisbury and London's St. Paul's, and part of the stone for Norwich, Rochester, Bristol and Exeter. The ooliths are small spherical grains the size of a pin's head or less, with an internal structure of calcium carbonate crystals. It is also calcite, acting as the matrix, that holds the rounded granules together. Not all the stones classified as oolites look equally oolitic,

2 St. Mary and All Saints, Fotheringhay, Northamptonshire

3 Farleigh Hungerford Castle, Somerset

4 St. John, Barnack, Soke of Peterborough (now Cambridgeshire)

for the proportion of ooliths to matrix varies and in some of these limestones there are other bodies such as oval pellets (which are in fact the excreta of water-snails) and irregular crumbs of calcium carbonate. The most perfect example of pure oolite is Ketton stone, quarried four miles west of Stamford, which has furnished much of the stone for the colleges of Cambridge. There is no need of a microscope to perceive that Ketton stone is almost wholly composed of tiny spherical fragments which look very like petrified herrings' roe. Here the shell fragments, which are such a prominent constituent of some of the other oolitic limestones, Barnack rag, for example, or Weldon, are wholly absent.

In some beds of Portland stone the ooliths are so small as to be not easily

5 St George, Hanover Square, London, W.1.

visible to the naked eye (although perfectly discernible with a lens), so the texture is very close and even, which makes it excellent for carving. It can attain a dazzling whiteness, as we are constantly being reminded in most parts of central London (**5**). Unlike the other oolitic limestones, therefore, Portland tends to rely for its effect upon contrast with other materials rather than on blending with them. This can be quite dramatic, as for example, in the Wren portions of Hampton Court Palace, where the bricks are a very bright red and the use of the white stone is lavish. But because of its whiteness Portland is, as a rule, not a good mixer, especially with other limestones. For a complete building it would look quite wrong, for example, at Oxford or at Lincoln.

Nevertheless, Portland stone is the king of the oolites, and a magnificent gift to the builder and the carver. It is also the variety for which there is still a fairly steady demand; on the Isle of Portland four quarries are still working. The output, it is true, is not what it was. But in a workshop which now employs 60 men where formerly there were 400, machinery in recent years has made such remarkable strides (cf. Chapter 10) that this could represent no diminution in the total quantity of work performed.

Oolitic limestones occur at various levels in the sequence of Jurassic rocks. The youngest are Portland and its contemporaries Purbeck-Portland, Chilmark, of which Salisbury Cathedral was built, and its neighbour Tisbury. (The two latter are more sandy). They ought to be known as the Upper, or Superior, Oolite; but these words are not used. The terminology employed by geologists for these limestones is indeed very confusing for laymen. The limestones around Bath, in north-west Wiltshire, western Oxfordshire and the whole of the Cotswolds are classified as belonging to the Middle, or Great, Oolite. Their colours vary considerably, but they are almost all beautiful stones, without the durability of Portland.

Finally, at the bottom of this section of the Column, are the stones which the geologists call Lower, or Inferior, Oolite: the stones of Northamptonshire, Rutland and Lincolnshire. This is a terminology which to the stonemasons of that area is wholly unacceptable, and since it includes such stones as Barnack, Weldon, Ketton, Clipsham, Ancaster and Collyweston, all of which are extremely superior and will figure prominently in this book, it will be understood why. It is important that everyone should realise that Inferior Oolite is a geological term (and, it may be thought, an unfortunate one) which carries not the slightest implication of inferior quality.

Immediately below these oolitic limestones come the Liassic rocks, which also comprise Upper, Middle and Lower strata. The Lias makes another almost continuous belt, outcropping to the west and north-west of the Oolite throughout its entire length from West Dorset to the Cleveland Hills. The Liassic limestones are very variable and it is not easy to generalise about them, but as a whole they are not the equal of the oolites for building purposes. The products of the Upper and Middle strata tend to be more sandy, and less durable. Many quarries only yielded rubblestone, and none is any longer worked for building purposes.

Undoubtedly the most prestigious of these stones is Ham Hill. This used to be regarded as one of the Lower Oolites which it closely resembles; but modern geology has reclassified this stone as belonging to the Upper Lias. Small towns on the Somerset-Dorset border such as Sherborne and Martock, famous houses like Montacute (**153**), and many churches in the vicinity bear witness to the charm of this seductive golden brown stone, which is due to iron oxide staining. Sometimes, it is true, the iron content causes it to weather very dark and the natural striations within the stone to show

6 (left) Abbey Farm, Preston Plucknett, Somerset

7 (below) Wroxton Abbey, Oxfordshire

8 (right) The Town Hall and Market Cross, Somerton, Somerset

conspicuously. Ham Hill roofing slates were also made in substantial numbers, as can be seen to good effect at Abbey Farm, Preston Plucknett, near Yeovil (**6** and **98**), one of the most venerable examples of Ham Hill stone in a secular context. This was a grange (farmhouse) which would seem to have belonged to the once very rich Priory of Bermondsey. Now a

private house, it has not only a remarkable early fifteenth century chimney, which will be described later, but, set at right angles to the domestic building, a splendid barn.★

Otherwise it is the Middle Lias (or Marlstone, as it is often called) which provides all the most enjoyable buildings in this group of limestones. Many of them are rich in iron, notably in the area around Banbury, where villages like Adderbury and Bloxham and houses like Broughton Castle, Wroxton Abbey (**7**) and Farnborough Hall seem to soak up and store the sunshine within their rich tawny brown carapace. Here and there greenish tints also occur. The principal quarries were at Hornton, long since closed, and Edge Hill. The latter is still working. Similar stone used to be quarried at Lyddington in Rutland. Most of this village is built of it, and so is much of Uppingham.

The Lower Lias spreads down into the valleys of the Severn and of Shakespeare's Avon; at these levels the thinly bedded argillaceous limestones alternating with the heavy clays yield excellent hydraulic lime. The only building stone from this stratum is the so-called Blue Lias, which is grey rather than blue, and a cold grey at that: no iron staining here! Blue Lias is seen intermittently in the Midlands from Nottinghamshire southwards, but is commonest in central Somerset and west Dorset; the older parts of Lyme Regis, for example are almost wholly built of it. So is Somerton, where the mediaeval Market Cross was reconstructed in 1673 and the Town Hall a little later (**8**). Blue Lias is very narrow-bedded, so the

★An outstanding feature of this barn is the series of long vertical slits or embrasures. Despite their military look, it is unlikely that they had anything to do with defence. Their probable purpose was for ventilation and to facilitate the entry of owls, which were very welcome in mediaeval barns as they would catch the mice and so save the precious corn. (Hence, presumably, the name Barn Owl).

walls are closely coursed. Nor is it a freestone. It is not the most beguiling of the English limestones.

The Magnesian limestone of Permian age is an older rock which also outcrops in a belt, but much narrower and shorter than its Jurassic counterpart. It runs more or less continuously from Nottingham due northwards to Doncaster, and thence in a gentle curve which passes Wetherby, Ripon and Darlington and ends at South Shields. The best known quarries were at Thevesdale, near Tadcaster, and at Huddleston, near Sherburn-in-Elmet. In the country, as, for example, at Howsham Hall in Yorkshire (**9**), this is a beautiful creamy-white stone, fine-grained and distinctly crystalline in texture, which in aesthetic quality vies with the best oolites. Unfortunately, however, like some but not all the oolites, it is chemically unable to withstand smoke pollution. This has caused much trouble and expense in towns, not least in London, for Magnesian Limestone was the stone selected by the Royal Commission in 1839 for the new Houses of Parliament, and some of it began to fail almost as soon as the building was finished. But in the unpolluted atmosphere of today, all is well: York and Beverley Minsters, both recently cleaned, show it to splendid effect; the west towers of Beverley, since their recent restoration, display the quality of this beautiful stone to perfection (**10**).

These, then, were the limestones used for buildings of the highest quality. Our debt to them, and to those who worked them, is beyond computation. Yet they were not as difficult to work as might appear.

9 Howsham Hall, Yorkshire

10 Beverley Minster, Yorkshire: the west towers

While the stone lies in the quarry, the pores between the grains contain natural moisture. When it is lifted out, the moisture moves towards the surface of each block, and, by the absorption of oxygen, the calcite within the stone gradually crystallizes and hardens.

So limestone can be worked and dressed much more easily while still 'green': that is to say, when it has just been quarried. Masons, of course, have always known this, even if they did not fully understand the chemical changes that the stone was undergoing. They called the pristine dampness 'quarry sap'.

Some limestones are more vulnerable than others; but in the first weeks after quarrying the calcite matrix should be treated with care, or the stone may eventually fail. Freshly worked, unseasoned stones should not be set in high, exposed places, because calcite is soluble in water, and can be leached out if in such situations these stones have to stand up to continuous rain. Nor should this calcite be exposed to frost damage. The time for maturing varies both with the weather and the stone. In warm sunny weather the moisture may have dried out within a week or two, but crystallization may continue for several years. Until this is complete the stone is not properly seasoned.

There is an old masons' saying that limestone should not be moved north of its place of origin: to do so can be risky. For example, Bath stone in the Northern counties may easily perish in less than a hundred years. To this dictum Portland stone is the one great exception: this will survive anywhere.

This brief survey of the finest limestones by no means exhausts the list. The others have mostly been used only in the areas in which they occur, but the Carboniferous limestones – or Mountain limestones, as they used to be called – play a very important part in the landscape of the northern counties, as also of the Peak District and the Mendips. It is right to mention the landscape first in relation to these ancient stones, for they belong to the remote places, mostly very sparsely populated. On the Jurassic belt, over and over again the buildings 'steal the picture', for which the landscape provides no more than a quietly anonymous background. But in the Yorkshire Dales and in much of Durham and Northumberland away from the industrial areas, liberally dotted with steep cliffs and scars, gorges and waterfalls, and mile upon mile of dry-stone walls, the landscape *is* the picture; the buildings, lonely farmhouses or barns, are frequently no more than tiny 'incidents'. They are often roughly built, and that is exactly as

they should be: thereby they 'belong'. There are also some small towns
built of this stone: Kendal is one of them. Most of its stone came from
Pennington quarry, a mile to the west: the track was all downhill. And
there are a few greater houses – although at Haddon Hall (11) the dressings
and the whole of the facing stone of the central tower, as well as the steps,
are of the more amenable gritstone, which was also quarried locally.

Even older (about four hundred and twenty-five million years) are the
Silurian limestones, which are more important in Wales and the Lowlands
of Scotland than in England, where they occur only in southern
Shropshire, and small areas of Herefordshire. Ludlow Castle is built of this
chunky rough-textured stone, and so is much loved Stokesay Castle (92), a
few miles to the north-west. Needless to say, it could not be ashlared. The
quarrying of this stone on Wenlock Edge, mainly for agricultural lime, is a
matter of continual concern to country lovers and conservationists.

At the other end of the geological time-scale are the limestones of the
South-East: mainly Tertiary in the Isle of Wight, Cretaceous on the
mainland. These stones have many limitations; most of them are not
freestone and some weather badly. The Cretaceous limestones vary
considerably in character. The most widespread is the Chalk, much of
which is too soft and lacking in durability to be suitable for building, at least
for external use. There are, however, in the Lower Chalk, some more
compact beds which contain tiny fragments of shells and other impurities
including calcium phosphate and occasional sand grains, producing a gritty

12 and 13 The Archbishop's Palace, Maidstone, Kent; with (right) detail of ragstone walling

texture which can be quite hard on the tools. This is the kind of chalk which is properly termed clunch; but in practice that word is often applied loosely to all forms of chalk-stone. Clunch was obtained at a number of places in Cambridgeshire – Burwell, Barrington, Orwell and elsewhere – and also from Totternhoe near Dunstable in Bedfordshire, where some of it was mined. This last quarry is still in operation for building conservation work at Woburn and elsewhere, as well as for agricultural lime.

The shelly chalk-stone quarried at Beer in the eastern corner of Devon is somewhat harder. This is of the same age as the Upper Chalk, but has a more granular texture, having been formed in shallow coastal waters rather than in the deeper seas in which most chalk was laid down. It was used extensively for the Cathedral at Exeter (150).

The toughest of these 'young' limestones, occurring in the Lower Greensand, is Kentish ragstone, of which a good example is the much restored Archbishop's Palace at Maidstone (12, 13). Though coarse-textured and brittle, and treacherous too, for it includes sandy patches which can be decidedly soft, this is a stone with a very long history; it was worked by the Romans, and unfortunately, because of its relative cheapness, was much patronised by Victorian church architects in the London area. We say unfortunately because Kentish rag is an unaccommodating stone, difficult to dress, and even to square at all precisely, so its uneven surface is all too prone to harbour dirt. The Palace at Maidstone has responded well to cleaning, but the random character of the masonry will at once be evident; even to course this stone was difficult, and seldom attempted. Ragstone buildings include Rochester Castle, many Kentish churches, and Knole.

Still younger, and not worthy of more than a passing mention, are septaria, which mainly consist of nodules of calcareous clay or marl. It was formerly thought that these nodules were usually seven-sided, which is the explanation of the name. They are widely distributed in those parts of the country lying to the east and south of the limestone belt, but recourse was only had to them in the Thames estuary and along the coasts of Essex and Suffolk, and they must always have been a 'last resort' building material. Nevertheless they were used for many centuries, from Roman times onwards. They can be well seen on the keeps of two Norman castles: Colchester and Orford. In the first half of the nineteenth century they were in great demand for making, by a process of burning, the stucco known as Parker's Roman cement, so much used by John Nash.

The limestones experienced their greatest period of danger during the nineteenth century, for without doubt their direst enemy is polluted atmosphere. It was the first century of the Industrial Revolution which saw clouds of black, sulphurous smoke belched forth from countless factory chimneys; nor did the coal fires of a million houses help. The sulphur released into the atmosphere, coming into contact with the soot and dust already deposited on the stone, was converted whenever it rained into sulphuric acid, a highly corrosive agent. Salt can also be a danger, whether it comes up from the ground where there is no damp course (for some soils are slightly salty) or, in locations near the sea, is airborne. If from defective gutters or rainwater pipes, or some other cause, stone is allowed to become saturated, frost will also be a hazard. But so long as it stays dry, limestone can withstand the most severe frosts, nor does driving rain do any harm, because stone walls quickly dry out again.

THE SANDSTONES

The dividing line between the sandstones and the limestones is not always sharply defined. There are limestones with a high sand content, and sandstones that are markedly calcareous. The essential point is that the sandstones, too, are all sedimentary rocks, built up in layers.

There are abundant sandstones in the South-East, but for building their importance lies principally in the Western and Northern counties. There are even more kinds of sandstone than of limestone, and still greater variations in durability and in colour. But they all consist mainly of grains of quartz, sometimes with the addition of small quantities of felspar, mica or some other mineral, and, always, a cementing material, known as the matrix of the stone. This varies considerably, but it is on the character of the matrix that the strength and durability of the stone really depends. The strongest cement is silica; the weakest just clay. In between these, in strength, come calcite (calcium carbonate), dolomite (calcium–magnesium carbonate) and oxide of iron.

Siliceous sandstones are chemically inert, which no limestones are; this enabled them to withstand better than any limestones the smoke-laden air of the industrial towns in the grimy decades which are happily now, in England, little more than a memory. The structural homogeneity of sandstone with a siliceous matrix is proof against the most rigorous weather conditions and the most smoke-polluted atmosphere. There is, however, an obverse side of the coin. The inhalation of dust containing grains of glassy silica can be very dangerous for the lungs; protective masks must therefore be worn by the workers, and, to allay the dust as much as possible, these stones are now usually only worked wet. Even so, they are very hard on the tools. The wear and tear on the chisels and on all the cutting tools is considerably greater with the siliceous sandstones than with any of the limestones.

The methods of quarrying, machine cutting and hand working the sandstone are almost exactly the same as those now used for the limestones; these will be fully described in the next chapter. Exposed faces of sandstone in the quarries can be as much as 40 ft. from top to bottom, which is economically very advantageous.

The most important building sandstones are from the Carboniferous series: the stone from the Coal Measures, the Millstone Grit and what are known as the Lower Carboniferous sandstones. These form the stone of a large part of Northern England, including the whole length of the Pennines. There are extensive deposits in the Midlands, especially the North Midlands, also in the Forest of Dean, around Bristol, and in Devon and Cornwall. These sandstones can sometimes be quarried in enormous blocks which have no parallel in English limestone, except perhaps at Portland. But the colours are sober; brown or buff when first quarried, settling down to darker shades of both. Since the advent of the railways, these sandstones have travelled widely. Coal Measures sandstone from Bramley Fall quarry near Leeds can even be seen at Stamford, in the Town

14 Disused engine house, Mary Tavy, Devon

Bridge over the Welland (**77**). When employed in conjunction with Carboniferous limestone, as at Haddon Hall (**11**), the sandstone (here gritstone) is easily distinguishable, because it is browner and in much larger blocks.

By 1900, much of this sandstone in the industrial districts was jet black, and under their mantle of soot the buildings could only be appreciated as silhouettes. In recent years many of them have been cleaned; there will be more to say about that later. What a transformation the cleaning has effected can be well appreciated at Heaton Park near Manchester (**136**) by anyone who knew the house before the 1970s.

The Culm Measures sandstones of central Devon and North Cornwall are very much the poor relations of the lordly Carboniferous sandstones of the North. Unlike them they are not freestones, and are only obtainable in small, hard somewhat rubbly pieces, often of a dark brownish-red. But they too look absolutely right in their own locality, as demonstrated by the old bridge over the Tamar near Stoke Climsland (**123**) and the ruin of the engine house of the Devon and Friendship lead mine (**14**) at Mary Tavy, on the western fringe of Dartmoor, near Tavistock.

Beneath the Carboniferous rocks are the Devonian and the Old Red sandstones, which are among the oldest to have been used on any considerable scale. The Devonian rocks are not confined to Devon, nor are they by any means all sandstones: some, in South Devon, are limestones and a great many are slate. But there is plenty of sandstone too, in west Somerset, in the coastal areas of north and south Devon, and in Cornwall. The Old Red sandstones are differently constituted but of much the same antiquity. These occur mainly in Herefordshire. The colours vary considerably: the pinks, greys and purples are less dense and therefore more enjoyable than the red. But freestone, as seen on parts of Hereford Cathedral, at Berrington Hall, and on the porch at Dilwyn (**15**) is not typical; most of this stone consists of rubbly pieces, usually rather small, as is apparent on the main wall of this church.

The most beautiful English sandstones, but unfortunately by no means the most reliable, are the Permian and the Triassic, often grouped together, for they are closely similar, under the name New Red. This is the characteristic stone of the West Midlands, but is distributed far more widely than that: in fact, in the area of solid rock (as distinct from drift) exposed in England, this stone comes first. It is an important building material in almost every western county from Devon to the Scottish Border, and there is also a long north-eastern arm stretching through Nottinghamshire and the whole length of central Yorkshire. Often it lies under a considerable depth of clay and marls, which rendered quarrying impracticable; this is the stone associated with some of our richest farmlands. New Red sandstone is, like the Old, of many other colours besides red: the range of

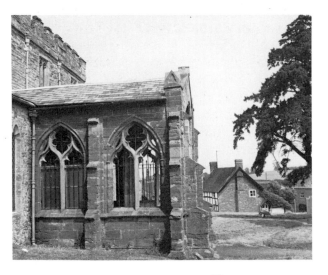

15 St. Mary, Dilwyn, Herefordshire: south porch

hues also embraces pinks and subtle greys, deep purples and pale lavenders, the warm browns of chocolate and cinnamon, and every shade of yellow and buff from ochre to honey. In country places New Red sandstone buildings are often gloriously right, and wherever the soil is ploughed there is a harmony of colour between earth and stone which is a continual delight. At some of the quarries it can be cut like cheese, and ashlar is no problem at all. But structurally, alas, much of it is very deficient in strength, reacting badly to the rigours of the English climate. Blistering, flaking and crumbling are all too common. So our New Red sandstone cathedrals, Worcester, Lichfield, Chester and Carlisle, are the most restored of any, and seldom wholly free from scaffolding.

Nevertheless this is the stone used for the two best known Anglican cathedrals of the present century: Liverpool and Coventry. Liverpool Cathedral, which took seventy-four years (1904–1978) to build, is of load-bearing masonry throughout, from the nearby quarries of Woolton and Rainhill. (At Woolton there is now a hole in the ground about the same size as the cathedral itself). It is likely to be the last great building to be constructed in this way. The dull red sandstone is rather sombre, for it does not reflect light. It is very much to be hoped that it will weather satisfactorily, for this cathedral embodies a great deal of traditional hand craftsmanship. It was only towards the end that modern stone cutting machinery was introduced on a limited scale. Coventry Cathedral (1958–62) is a ferro-concrete structure which was faced externally with a thick ashlared cladding of Hollington sandstone from Staffordshire, together with a certain amount of Westmorland slate-stone from Little Langdale. It was intended to sheathe the interior too, but unfortunately this proved too expensive.

Woolton and Rainhill quarries are now closed and today the only important production of Triassic sandstone for building comes from Hollington near Uttoxeter. There is a red variety and another known as white, which is in fact light grey, tinged here with green and there with a blush of pink. Red Hollington is the stone now used to replace decayed Old Red sandstone at Hereford Cathedral.

Grinshill, near Shrewsbury, also produced both a 'red' and a 'white' variety: the latter, the better of the two, was used for Attingham Park (**134**). These quarries, which once supplied most of Shropshire with its building stone, were closed in 1914, but both were reopened in a small way a few years ago. White Permian sandstone is still worked at Mansfield, red Permian (**62**) near Penrith, and red Triassic at St. Bees, on the Cumbrian

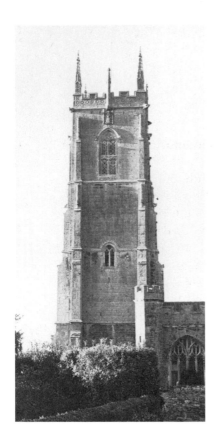

16 St. John, Broad Clyst, Devon   17 St. Laurence, Chobham, Surrey

coast. St. Bees stands with Hollington as probably the most uniformly reliable of these Triassic sandstones. Mansfield provided most of the stone for Southwell Minster, including the famous 'leaves' (**147**).

Another long arm of this stone stretches, with a few interruptions, from the West Midlands down the Severn valley into Somerset and Devon. The rich red soil of east Devon and the fantastic coast scenery around Dawlish are much loved features of the train journey from London or Bristol to Plymouth. The building stone, once again, is absolutely in tune with the landscape. Devon churches are noted for their lofty towers, of which a fine example is at Broad Clyst, near Exeter (**16**). On the south and west faces there is now plenty of grey lichen, which combines with the red stone to endow this tower, particularly towards evening, with an almost magical beauty: the colour is a delicate grey-pink.

The Jurassic rocks, as we have seen, are mostly limestones, but there are a few which are classed as sandstones; they are in the Northampton area and in North Yorkshire. Here the most important quarries were at Aislaby, high above the Esk valley four miles west of Whitby. Hence, in the 1720s, went the stone for one of England's most magnificent houses: Houghton Hall in Norfolk. It was shipped from Whitby to King's Lynn and from there dragged overland: a very costly proceeding. Castle Howard presented no

34

such problem, for there was a quarry of equally good Jurassic sandstone on the estate.

The Cretaceous sandstones occur only in the East and South, but spread over a wide area from the fringes of the Lincolnshire Wolds to Wiltshire and Dorset. Some of these stones are also beautiful in their colouring: here and there light grey but usually, owing to staining with iron oxide, some shade of brown, from dark chocolate to the palest gold, and with some greenish tints. Many of them, however, are deficient in strength. Perhaps the best is the so-called Wealden stone of Sussex, a fine-grained sandstone which can be ashlared, and which can be seen to perfection at Bodiam Castle. Some of the beds are fissile and yield the splendid roofing stone known generically as Horsham slates, which never fail to give distinction to any house fortunate enough to be roofed with them (**161**).

Bargate stone, quarried in the neighbourhood of Guildford and Godalming, is West Surrey's equivalent of Kentish rag, and, like that stone, cannot be ashlared (**94**). But in a part of the country poorly supplied with stone of much durability, Bargate proved very useful: Lutyens employed it at two of his best known houses, Tigbourne Court and Munstead Wood.

Elsewhere, many of the Cretaceous sandstones come from outcrops of the Upper and Lower Greensands. One of them is the so-called 'gingerbread stone' still quarried (though now mainly for roadstone and hardcore) at Snettisham in north-west Norfolk. At Houghton Hall it is instructive to compare the stables, built of brick faced with this yellow-brown carstone, with the elegant light greys and buffs of the Aislaby stone ashlar employed for the mansion itself. The stables are appropriately modest by comparison. These stones have a very long history in the South-East; Reigate stone was the principal material of Edward the Confessor's Westminster Abbey. Besides Carstone, other terms applied to them include Malmstone and (mainly in Surrey) Firestone.

Still more recent, products of the Tertiary system, are two freaks: sarsens and pudding-stone. Both (together with just four courses of Horsham-type slates at the eaves) are very well seen at Chobham church in Surrey (**17**): and it is safe to say that builders in most other parts of England would not have thought much of either of these materials. But in north-west Surrey there was nothing else.

Pudding-stone is a conglomerate: that is to say, a stone composed of fragments, generally rounded by contact with water, of previously existing rocks, held together by natural cement. Here the fragments are of dark brown sandstone, some of it very soft and crumbly, interspersed with little

pebbles of flint. The matrix is iron oxide. It made a very coarse mixture (**18**), and of all English stones is perhaps the least enjoyable: but it was better than nothing.

Sarsens, of which there will be more to say in the next chapter, are very much more pleasing. They are boulders of grey siliceous sandstone varying a lot in size and shape, which were for centuries a great geological mystery, because they bore no relationship to the other stones in the regions where they were found. Hence the name they were given: a variant of 'saracen', for there was a time when any stranger was dubbed a Saracen. It is now realised that these boulders are the remnants of sandy strata of Tertiary age, otherwise eroded away. In the Middle Ages their siliceous character rendered them very difficult to work: they were broken into what were often nearly square-shaped blocks, and only roughly coursed, as can be seen in the low wall at Avebury (**19**). Ashlar was, of course, out of the question. Unfortunately the old dovecot here, also built of sarsens, was at one time rendered.

The best place to see sarsens is on and around the Wiltshire Downs. Villages such as Avebury and Aldbourne abound in them. By the beginning of the nineteenth century, shaping had become much more skilful (**20, 178**). But there is no longer any call for them.

GRANITE

The sedimentary rocks, formed in layers, cover most of England but much less of Scotland. The other principal group of rocks, the igneous (from the Latin *ignis* = fire), came into existence in quite a different way: by cooling and solidification of once molten material. Of these rocks, the only one that has been of much importance to English builders is granite.

18 (left) **St. Laurence, Chobham, Surrey: detail of pudding-stone**

19 (above) **Mediaeval dovecote, Avebury, Wiltshire**

20 (right) **The Old Manor, Aldbourne, Wiltshire**

Granite solidifies under high pressure deep beneath the earth's surface. As the molten material cooled, so this stone was formed. The process was coterminous with the emergence of some of the older sedimentary rocks. The granites of Devon and Cornwall were formed about 290 million years ago; those of Cumbria and the Charnwood Forest are older.

The three essential components of granite are all minerals with a markedly crystalline character: quartz, which is intensely hard, felspar, which is only slightly less so, and mica, which though comparatively soft is chemically inert. Hence the distinguishing characteristics of this stone: tremendous strength, a compact and generally uniform structure, and usually a mottled or speckled appearance. Granite can withstand the most severe weather conditions and is also impervious to water, so it has been a great boon to builders of embankments, breakwaters and lighthouses. It has also been invaluable for kerb-stones and, as we shall see, was once in great demand for setts. By the use of abrasives with water, all granites can be polished, but before the machine age this was a very slow and laborious process.

The number of Cornish buildings in granite is far greater than anywhere else in England, because in parts of that county there was no other material available. But in pre-industrial days, particularly before the advent of

21 St. Protus and St. Hyacinth, Blisland, Cornwall: nave

22 The Vicarage, Lostwithiel, Cornwall

gunpowder, the task of quarrying and working this intensely hard stone was formidably difficult. So whenever they could, the builders availed themselves of what is known as moorstone – blocks lying about on the moors and hills just as the sarsens lay on the downs and heaths farther east. Before the end of the Middle Ages the masons had learnt how to dress their moorstone, as well as blocks which they had prised out from near the land surface, sufficiently well for rough church-building. The granite arcades of Cornish churches such as Blisland (**21**) are not lacking in charm, but profiles had to be kept comparatively simple, with no undercutting and, as a rule, rather plain capitals.

Regular coursing only appeared very gradually; the (by Cornish standards) lavish Perpendicular south aisle of the church at St. Neot (dedicated to one of that large band of totally obscure Cornish saints, St. Anietus) is an early example. Because cutting the stone was so difficult, the individual blocks are usually, by comparison with limestone, very large (**89**). At the Vicarage at Lostwithiel (**22**) there are only thirteen courses of stone from base to cornice, which endows a modest Georgian house with a monumentality that has nothing to do with the design itself. Only with the development of modern saws was it feasible to introduce quite narrow courses of granite among the broader ones, as Lutyens did at Castle Drogo (**86**). The sharp arrises here also depended on these new saws. (It is said that the two chief masons, in the best tradition of the Middle Ages, stayed on this same job for nearly twenty years).

More will be said later about the frame-saws, and finally, very recently, the thermic lance for cutting granite. Although the sawing processes are always slower with granite than with the sedimentary rocks, their introduction in the nineteenth century was vital to the health of this branch of the stone industry. For the demand was, and still is, increasingly for big slabs no more than 2 ins. thick, to be employed as a facing material, nowadays over ferro-concrete. When all the masons had were picks and hammers, the large-scale use of granite in this way would have been an impossibility. So also with polishing. The ancient Egyptians had polished their granite statues, and so had the Romans. Then, it would appear, the methods were forgotten; there was no more polished granite until 1803. Nowadays the demand for highly polished granite for cladding is considerable, and in the right place it is certainly an embellishment. The wrong place is the English churchyard, from which, unfortunately, all the Diocesan Advisory Committees have not yet succeeded in eradicating it.

Unpolished granite can also look very dignified when employed with circumspection. Except sometimes for plinths, it does not usually blend very happily with limestone or sandstone: this is specially true of those granites with a markedly speckled or mottled composition, and, still more obviously, of those with huge porphyritic crystals of pink felspar, which are characteristic of Shap granite.

The colour range of the English granites is somewhat limited. In the South-West they are generally some shade of grey, ranging from the 'pepper and salt' stone at the De Lank quarry on the edge of Bodmin Moor to the light oatmeal-grey seen at St. Buryan on the Land's End peninsula. But in Cumbria the pink shades predominate: the pale pinks of Eskdale are visually perhaps the most pleasing that we have. Threlkeld granite, quarried near Keswick (and now, alas, only for roadstone), has pink patches but is mainly bluish-grey.

Several granite quarries are still producing building stone in Cornwall. Elsewhere there are now only two: Merrivale in Devon and Shap in what used to be Westmorland. Regrettably, a good deal of granite is now being imported from abroad. Nor was this stone ever used extensively in Devon, Leicestershire or Cumbria, for all these counties had plentiful supplies of other stones which could be worked a great deal more easily. The centre of the industry in Leicestershire was at Mountsorrel, on the eastern edge of the Charnwood Forest, but not all the granite buildings there have survived. At Shap in Cumbria quarrying only began about 1870, and all the stone went elsewhere: this was inevitable, for on this remote moorland site there were no local needs. Fortunately it was possible to erect the works beside the main London to Glasgow railway line.

OTHER IGNEOUS ROCKS

The term granite is often used in the stone trade to describe other igneous rocks which are geologically somewhat different. Most people will be able to recognize porphyry and some will know serpentine, but who among our readers, we wonder, will be familiar with diorite and dolerite, syenite and basalt, gabbro, the elvans, polyphant and catacleuse? Several of these have played no part in the history of English building. Others, occurring mainly in Cornwall and hardly anywhere else, deserve a mention.

Porphyry is found in Northumberland, Leicestershire and Cornwall, but only in the South-West was it used as a building stone. In its familiar red form we can only point to a single example: the wall-facing of the hall of the house called Place, at Fowey, constructed in the 1840s. With its polished red walls this is certainly a great curiosity, but few would call it beautiful.

Much more important, in Cornwall and south-west Devon, is the stone known as white elvan, which is the local name here for a pale buff-grey quartz-porphyry, fine grained with very small felspar crystals. This excellent stone, which could be ashlared, is seen at St. Austell and at a number of other churches in its vicinity, and also at Antony House, Torpoint. The principal quarry, now completely worked out, was at Pentewan, a mile or so north of Mevagissey. The stone for the charming, partly Elizabethan manor house of Trerice (**23**), near Newquay, is very

23 (left) Trerice, St. Newlyn East, Cornwall

24 (above) St. Merryn, Padstow, Cornwall

similar: it came from a small and long abandoned quarry only a mile away.

Elvan is a word not heard except in the South-West; it was an old miners' and quarrymen's term, and they were not concerned with the niceties of geological classification. White elvan looks not unlike Devonian sandstone, and is decidedly easier to bring to an arris than granite. But Cornwall also has a stone known as blue elvan, which is geologically quite different. This is a form of gabbro, which is an exceedingly hard stone, tougher than granite, which could only be quarried in rough, chunky pieces that no builder would use unless he had nothing better. The colour of blue elvan after weathering, when the initial blueness fades, is a rather sombre grey-brown. It cannot be dressed, and today is only employed for roadstone. It can be well seen (with no trace of any blue tint) at Restormel Castle, which was entirely built of it. It is also one of a *potpourri* of unfamiliar stones that constitute the fabric of the church of St. Keverne on the Lizard peninsula. (This church is dedicated to St. Akeveranus, which must be a prizewinner even among Cornish dedications!)

Some of these Cornish stones are much more amenable; white elvan is one of them. The village of St. Keverne also has plenty of serpentine, and so have the nearby parishes of Landewednack and Ruan Minor, where the low tower of the church displays great blocks of it. This is a beautiful stone, but employed externally it may be treacherous. For internal use it can be polished. It is usually dark grey, with hints in places of dark red and olive green, but elsewhere it is mainly green, shading to grey-green and grey-blue. A modern bungalow at St. Keverne has been entirely built with lumps of stone gathered from the nearby beach, of all the three kinds just mentioned: blue elvan, gabbro and serpentine.

Polyphant and catacleuse could also be worked quite easily. Polyphant stone takes its name from the eponymous hamlet, close to Altarnun, which

is about nine miles west of Launceston. The quarry is still worked from time to time as required: the stone is popular with sculptors. The predominant colour is grey-green. Catacleuse also occurs at one place only: just to the west of Padstow. It is best seen in the arcades of the church at St. Merryn (**24**): a medium-toned bluish-grey. The abaci have rather crudely carved leaves. In Padstow church the font is of catacleuse stone: here it is dark grey, and very well preserved. This delightful object has the twelve Apostles, among whom St. Thomas is holding a builder's adze and St. Philip a saw.

Catacleuse is akin to dolerite, mention of which takes us at once to the other end of England, for, apart from a few farms on the slopes of the Clee Hills in Shropshire, it is only in the counties of Northumberland and Durham, where it is known as whinstone, that it has been employed for building, and then only rarely. It was, however, used by the Romans for parts of Hadrian's Wall: many of the big blocks are still *in situ*. It is also in evidence farther north, at Craster. The main front of the big house, Craster Tower, is faced with it, and it was also employed for the perimeter walls of the estate (**85**). Dolerite is not an attractive stone; it is iron-brown or nearly black.

Basalt, diorite and syenite are also dark rocks, finer in grain than granite.

They all contain plenty of felspar but little or no quartz. They belong more to Wales, Scotland and Northern Ireland than to England. They have occasionally been used for roadstone, but have no importance in the story of English building.

SLATE

True slate, like marble, is a metamorphic rock, which means a substance transformed from its original character, whether sedimentary or igneous, into something different by great heat or pressure or both, far below the earth's surface. During this violent process, which was sometimes sufficiently powerful to have thrown up great mountain ranges, the physical character of the original rock was changed, usually into a laminated condition which could be split quite easily into thin layers.

This property rendered it highly suitable for roofing, and as a building material slate has had much more importance for roofs than for walls. The number of slate roofs in our island goes into millions, and the large majority date from the nineteenth century and are Welsh. This is a subject to which much fuller consideration will be given in Chapter 8.

But in the slate areas – which in England are much the same as those of the igneous rocks: Cornwall and South Devon, the Lake District and the Charnwood Forest in Leicestershire – this stone was used not only for roofs but also for walls. Seldom was this walling stone specially quarried. The production of roofing slates has always involved enormous wastage; it was from this waste that the walling material was normally obtained, and at a very low cost. The resulting appearance is quite distinctive. Many of the stones are long and narrow, tapering from a wider central part to almost a point at one or both ends. Walling masons in slate had therefore to build in quite a different manner from other masons, and this is instantly recognizable (**25**). The hunks of slate had to be fitted together with very little further shaping or dressing.

In the South-West and in Leicestershire the walls were pointed with mortar in the usual way, but in the Lake District, possibly because sand for mortar was not readily available, most of the old walls were bedded into clay. This was kept so well back from the face of the wall, perhaps to protect it from being washed out by the heavy rains, that it is frequently mistaken for dry-walling. It is usual in the Lake District, as also in Wales, to limewash the walls of the house or cottage, but not of the outhouses or farm buildings.

43

The most difficult problem for a builder in slate is how to manage the angles, the window and door openings and especially the quoins. The stone splits very easily along the lines of cleavage, but to cut across the grain is quite a different matter. So, wherever it was feasible, another kind of stone was used for the angles, or, as at Woodhouse Eaves (**25**), the builder resorted to brick.

Level courses also presented a problem. Shaped blocks of slate can be produced, but only with much labour and expense, so they are seldom seen. They really run counter to the nature of the material. Thus there has never been much demand for slate as a building material outside the slate-quarrying districts.

For dry walls, which will be considered in Chapter 4, slate is of course ideally suited, and in the slate areas there are many miles of them, which fit admirably into the landscape. Some of these were also built with the quarry waste, but another convenient source was the quantities of slate scree often found on the surface of the land in hilly districts.

Slate has many other uses, some but not all in relation to buildings. It is from its nature very suitable for paving floors, for steps, window-sills and surrounds, lintels, shelves, chimney-pieces and sinks. Before the days of galvanized iron it was the usual material for water tanks. Where it is the local stone, gate-posts are often of slate, and sometimes whole fences, as will be described later. It is an excellent material for memorial tablets, particularly when there is an opportunity for fine lettering, but for gravestones its use should be confined to the slate areas. In the eighteenth and nineteenth centuries Swithland slate was used for headstones far beyond the confines of the Charnwood Forest, and, despite the beautifully incised lettering, it cannot be said that, where the church is of sandstone or limestone, its presence is very welcome.

In the later Georgian period and especially during the Regency there was a great vogue for hanging slates vertically on walls. This was done partly to provide additional protection from the weather and, at coastal places, from the salty air, and partly in order to mask timber-framing, which in this period was very much out of fashion, being regarded as too 'folksy'. Slates were also hung over rubblestone, to give such buildings a more urbane appearance. Generally, as in the two buildings at Launceston (**26**), the slate-hanging is confined to the upper storeys.

The usual method of attaching hung slates was by first fixing wooden battens on to the wall; on to them the slates would be hung with the aid of long nails, one or two small holes having been pierced near the top of each

26 The Bell Inn, Launceston, Cornwall

slate and sometimes another about a third of the way down each side. The nails are concealed by the overlap, as is the mortar into which the upper ends were often bedded. With brick walls battens were not usually necessary, as the slates could be nailed directly into the mortar courses; but with rubblestone this did not work, for level courses are essential.

Slate-hanging in England can sometimes be seen in the Lake District, and now and again in non-slate areas too, for in the nineteenth century slates could easily be transported; but the principal counties in which to find it are Devon and Cornwall. Hung slates vary considerably in size, but are usually on the small side, to reduce the weight on the nails. Generally, too, they are plain; shaped slates provide a delightful variation, but are not nearly as frequently seen in England as could be wished. In this direction France and Germany have been much more resourceful.

Sawn or riven slate is now very much in demand as a facing material for structures of steel or ferro-concrete, for which it is more suitable than any other English stone. This will be considered in our final chapter.

MARBLE

Marble, no less than slate, is a metamorphic rock. Here the starting point is limestone. When subjected, deep below the earth's surface, to great heat or pressure or both, the calcium carbonate of the limestone is converted into crystals of calcite. All traces of fossils disappear, having been replaced by crystals which, if no other material is present, are pure white. In practice these white crystals are often stained by impurities to a different colour; and when, under stress, fissures are revealed, these may become filled with some other mineral which produces the effect known as veining.

True marble is the one major stone in which England is totally deficient. There are true marbles, never very much exploited, on Iona and Skye and near Clifden in County Galway (Connemara marble), but in the British Isles that is almost all. When marble was required, therefore, it had to be imported, usually from Italy. Very little was used before the Georgian period. It was then in great demand for statues and memorials, and also for architectural details such as fireplaces; but before the middle of the nineteenth century it was always a luxury material here, standing aloof from the native stonemasonry tradition. Nor, externally, does white marble ever look right in England, a fact to which far too many churchyards (140) and every cemetery without exception bear deplorable witness. As used by the Georgians it is undeniably a very 'classy' stone; the fireplaces are so chaste, the urns and vases so elegant, the statuary so immensely urbane. Marble sculpture in England is often arrogant and not infrequently ice-cold, but sometimes irresistible in the brilliance of its accomplishment.

The appeal of marble, both to sculptors and to architects, ever since the days of Classical Greece, had been due to its fine-grained, compact, even structure, to its relative softness when freshly quarried, making it easy to carve, and to its being able to take a high polish. Polished surfaces appeal to some people as conveying sensations of luxury. Hence the term 'marble' has come in popular usage to be applied, loosely and incorrectly, to any very hard limestone which can be ground and polished. Limestone, note: granite and most of the other igneous rocks can also be polished, but these are never now described as marbles, although they were in Roman times.

Much the best known and, historically, most widely used of the so-called English marbles is Purbeck. The limestones of what is known as the Isle of Purbeck (it is, in fact, a peninsula) lie in a succession of beds which differ considerably. In the upper beds the stone mostly consists of fossilized shells, the tiny shells of a water snail. It was from two of these beds that the so-

46

called marble was taken. Partly, perhaps because several of the quarries were the property of the Crown, and also because, being close to the sea, shipment was easier than with most stones, Purbeck marble won immense popularity in the thirteenth century; there was scarcely a major church in England which did not use it. In its unpolished state it is light grey, often with hints of green and brown. With polishing it darkens (**147**), and if, as happened at Salisbury Cathedral, Beverley Minster (**27**) and elsewhere in the Victorian period, the shafts are for reasons of preservation given a coat of varnish, they become almost black.

The stone was taken to the village of Corfe Castle, where most of the masons lived and where the work of carving and polishing was all performed. It was then carried to Ower Quay, at the tip of a peninsula jutting out into Poole Harbour, where loading was much easier. The vogue

27 Beverley Minster, Yorkshire: double stair to the former Chapter House

for this stone endured until about 1330, and continued throughout the Middle Ages as a favourite stone into which to set brasses; then the taste for it disappeared until a small revival occurred under Queen Victoria.

Like all these polished stones, it could only be used internally. Exposed to the weather it quickly lost its polish and its appeal. Even internally it may eventually show signs of serious decay, as can be seen, for example, at Lincoln. Whether the lavish use of this stone in the early Gothic churches was aesthetically an asset or an aberration must always be a matter of personal preference. There are good arguments both ways.

Dark polished shafts are not always Purbeck 'marble'. But none of the others acquired more than local recognition. The two best were Alwalton, another oolitic 'marble', found beside the Nene south-west of Peterborough, and Frosterley, a carboniferous limestone with many extremely large, pale grey fossils, quarried close to the Wear in Co. Durham, and seen in the Chapel of the Nine Altars in Durham Cathedral (**28**) and in the Chapel of the Bishop's Palace at Bishop Auckland. By dint of the most arduous labour, mainly in Somerset, Blue Lias could also be polished.

Broadly speaking, the harder the limestone the better the chances of obtaining a high polish, which implies that the Carboniferous and Devonian limestones were at an advantage compared with the Jurassic. In practice, however, in the Middle Ages this was not so, because good tools for grinding and polishing were not yet available. When these were developed, other English 'marbles' made their appearance. The two most important groups came, and to some extent still come, from Derbyshire and from South Devon.

Of the Derbyshire limestone marbles, the most familiar is Hopton Wood, obtained from Middleton near Wirksworth. Not long ago the quarries changed hands, and this handsome stone is, after over thirty years, now again available, and in large blocks. Other interesting varieties include Derbyshire Fossil and Ashford Black: both were at one time in considerable demand for fireplaces and paving, and Derbyshire Fossil marble was extensively used in London for wall covering at the Royal Festival Hall and for flooring at Terminal 1 of London Airport. Still more 'dressy' are the Devonian limestone marbles, which, when polished, are the closest we have to true marble, of the veined and patterned as distinct from the pure white kind. Ashburton is perhaps the best known: this is almost black, with thin pink and white veins, and has a texturing of fossil corals. It was used to pave the Queen's Chapel in Guildford Cathedral. The more florid varieties were popular in the Victorian age for reredoses and fonts, and look painfully out of place in a mediaeval church.

These English 'marbles' are seen at their best, perhaps, when used for paving: and many have been so used, from Bethersden in Kent to Orton Scar in Cumbria. Robert Adam employed Hopton Wood, in combination with a white marble from Italy, for the fine patterned floor of the great hall at Kedleston. Recently this stone has provided a new floor for the Cathedral at Birmingham. Basil Spence used a somewhat similar Derbyshire marble on the floor of Coventry Cathedral, at a time when Hopton Wood itself was not obtainable.

Some of these limestone marbles have also been highly regarded by sculptors, carvers and lettering artists: Hopton Wood in particular. The less intractable ones, such as Bethersden and the so-called Sussex marble from the Petworth neighbourhood, were used in the Middle Ages for tombs and fonts, and later for chimney-pieces. Big slabs sometimes serve as altar tops or as the top slabs of box tombs. It must, however, be emphasised that all this work is internal. Employed externally, the English 'marbles' lose their point.

ALABASTER

Alabaster is another stone which in England can only be used indoors. It is much too soft for external use.

Geologically, alabaster is a compact form of gypsum, which is sulphate of lime. It occurs at various places, principally in the Triassic formations of the north Midlands. Some of it was quarried, some mined, as at Hanbury near Tutbury it still is. The sole source of production in any quantity was the valley of the Trent.

Gypsum has long been a mineral of commercial importance; it is the raw material of plaster of Paris and indeed of most of our patent plasters. In the course of quarrying, large compacted blocks will sometimes be encountered. These are alabaster. If their texture is good and their colour satisfactory, they are carefully reserved. Creamy white alabaster has generally been the most highly prized, for this beautiful stone is translucent. But other colours appear, for example honey, which may be threaded, not usually to its advantage aesthetically, with veins of pink or reddish brown.

Alabaster has been used much more for sculpture than for architecture. It was the material for many of our best tomb monuments and effigies in the later Middle Ages, beginning shortly before the Black Death. But the ease with which it could be carved encouraged commercial development too. From the latter part of the fourteenth century until about 1500 small statues, together with vast numbers of reredoses, triptychs, retables and panels were produced in and around Nottingham, not only for English churches and private patrons but for export abroad. Although the best were good, the general standard was poor; the panels are often overcrowded and mannerisms like the bulging eyeballs are decidedly ugly. There was a revival of alabaster carving in the Victorian period, for pulpits, fonts, reredoses and recumbent effigies, many of which are now the great eyesores of the churches that harbour them.

In architecture it was used sparingly. This is another very 'dressy' stone, only suitable for interiors of real splendour. Two such exist, both dating from the middle years of the eighteenth century. The great hall at Kedleston has twenty stately (but not monolithic) columns, each nearly 25 ft. high, in a veined ivory white alabaster from a quarry close to where the Soar joins the Trent. This was about twenty miles away, but was a family property, and accessible by the River Derwent. For the slightly earlier hall at Holkham in Norfolk a much longer journey by barge was required. But expense here was no object: a sumptuous alabaster was used, with red markings on a ground of almost pure white, quarried at Castle Hay near Tutbury. The outcome was one of the most magnificent rooms in the country.

FLINT

Flint is among the strangest of all building materials, and no other country has made so much use of it as England. As a building stone it is quite unlike any other, and, although readily portable, is not easy to handle. It is improbable that anyone would have chosen it if any other stone had been available, but over large parts of the East and South-East there was, until the advent of brick, no alternative but wood. It is one of the hardest of all the minerals, since it is composed of almost pure silica. But it is also brittle, so can be fractured quite easily. This is the process known as knapping, which will be described in the next chapter. Knapped flints were first used in walls about 1300.

Most flint occurs in nodules or in continuous beds in the upper layers of the Chalk formation. Chalk, as we have seen, is widely distributed over the area to the south-east of the limestone belt; in fact, from Norfolk to Dorset there is no county without it. Essex and Middlesex have less than the other south-eastern counties, but no other building stone to compensate for this deficiency. Norfolk and Suffolk are the counties which used flint with the greatest resource in the later Middle Ages; most of the churches in these two counties, some of which are very large, were built of it. In Norfolk, as in Sussex and Kent, the chalk reaches the sea, the action of which not only dislodges the hard flints but washes them smooth. In this state they could be collected from the beaches as cobbles.

The smoothed and often rounded shapes were certainly more amenable; for normally the special difficulty of building with flint was that the shapes were so amorphous. This entailed the use of a great deal of mortar. The quality of the mortar was therefore of prime importance. In this respect the Romans, who made considerable use of flint and who liked to lace their flint walls at intervals with courses of tile-like bricks, excelled. Many of the later builders were not so skilful. Sometimes in the eastern part of England, as at the church of Great Gransden (**29**) in Huntingdonshire (now Cambridgeshire), the walls will be faced with 'any old thing': pieces of stone and broken brick, lumps of flint, and here, mainly, cobbles. These are fragments of other rocks differing substantially from flint in structure, which have been rounded by the action of glacial ice or water and carried far from their place of origin (**40**). They are usually larger than flints.

Flints themselves can weigh up to ten or twelve pounds each. They are virtually indestructible, but for a flint wall to endure, a strong hydraulic lime mortar (cf. p. 128) is the best. It needs to be stiff, as flints have a tendency to roll out of position, but it must also be able to 'breathe', for if water penetrates it must dry out. That is why modern cement pointing is wrong, quite apart from the fact that it is also very ugly.

The natural colour of flints is black, or nearly so, but millions of years in the chalk have usually left them with a cortex of white lime, which may be as much as $\frac{3}{8}$in. thick. In places contact with iron in the soil has stained them brown. Add grey, and that is the full colour range. Where white is predominant, and no attempt has been made at coursing, the effect is undeniably very 'busy' (**30**). But nobody could say that it is deficient in texture!

As with slate-stone, the corners always presented the flint builder with a problem. It was in order to avoid angles that so many church towers in East Anglia, in the Saxon and Norman periods especially, were circular. If angles were required, as for door and window openings and quoins, resort had to be made to stone or brick (**31**). Of the two, stone is always preferable. If this is not available, 'white' (pale yellow or dun-coloured) bricks undoubtedly look better with flint than red.

In the fourteenth and especially in the fifteenth centuries the standard of craftsmanship improved. The smaller flints were embedded in the core of the wall, and on the face the flints were more often coursed, at least roughly, and less mortar was in evidence. But the process of building in this material was always slow, because after every few feet it was necessary to pause to enable the mortar to achieve a firm set. No building could be done in wet weather, nor at all in the winter months. Nevertheless, partly because of the increasing scarcity of wood from the Tudor period onwards, flint remained a popular material for small houses and cottages until at least

29 (below) St. Bartholomew, Great Gransden, Huntingdonshire (now Cambridgeshire)

30 (right) Newmarket, Suffolk: flint wall

31 Buckland, Hertfordshire: flint with brick dressings

33 No. 3 Old Steine, Brighton,
Sussex

1700. For big houses it was not usually considered to be urbane enough in the Georgian period, a view reinforced rather than invalidated by the fact that in the 1790s the third Duke of Richmond insisted that his architect, James Wyatt, should use flint for Goodwood: a rare example of the local material being the wrong one. For this house the flints were not even knapped nor squared.

Elsewhere, by this time, squared flints had become familiar, and for a classical building like the little Sussex church at Glynde (32), built in 1763–5, they are certainly far preferable. Here, too, there is plenty of freestone in evidence, including the charming coat of arms in Portland stone in the pediment. Our view is that the more flint is accompanied by freestone the better: the latter is always an embellishment. The resourcefulness shown by some builders in the use of flint and stone together, arranged in bands and chequers, and in the evolution of flushwork, a still more sophisticated development, will be considered in our fourth chapter.

In Regency and Victorian times there was a revived interest in flint, particularly along the Sussex coast. The source of supply, again, was the sea-shore. There were so many that it was possible to pick out large numbers of smooth, ovoid-shaped flints of very much the same size. They could then be carefully coursed in a much more orderly fashion than usual. Towns like Brighton (33) and Shoreham can show many examples. In the house illustrated, the window-frames and quoins are of brick, whitened: this was

34 (below) The Gatehouse, Shute Barton, near Axminster, Devon

35 (right) Shute Barton: chert and greensand

36 (far right) The Grammar School, Chard, Somerset

the normal practice here. Sometimes a boldly contrasting colour effect was obtained by tarring the flints.

The Victorians were responsible for some excellent flint buildings, which included country railway stations, few of which, alas, are any longer in operation. And even today, especially in Norfolk, flint-faced buildings still go up here and there. A notable example is the church at Bawdeswell, rebuilt in 1953–55 after bombing: the architect was J. Fletcher Watson of Norwich. This charming building is mainly faced with uncut water-worn egg-shaped flints of various colours (principally white, grey-blue and light brown), uniform in size and carefully laid, in herring-bone fashion, with quite regular courses. The flints all came from a pit about ten miles away. Most of the Norfolk builders employ craftsmen with a good understanding of flint. More use could be made of it.

CHERT

Not many people would seem to know about chert, which is understandable, since its use for building, although widely distributed, has always been on a small scale. So first, what exactly is it? It is properly defined as a

siliceous microcrystalline substance occurring in nodules, or sometimes in narrow beds of its own, in almost any sedimentary rock other than chalk: in the Chalk this material is flint. Chert is therefore rather similar to flint: the nodules are all silica, and extremely hard. They tend to be somewhat larger than flints but, like them, brittle.

The best area in which to see chert is around Axminster, Colyton and Chard: where Devon, Somerset and a corner of Dorset meet. Here it occurs in the Upper Greensand. The beautiful Elizabethan gatehouse of Shute Barton, near Axminster (**34**, **35**), is faced with a rough chequer of grey ashlar from the Upper Greensand and unworked chert. But a more striking example, also Elizabethan (1583), is the Old Grammar School at Chard (**36**), which was built as a private house and converted into a school in 1671. Here the dressings are of Ham Hill stone but otherwise the entire building is faced with chert, which was dug out of the hill at Combe St. Nicholas, a couple of miles to the north-west. Here, furthermore, the

37 The Grammar School, Chard: squared chert

lumps of chert have all been roughly squared (37), which must have been a most laborious undertaking. The analogy with knapped flints will be at once apparent, but the blocks are larger. Another notable example is the church at Colyton, where again the blocks of chert are roughly squared; some here are as much as 10 ins. long and others 5 ins. high, sizes never found in flint buildings. In both these instances the predominant colour is milky brown, with suggestions of amethyst, and some toffee brown; there is also something of the shiny, semi-transparent appearance of polished horn.

Along the northern fringes of the Weald chert occurs in the Lower Greensand and can be found in buildings at Westerham, Ide Hill and elsewhere. At Richmond in North Yorkshire it comes from the Carboniferous limestone, and many lumps of it are incorporated into walls of limestone rubble. There is also one house, 15 Bridge St., which is mainly built of it.

At Portland the chert occurs in nodular bands immediately below the lowest stratum of the building stone. Some of the nodules here are large. Until recently this stone was ignored, but now it is being dug from the floors of abandoned quarries and taken to the crushing plant, to be converted into roadstone or concrete blocks. Chert from the Culm Measures is also being worked on a small scale in west Devon, mainly for walling.

This is a far from detailed survey, but will have given, it is hoped, some idea of the immense variety of building stones that our relatively small island has the good fortune to possess. It is sad that so many of them are no longer worked, but they have yielded an enviable inheritance.

3

METHODS OF WORK

FINDING THE STONE

We have painted a picture of a country exceptionally well endowed with building stones. Not all, of course, were equally good, but at many places where buildings were required there was stone, of one kind or another, on the site or not far away.

Before the arrival of the Normans little of this stone was used, because England was also abundantly, indeed in some parts superabundantly, supplied with timber, and wood could be worked much more easily. Moreover, a great deal of this stone needed finding, and when found required tools to get it out and to work it.

The most obvious exposures were along the coasts and on the flanks of some of the deeper river valleys. Where the exposed stone was comparatively soft, like chalk or some of the sandstones, it would no doubt have been possible for our ancestors to have prised out such small quantities as they might have required; but just because these stones were soft, no evidence has survived.

More readily accessible were the stones to be found lying around on the surface of the land, particularly on exposed hill-tops; and also in the beds of streams. These stones were of the most diverse geological origin and varied tremendously in size. Some were large and heavy, like those great boulders of sandstone known as sarsens (**38**), referred to in the previous chapter (cf. p. 36). Because their swelling and often roughly rounded shapes were thought to recall flocks of resting sheep, people often called them grey wethers. A profuse assembly can still be seen in the park of Ashdown House on the Berkshire Downs. Their removal and shaping must have presented formidable problems, yet our forebears succeeded in making use of them, as is attested by a number of their monuments, including Avebury and

38 Sarsen stone, near Aldbourne, Wiltshire

39 Stonehenge, Amesbury, Wiltshire

above all Stonehenge (**39**), where there can be little doubt that the monoliths, although undressed, were roughly shaped by the primitive method of beating the block with a rock or heavy stone until all the unwanted material had been bruised away. The lintels, dragged up sloping banks of earth which were afterwards removed, were held in position by mortices which fitted over tenons on top of the monoliths. These projecting pieces, one of which is well seen at the centre of the photograph, were worked from the solid block.

Comparable with the sarsen stones, although geologically entirely different, are the granite boulders of Cornwall, South Devon and (though much less important here) Cumbria and the Charnwood Forest region of

60

Leicestershire. In the far west, where, exceptionally for England, trees are relatively scarce, granite was in use for building even in the Bronze Age. But here too the stones, some quite small, others very large, were lying about on the hills and moors; hence the name by which they were known: moorstone. No quarrying was required, but shifting the stones must have been a daunting undertaking, and not until the late Middle Ages did Cornish masons learn how to dress their moorstone sufficiently well for rough church-building. In the Lake District, where much of the stone is of volcanic origin, the beds of the becks provided a useful source of supply. Up here the Ice Age only came to an end about ten thousand years ago, and waters from melting glaciers served to smooth the surfaces of what are often known as cobbles. In all these areas the lumps of stone are so difficult to break that most of them were used unbroken and, needless to say, uncoursed.

Here and there we may be surprised to encounter large boulders unrelated to the geology of the area in which they are found, as for example at Lanchester in County Durham, where the walls of the church, mainly of warm brown sandstone, incorporate a few blocks of granite, a stone which does not occur anywhere in this county. The agent was, again, glacial action, carrying these blocks down, aeons ago, from the Cheviots: the mediaeval builders, who were never prone to look a gift horse in the mouth, salvaged them.

Elsewhere builders were able to resort to what might almost be called natural quarries. The slate districts, which in England are, as we have observed, in much the same areas as the granite, provide many good examples of these. Since slate fractures very easily, below every exposed rock-face large quantities could be found lying about as scree, and only waiting to be collected. It could be used both for walling and for roofs, even though it could only be very roughly dressed.

In the chalk areas of the South-East small, although unaccommodating, stones were abundantly available in the form of flint. Much of it lay about on the surface of the land, to be gathered up for the asking, but flints were also mined, notably at Grimes Graves near Thetford in Norfolk, even in Neolithic times. They were not wanted then for building, but for tools and for weapons. How the early people located these deposits, in the chalk which lies under the sands of Breckland, is as yet unexplained.

Another good place for finding flints, as already indicated, was the sea-shore, at places where chalk cliffs drop into the sea. The beaches yielded other stones too, often much larger than flints, such as the boulders of

40 St. Bartholomew, Great
Gransden, Huntingdonshire (now
Cambridgeshire): cobbles

Holderness or the 'cobble-ducks' of Cumbria. Cobble facing is not
constructional but merely an external surface for walls made of some other
material such as chalk (40).

From the Roman period onwards, deep wells were sunk to obtain
drinking water at places where no spring water was available. These wells
served as excellent trial holes, for in stone country their depth might be as
much as sixty feet or more. To reach the water every stratum through
which they passed was revealed; this was therefore another way of locating
workable stone. The sinking of wells manually continued even into the
present century; it was only in the nineteen-twenties that machine boring
became general, and piped water mains commonplace. Today special
machine-driven bore holes have enabled us to learn a great deal more about
the character of underground stone strata.

SELECTING THE STONE

In the remote past it is probable that little thought was given to choosing
the best stone. The structures required were very simple, and men just
used whatever was to hand. Having been exposed to the weather through
countless ages, all the visible stone lying on the surface of the land, on hill-
tops and in rocky outcrops, and in the beds of streams, would be in a state of
at least partial disintegration, but it was the obvious choice.

When stone is excavated from quarries deep below the ground,
however, problems arise immediately, once it is on the surface, for by no

means all natural stone will stand long exposure to the elements. In many quarries every bed (or layer) of stone will be of good durable quality, but elsewhere whilst some beds are excellent others are trash. How could the early quarrymen, masons and builders tell the difference? The broad answer is that they could not, because they had no scientific means of testing; they could only draw on their knowledge and practical experience, and observe how the stone they selected stood the test of time. If a stone was not durable, it would usually fail after the first few winters, so would not be used again. But mistakes were continually made, some of which were later to prove highly expensive. A glaring example was at Oxford. There was plenty of stone at Headington, only two miles up the hill from Magdalen Bridge, and more at Wheatley, three miles beyond. The mediaeval Oxford builders naturally used it; it was the principal source of their walling stone. But they only quarried the high-class material known here as hardstone, which could be squared and coursed in sizeable blocks but only with difficulty ashlared. For their freestone they went much farther afield, to Taynton near Burford, which involved a river journey by barge, at least from Eynsham. In this they showed much better judgment than the builders of Stuart and Georgian times, who drew heavily on the deeper beds which the mediaeval masons had carefully avoided. They failed miserably, and since the last war millions of pounds have had to be expended on replacing them. Another instance is Warwick, where the use of indifferent local sandstone has meant that nearly every Georgian building faced with it has in recent years had to have its stonework partly or wholly renewed.

The quality of stone cannot be judged merely by looking at it; inspection needs to be supported by great skill, long experience, and perhaps also a flair for the task. By observing the buildings standing around them, the old master-masons arrived at a deep understanding of the stones in their own localities. In the quarries, owing to the penetration of acidified ground water and frost, there is generally some indifferent stone near the top of the deposit and above the good stone; because the lower beds are too deep to be affected by the weather, they are usually better. But not always; there are many complexities and exceptions. A single quarry, like Portland or Ancaster, may well produce three or more varieties of stone, each of which has its own particular character and uses. Although the building stones of this country fall into well-known groups, in almost every one there are great variations.

A widespread fallacy which needs to be corrected is that the harder stones are necessarily the most durable. This is not so. Many hard stones are good, yet the records of others have been decidedly poor. Some softer stones are very durable while others are not; such are the complexities of untamable nature! Among the limestones, a stone which has an open texture will often be more resistant to frost damage than one of finer grain because when water is absorbed it will be able to dry out again more quickly through the cavities. On the other hand, a fine-grained, dense, evenly textured stone without fossil fragments, or one which is full of detritus, may not be so reliable, because in following the natural process of surface hardening common to most sedimentary rocks it can develop an almost impervious skin which prevents the stone from 'breathing'. Thereby moisture may accumulate behind the hardened surface, leaving the stone to meet the onslaught of severe frosts in a state of saturation. This can often cause damage, because the smaller pore spaces can be more easily forced open by the expansion of freezing moisture. Under these conditions even a good variety of stone, which has stood for many years and given no previous trouble, may suddenly fail.

Building stones are not usually damaged by either saturation or frost when these occur separately; it is when the two are combined that the troubles are likely to arise. And not even the best stone can be expected to stand up to years of neglect resulting from failure to devote proper attention to the repair of roofs, gutters, and down-pipes.

QUARRYING AND LIFTING THE STONE

What we now know as quarrying could scarcely have been undertaken before the advent of iron for tool-making, which in England is believed to have been about the sixth century B.C. The provenance of the first imported iron is not known for certain, but it was probably either Spain or central Europe. With charcoal as their fuel, the Celts gradually learned how to hammer, forge and temper the iron into a simple kind of carbon steel.

It was the Romans who first mined iron in this country, and they were also the first people to engage in large-scale English quarrying. On the continent of Europe they had had great experience both as quarrymen and as masonry builders, and with the conquest of England considerable quantities of stone were needed here too, both for building and for road-making. The native Britons supplied the labour force. Large blocks were wanted for the most important buildings, and also for bridges.

Locating these large blocks was not a difficult problem. In some places stone of this kind has been laid down by nature in very deep beds or strata: limestones can be as much as five feet in bed thickness, and sandstones much more than that. It was therefore always necessary to cut the stone as it lay in the quarry. There are said to be at least a dozen methods of doing this, some best suited to the hard stones, others to the softer varieties. The Romans employed a tool known as the *jadd*, jadd pick or racer (**41**), which is still occasionally used in some of our quarries. The late-twelfth century panel of stained glass in the west window of Canterbury Cathedral, showing Adam delving, gives a good idea of it. It is somewhat akin to a pick-axe or cross-mattock, with a cutting edge about $1\frac{1}{4}$ in. or $1\frac{1}{2}$ in wide that required frequent sharpening. With this tool a two inch groove would be chopped right through the block of stone. The process was extremely slow, and wasteful of the material.

The Anglo-Saxons made comparatively small use of building stone, but with the advent of the Normans the demand rapidly increased. But it gradually came to be realised that it was not necessary to chop right through the block. Instead, a number of vee-shaped slots were made along the line of the cut. These were chopped out, again with a jadd, to a depth of about 5 ins., and into each was inserted a pair of steel slats and a wedge, or plug, also of steel. Then, using a sledge-hammer, the block of stone could be split. This was the forerunner of the well known *plug and feathers* method, which is still in use today.

The feathers are a pair of steel plates of half-rounded section; the plug is a steel wedge which is driven down between them (**41**). The object of having the feathers is to distribute the pressure as evenly as possible and so prevent the stone from being bruised. The first stage is to drill the

41 Quarrymens' Tools

1 *Frig Bob Handsaw*
2 *Set of Plugs and Feathers*
3 *Walling Hammer (Northamptonshire)*
4 *Jadd, Jadd Pick or Racer*

42 Quarrying limestone at Weldon,
Northamptonshire

holes for them, about an inch in diameter and at intervals of from six to
twelve inches apart, along the line of the proposed cut. This used to be done
with *jumpers* or jumping bars, which were about an inch in diameter and
had a fan-shaped cutting edge. They were operated over the position
required for each hole by a laborious process of continuous lifting,
dropping and turning. The holes were kept filled with water to enable the
'scarf' (loose chippings and dust) to float up and out. The invention, early in
the present century, of the pneumatic rock drill was a great boon to
quarrymen for this as for so many other tasks. Pneumatic drills and jack-
hammers are connected by pressure hoses to power-driven compressors,
which usually have diesel or petrol engines. These are now standard
equipment in almost every working quarry. Plate **42** shows holes being
made with a pneumatic rock drill in the quarry at Weldon.

The plug and feathers are then inserted into the drill-hole, which can be
as much as 3 ft. deep or even more, and driven down with the help of a
pneumatic or sledge hammer. The stone will then fracture along the
required line. The half-holes, visible in profusion not only on the face of the
stone that is left (**42, 43**) but on that of every block which has been quarried,
are an infallible indication of the bedding plane, because they always run at
right angles to it.

The softer sedimentary rocks, and even those of medium hardness, could
also sometimes be sawn *in situ*. Until about fifty years ago the favourite
implement was a toothed saw known as a *frig-bob* (**41**). Although quite
heavy, it could be operated by one quarryman, often with water to clear
away the sawdust from the cuts.

Hard stones like granite have always presented greater problems for the
quarrymen. During the nineteenth century a Belgian engineer invented the
helicoidal cutting wire, operated with abrasive grit and water. This proved
of great assistance in the cutting of marble, slate-stones, and sometimes also

of granite, at the quarries.

The early granite quarrymen could only make use of natural fractures in the rock and their expert knowledge of the cleavage. Then came the introduction of gunpowder. This could not be made without saltpetre (nitrate of potash), which had to be imported, and its manufacture in England hardly began before the reign of Elizabeth I. What is known in the trade as black powder came to be extensively used, but blasting proved extremely wasteful of the stone. Today the most favoured implement in the granite quarries is the thermic lance, which will be described in Chapter 10. This is a type of flame gun which uses a mixture of oxygen and paraffin: the hardest rock can be severed with little damage or waste. The resulting textured surface is sometimes left as a decorative finish, which many people now regard as aesthetically preferable to highly polished granite.

Once the blocks of stone are detached, the next problem is how to lift them out of the quarry. The ancient peoples solved this in various ways, based on manpower (including slave labour), animal power, rollers, levers and other devices, all relatively simple. The fact that, to avoid cutting, many of the earliest buildings were erected with very large quarry blocks made their tasks all the greater. Few of these blocks weigh less than a ton and three tons is not uncommon, while exceptional blocks quarried for special purposes can weigh up to six tons.

By the Middle Ages, the practice of cutting the large blocks into more manageable units before they left the quarry floor became widespread. Even so, worked stones ready for 'fixing' as parts of columns, cornices, door and window heads and other architectural details will often weigh half a ton or more. So the evolution of some sort of crane became essential. Lifting gear was needed not only at the quarries but also on the building sites, and many of the appliances now to be described were common to both.

A Perspective View of the Centering of Waterloo Bridge

The simplest, and probably the earliest, are what are known as *sheer legs*. These comprised three long and strong wooden poles, erected into a tripod over the stone and lashed together at the top with a hemp rope. Below the lashing point lifting tackle would be attached; this consisted of ropes running over pulley wheels and carrying a lifting hook for the stone. Three sets of sheer legs can be seen in the engraving (**44**). With stronger ropes and larger pulleys, weights of up to about a ton of stone at a time could be lifted in this way, but only vertically: the lateral movement was limited to a foot or two. Equipment of this kind is nevertheless still occasionally used; sheer legs are very simple to erect and easy to transport.

Another very simple device was the *windlass*. This was in essence no more than a wooden cylinder mounted into a frame, round which the rope was wound. There were usually two handles, but never any gearing nor safety ratchets; some later examples did have brakes. By this method two men might lift up to about three hundredweight. Later, brakes and ratchets were introduced and the windlass became safer to use.

The next development was very interesting. In order to be able to raise heavier weights to greater heights, the windlass was provided with a large treadwheel; it was indeed an extension of the wheel's axle, originally shaped from a single trunk of oak. For lifting water and for other purposes, animals could be used inside the wheel, as can still be seen at Carisbrooke Castle, but for the raising of stone animals were not practicable, because of the lack of precise control. With two men inside the wheel, no such difficulties arose. Very few of these treadwheels have survived: none, in fact, that has not been extensively repaired. But remarkable examples can still be seen high up in the towers of Canterbury and Salisbury Cathedrals, Beverley Minster and the church of St. James at Louth. The Beverley wheel, which is nearly 15 ft. in diameter, was still in use until as recently as 1977: only then was it replaced by an electric hoist. At Louth the wheel, known locally as the Wild Mare, is also in good repair; the windlass is about eighteen inches in diameter. It is only the rope, $1\frac{1}{2}$ins. thick, which is no longer safe to use, and this could easily be renewed.

In the course of time the windlass was succeeded by the *winch*. The essential differences are that winches were made of cast and wrought iron and are now all steel, and that every winch incorporated gear wheels, a brake and a safety ratchet. The old hemp ropes of the windlass usually gave place to steel wire cables: occasionally to iron chains. All these rendered it possible to lift much heavier weights with greater safety. But, needless to say, those who had to face the problem of raising heavy worked stones to the great heights of some of the mediaeval cathedrals did not have these advantages.

The first cranes probably appeared in the fifteenth century, and sometimes required treadwheels for their operation. But they were from the outset partly of iron, wrought by the blacksmiths. Presently the *jib crane* appeared. A primitive one can be seen, perched aloft, in the engraving of Rennie's Waterloo Bridge in London under construction (**44**). This bridge was built between 1811 and 1817. Attached to the crane are cast iron toothed gear wheels. The name of the crane had a nautical derivation. Those who sail will know that the jib is the small triangular foresail which in operation swings from one side to the other as needed, and this is exactly what the arm of this type of crane does. It is designed to be able to lift a large block of stone from one position, swinging round and lowering it at any chosen place within its radius. Technically this marked a great advance. Jib cranes with cast iron gear wheels were still in use during the early years of the present century. Now, of course, all cranes are made of steel, and are power driven.

From about the middle of the nineteenth century jib cranes were increasingly operated by steam power. Steam has now been superseded wherever possible by electric power. But at quarries where electic power lines are not available, the powerful jib cranes are operated by diesel engines or compressed air motors.

Until comparatively recently cranes were always static. At a quarry the crane would be fixed in a place close to the working face, and as operations proceeded it had from time to time to be shifted, which was often difficult and time-consuming. So the development of the mobile crane marks another advance. This is usually mounted on caterpillar tracks and, powered by a diesel engine, can be easily moved from one quarry site to another as required. It must, however, be added that a mobile crane cannot lift such heavy weights as some of the more powerful static cranes.

At the quarry the crane will be employed in the first instance to lift the stone only as far as the working floor, which will be well below the surface of the surrounding land. Here it is scappled (rough-dressed) into rectangular blocks, generally with pneumatic jack-hammers but still, at some quarries, with the old-time jadds and other similar tools. Only then is it ready to go off to the masonry yards and building sites.

In our own time mechanization has simplified out of all measure the tasks of those whose work is to quarry and handle stone. A familiar sight on high rise buildings is now the *tower crane*, which is mainly used for other building construction but which may sometimes hoist stones too, on pallets, to near their fixing position. Tower cranes cannot be operated with sufficient precision for the actual fixing; this is done with smaller equipment operated by the masons themselves.

Another quite different type of lifting equipment much used today is the *platform hoist*. This is really a lift fixed alongside the scaffolding for hoisting stones from the ground up to the fixer masons operating at various levels as the work proceeds. Some of the larger platform hoists can lift a whole pallet of worked stone at one time, which reduces handling and the consequent risks of damage.

In modern masonry yards the jib crane is still an essential piece of equipment. Some of the larger yards also have travelling *gantries*. These powerful machines consist of frames of steel mounted on elevated rail tracks some distance apart, which can also move laterally over the whole area enclosed within the elevated rails. Fitted with electric lifting gear, these machines can load and unload the lorries, stock-pile the stone quarry blocks, and move them as required to the various sawing machines and to the banker masons' workshops. Nowadays the masons, both in their workshops and on the building sites, frequently have the assistance of travelling electric hoists, also fitted to run on overhead rails.

TRANSPORTING THE STONE

If consideration is given to the quarries known to have been worked by the Romans, it will be found that most of them were situated close to their roads. The Clipsham quarry area in Rutland, for instance, is only about a mile to the east of Ermine Street, and a few years ago good evidence of Roman quarry workings for large blocks of stone was found there. Also close to Ermine Street were the quarries of Ancaster and Barnack, both believed to have been used by the Romans; the latter was only six miles distant from Durobrivae, today Castor, which was the site of a station of some importance. Corinium, today Cirencester, a major centre, both civil and military, during the four centuries of the Roman Occupation, was built of Cotswold stone. It was at the point of intersection between the other Ermine Street, running from Winchester to Gloucester, and the Fosse Way, and several of the Cotswold quarries were contiguous with the latter.

Short hauls, both in Roman times and in the Middle Ages, were made by loading the stone on to very strong and specially built low wagons or sledges, usually drawn by teams of horses. But for very heavy loads, requiring a number of animals, oxen were preferred, because of the steadiness of their pulling power and their superior team-work. More than two pairs of horses were much more difficult to control, for they tend not to heave together and there can be a certain jerkiness about their action which may break the gear or harness, whereas teams of no fewer than six pairs of oxen were not uncommon.

For longer distances, before the days of mechanical transport, access to navigable water was essential. Flat-bottomed boats which could operate in shallow water were indispensable, and vast quantities of building stone were carried in this fashion, sometimes over very long distances, especially to East Anglia, where there was practically no durable block stone. Records are unfortunately scarce, but there was absolutely no other way in which the stone for the great cathedrals, abbeys and churches of Fenland could have been transported to the building sites. Use was made of the natural rivers wherever they existed – Barnack quarry, for instance, as well as being near Ermine Street, was still closer to the Welland and not very far from the Nene – and there were also a certain number of canals specially cut, of which the best known are in Lincolnshire: Car Dyke and Foss Dyke, dug out by the Romans. The former was navigable well into the mediaeval period; the latter is still in use.

Until the Dutch irrigation engineer, Cornelius Vermuyden, undertook the drainage of the Fens in the 1620s, this region was dotted with meres and broads; one of the objects of the early canals, called in this region 'lodes' was to link these meres into a continuous waterway. At least one of them continues to exist in Huntingdonshire (now called Cambridgeshire): this is still known as Monks' Lode, and its purpose was to provide access from Whittlesey Mere for craft carrying stone to the site of the Cistercian Abbey of Sawtrey.* It ran, over land only just above sea level, for a distance of about three miles.

Many records could be cited of the transport of stone along the English rivers, usually downstream. Even quite small rivers, like the Glen, a tributary of the Welland, which happens to flow within a few miles of Holywell and Clipsham, were brought into service: records exist of its use for the movement of stone in the fourteenth century. On the Welland itself the annual value of the limestone being carried by barge during the middle years of the nineteenth century averaged fully £10,000 a year. But the advent of the railways wrought great changes, while today the all-pervasive motor lorry holds the field. Even Portland stone, quarried just above the sea, is now all transported by road to destinations in England, for only by motor vehicles can the stone be brought right to the required site. At Portland there used to be at least a dozen quays on the east side of the peninsula, from which the stone was shipped. Now there is but one, inside the Harbour, and it is only used for the shipment of Portland stone abroad.

THE STONEMASONS

The key figure in any building enterprise was for many centuries the master-mason. The master-masons were the chief organizers and supervisors of the works, taking instructions from their clients, and often acting as architects before architecture became a separate profession. They were under the direct control of the Crown, high dignitaries of the Church, heads of noble families, city authorities, heads of colleges, or whoever the clients might be, working in consultation throughout, making payments and keeping accounts. In baronial times they sat at the high table above the salt, and wore a distinguishing robe.

Among the many duties of the master-mason none was more

*Sawtrey Abbey was also close to Ermine Street. Nothing now survives except excavated foundations.

important than the supervision of the quarrying of the stone or of its purchase if already quarried. Then he had to select the blocks and arrange for their transportation to the building site. He was also responsible for preparing the full-scale layouts (drawings) which were needed for all the special details of a building. Today this is the task of the masonry draughtsmen, and it requires great skill and experience. Full-sized working drawings, known in the building trade as 'setting-out', are required by every man who has to cut the stone, whether by hand or machine. Nowadays these drawings are prepared on very large sheets of paper laid out on horizontal drawing-boards, one of which can easily measure 20 ft. × 15 ft. and fill a room. But in the Middle Ages this work was done on whitewashed floors, either in or near the workshops or within the building itself. A few, a very few, still survive; one can be seen on the floor above the north porch of Wells Cathedral, and another is over the passage leading to the Chapter House at York Minster.

When the blocks of stone reach the stockyards of the masonry works, they are selected, usually today by the yard foreman, to suit the particular pieces of work for which they are required. Dimensions are now a very important factor. There are also, at this stage, final checks for quality, colour and texture.

The blocks then have to be sawn. This is now done by machine, and of the remarkable mechanical saws which have become available in recent years there will be more to say in our final chapter. In the past, however, there were only hand-saws. In most quarries and masons' yards the favourites were the *fish-bellies*, large saws operated by stone-sawyers working in pairs. These saws were about six or seven feet long, and, as their name implies, the lower cutting edge had a pronounced downward curvature, which carried teeth cut at about two to the inch. Similar saws with a straight cutting edge were also used. There was a special skill in marking out the blocks so that the resultant cuts were not twisted. For the smaller cuts, as at the quarries, a *frig-bob* (see p. 66) saw was used. This was six feet long and one foot wide, usually with two or three teeth to the inch. Sometimes a six or seven foot saw-blade would be mounted in a heavy wooden frame, which had guides and supports enabling the cutting to be done more rapidly.

The masons were always trying to devise ways of economising in time and labour. But, until the advent of steam power, building stone had to be worked entirely by hand. The tasks of cutting, dressing and carving involved a formidable amount of labour and application. Few of the exposed stones in, say, one of the great mediaeval cathedrals would have required less than a whole day's effort to prepare; many would have needed a great deal more time than that.

The weight of the blocks was always a very difficult problem. Quite recently, at Portland, we saw a block measuring about 9 ft. × 4 ft. × 4 ft. This could weigh eight or even ten tons. Ten ton blocks are now rare, but those weighing six tons are not uncommon. So, until the early years of the present century, in order to reduce their weight and simplify their handling, the usual practice was to saw these very large blocks at the quarries. At a few quarries this is still the usual practice. But with modern machinery, the larger the block the better: handling is thereby accelerated, and waste much reduced. Thus, in this respect also, modern practices have changed dramatically.

THE BANKER MASONS

Experienced masons can often work effectively in every branch of the stone trade, although each has its own distinctive skills. But the tendency today, here and elsewhere, is towards specialization.

First come the banker masons, as important today as ever they were. The word was originally written 'bancr', and is derived from the French word *banc*, meaning a bench. The term banker mason has been employed ever since the Norman Conquest to distinguish the craftsmen who shape the stones on their bench from those in other branches of their trade. Today machines have rendered it possible to dispense with much of the 'donkey work' of the past, but the banker mason, whose concern is with the most elaborate and complicated aspects of stone-cutting, still has to do much of his work by hand processes.

For him the work starts when a piece of stone, accurately sawn to prescribed dimensions, and known as a *scant*, is brought to his bench. It will be accompanied by the necessary moulds, job cards, perhaps a perspective sketch, and sometimes other instructions, always including the relevant code number, which he must cut into the top surface – or, as he would say, bed (see Glossary) – of the stone. Before the days of specialization he would have had himself to know how to handle the heavy quarry blocks, and with very simple tackle; in the smaller yards he would also have had to supervise the hand sawing, and sometimes even to do it himself. But these tasks now fall to others. On the other hand the moulds – which are sometimes known as

74

templates – remain for him indispensable. They are full-sized shapes of mouldings, sections, tracery and other details, which are now usually made of zinc by the masonry draughtsman or his assistant. Formerly the material was thin wood and it was the carpenters who produced them. A large collection is preserved at York Minster.

Most stonemasons, and banker masons in particular, are quiet and thoughtful men, absorbed in their work. Some of the old banker masons were heard to affirm that for them there were only three things that mattered: their mates, the quality of the work, and the nature of the stone. Unless the stone was 'right' (by which they meant not too difficult to cut), they would not willingly stay very long on the job. But if it was, some masons could show a real sense of dedication. That no doubt is what Wren felt about Christopher Kempster of Burford, who worked on St. Paul's. 'He is very careful in his work to keep true to my design', wrote the great architect. 'I can rely on him, and recommend him to your Lordships; I am confident he will promise little to himself for he may have the honour of the worke'. In our century it is recorded that a distinguished visitor was going round the masons' yard of the Anglican Cathedral at Liverpool. He asked several men in turn the same simple question: What are you doing? The first man said 'Well, I am a stonemason who has been working here now for seven years, and as they pay me 10p. over the hourly rate, with some overtime and bonus, I reckon I am really doing quite well'. The second mason replied, 'I am dressing this piece of Woolton sandstone, and have spent more than a day on it already; when it is finished it will form a section of the window tracery'. The third man was less specific. He simply answered, 'I am helping to build Liverpool Cathedral, and am proud to think that it will live long after me'.

THE FIXER MASONS

In old accounts the masons who fixed the stone are sometimes described as setters or layers, whereas the banker masons were hewers.

The fixer masons are concerned with the actual placing of the stones on the building. They work in teams, with additional help to get the stones up from the ground, and to assist in setting the very heavy ones.

On many buildings, however – indeed, on virtually all the best – almost every stone differs in dimensions and shape, and often also in detail. When there are literally thousands of them, how, it will be asked, is it possible

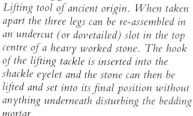

Three-legged Lewis
Lifting tool of ancient origin. When taken apart the three legs can be re-assembled in an undercut (or dovetailed) slot in the top centre of a heavy worked stone. The hook of the lifting tackle is inserted into the shackle eyelet and the stone can then be lifted and set into its final position without anything underneath disturbing the bedding mortar.

quickly to identify each one as it is needed by the fixers, and to bring it to the exact place on the building where it must be set? The answer is: by the most elaborate code-marking. This starts with the masonry draughtsman, who must have large scale drawings of every elevation of the building. On these, every stone will be indicated with a code number, which will give the name or location of the building, the particular elevation, the course, and the position of the stone in that course. For instance, WANE D26 could mean Westminster Abbey, north elevation, and no. 26 in the fourth course. (To avoid confusion, the courses are indicated not by numerals but by letters of the alphabet). These code marks, like the true masons' marks, are cut into the top surface of each stone: often Roman numerals are used. The fixer masons need to have copies of all these drawings, with the code numbers clearly indicated.

Most of the stones in structural masonry are much too heavy for the men to lift unaided. In order to raise them from the ground, recourse is had to cranes and strong slings. But it is also necessary to have some means of placing them on to their bed on the wall, without any part of the gear passing underneath. This is done with various kinds of *lewis*. The best-known is the three-legged lewis, which when in use is fixed into a special dovetailed mortice cut into the top centre of the block of stone to be hoisted, leaving the bottom bed and sides clear. This mortice may be up to four inches deep according to the weight of the block. The lewis was a very early invention: its special mortices are often found in Roman masonry. Formerly iron, this ingenious device is now made of steel. It has three main parts (*see illustration*), which, when assembled, fit so tightly into the mortice that they will sustain the weight of the stone without pulling out.

But what if the top surface of the block and all four sides need to be exposed? This can happen. What then? No problem is too teasing for the ingenuity of the masons. What they may do in a case like this is to lift the block with hoist and sling and then lower it on to a suitable number of ordinary cubes of sugar! These offer temporary support while the sling is pulled out. Then, with hot water, the sugar is melted so that the stone can settle down into its proper place. Often, in such cases, a permanent seating is provided by placing pads or strips of sheet lead, all of uniform thickness, under the heavy stone; these are of course kept well back from the corners and arrises.

76

45 and 46 Haigh Hall, near Wigan, Lancashire; with (right) detail of ashlar masonry

Skilful jointing plays a vital part in a building's aesthetic success. The jointing of good ashlar masonry is seldom more than $\frac{1}{8}$ in. thick and sometimes even less, so the joints are made 'flush' and pointing, as the term is generally understood, is unnecessary. A common practice for the best work is to set the stones on very thin beds of putty mortar. The vertical joints – the horizontals are known as bed joints and the verticals as perpends – are then 'grouted' (using liquid mortar) with the aid of 'joggles'. These are vee-shaped grooves cut into the meeting surfaces of the stones to ensure the free passage of thin mortar grout into these joints. All this is also the responsibility of the fixer masons.

There are some superb examples of jointing in the fossil-free limestone of Ketton. In the Coal Measures sandstone from Appley Bridge a very fine specimen can be seen at Haigh Hall, near Wigan (45, 46). So true is the cutting of the stone that there would appear to be no mortar at all here: in fact it is likely that a very soft mortar, made from a mixture of putty-lime and fine stone dust with a lot of water, was used as a bedding. Such cutting would not be difficult today, using machines, but by hand, in this hard stone, it was a very skilful achievement. Another remarkable feature of this masonry is that there are no joints at the angles: every angle stone was cut to turn the corner in a single piece. This is rare indeed. Yet artistically the Haigh Hall stonework leaves something to be desired; the fault is that it was cut to a uniform size throughout.

Where some additional security has been needed, the fixer masons have always resorted to the use of cramps and dowels. On the higher parts of Gothic buildings, in particular, such additional safeguards are a *sine qua non*. Finials, pinnacles and above all the tops of church spires have to withstand severe stresses from wind and weather, and so do projecting cornices (which may oversail the wall face by as much as three feet), parapets, copings and heavy chimney caps. It is also sometimes necessary to prevent movement between one stone and its neighbours in columns, arches (especially flat arches, or where there are heavy keystones), window tracery and vaulting. And, commonest of all today, there is the problem of tying back the thin facings known as cladding on to cores of rough stone, brick or concrete.

Cramps are bars of metal with bent ends, which can be bedded into two adjacent pieces of masonry. They always used to be made of wrought iron, which in the course of time has proved disastrous. For iron rusts right through its thickness and in so doing may expand to as much as twice its original volume. This places a strain on the stone which gradually becomes intolerable: the blocks crack, split and spall, and sometimes quite large pieces are displaced and fall out. Thus, instead of increasing security, iron cramps may come to constitute its greatest danger. During the present century, millions of pounds have had to be spent on repairing the damage caused by the over-enthusiastic use of wrought iron cramps in the eighteenth and nineteenth centuries on masonry which is otherwise excellent.

Dowels are headless pins or bolts which are also made to fit into holes made in contiguous blocks. The ancient Greeks, who used very little and wherever possible no mortar, either for wall facings or in fitting together the drums of their columns, reduced the dangers of rust by grouting their cramps and their dowels with molten lead, which also served to prevent movement between the stones.

Mediaeval builders did this too: but in time rusty iron will even break through the lead. Later builders usually omitted this precaution.

So wrought iron is now absolutely taboo. Cramps and dowels must be made of metals that are neither corrosive, expansive, staining nor prone to rust. The usual ones are Delta metal (a non-expansive, non-corroding alloy), phosphor bronze, stainless steel and, in some situations, galvanized mild steel. Because of the risk of staining, copper, which in other respects is also appropriate, can only be used in positions well away from the facing.

Nowadays, for attaching cladding to the structural frame of a building, cramps and dowels have to some extent been superseded by masonry fixings or holdfasts. These are specially made devices, usually of galvanized steel but sometimes of stainless steel or phosphor bronze. Some of the many variants incorporate cramps and dowels. Large panels of stone used as cladding may require as many as four or more holdfasts each; thus the total number on a tall building can be enormous. In addition, the panels will need to be supported at intervals by load-bearing corbel plates.

For dowels pieces of sawn slate up to about an inch square are very suitable too. Where bent forms are required, as with cramps and holdfasts, slate cannot of course be employed, but it is much in favour for joining sections of coping in damp situations and for the joints in window tracery. Oak dowels about two inches long were also occasionally employed.

THE WALLING MASONS

In the last two sections our concern has been with freestone, the material quarried in large blocks which can be sawn and worked freely with chisels: most of the freestones are limestones or sandstones of one kind or another. But a great number of natural rocks have been used for building which cannot qualify as freestone at all, because they are usually too hard and refractory to saw and work in the ways so far described.

These stones have to be rough-dressed with tools that vary considerably in different parts of the country, to suit the local materials and the practices of the local masons. But all are the responsibility of the walling masons, men who at various times and in different places have also been described as wallers, rough masons, hard hewers and dykers. They have to work in the most varied kinds of material but have nevertheless developed remarkable skills and techniques.

One of the best known of these walling stones, and certainly most loved, is the coursed rubble limestone of the Cotswolds. But much of the material from the limestone belt, all the way from Dorset to North Yorkshire, is of a similar type. Laid down by nature in shallow, flat beds, yielding course heights – where it is coursed at all – of only between 2 ins. and 5 ins., it can be much harder than the freestone. Although seldom more than two feet across when quarried, the stones vary considerably, and heavy sledge hammers have to be used on some of them to reduce them to the sizes required. The further preparation is known as hammer-dressing, and when the stone is ready for use it is often described by the masons as having been

47 Field barn, near Hawes,
Yorkshire

'knocked and chopped'. The walling masons use special walling hammers,
also stone hammers and stone axes, which have many regional and local
patterns. Many buildings in the stone areas, of which Poulton Manor (**60**) is
but one example, have freestone dressings, by which is meant such features
as the door and window frames, plinths, string-courses, quoins, cornices,
copings, parapets or balustrades and chimneys. This was the normal
traditional practice wherever freestone was available, and is aesthetically
very satisfying. The dressings are usually prepared at the masonry yard by
the banker masons.

The harder the stone, the more difficult is it to achieve regular coursing.
With the limestones, however hard, coursing is usually possible, but less
often with other varieties of hard stone. A field barn near Hawes in North
Yorkshire (**47**) provides a good illustration. The grand roof here is
gritstone, and the walling stone, laid without mortar, probably came out of
the same quarry. The walls to either side are wholly irregular, but for the
barn itself some attempt was made to shape and, especially at the angles, to
square the stones, and even to achieve very rough coursing. Another
feature, characteristic of the Pennine country, is the use of what are known
as *throughs*: large flat stones which are allowed to protrude beyond the wall-
face. There will be more to say about these in the section devoted to
dry-stone walling (pages 95–100).

Sometimes the walling masons resorted to what is known as *snecking* or *jumper-work*: the insertion here and there of large stone which jump two or three courses. It might happen that there were insufficient stones of the same height to run the full length of the wall; if so, a jumper-stone was the neatest looking way of altering the course level. That was the true reason for this practice; but fashion sometimes dictates nowadays that these larger stones shall be introduced simply to achieve what are felt to be interesting surface variations.

When Edward I's army marched into Scotland in 1301, they took twenty stonemasons with them, most of whom would have been wallers. Their function was to help breach and undermine the rough stone walls of the castles and other defences besieged, and to make them good again at the conclusion of each operation. There would also have been bridges to repair, in order that essential supplies could be brought up.

THE FLINT KNAPPERS

Reference has already been made to the strange character of flint as a building material. Very often, because of their intense hardness and intractability, flints were used as they were found, bedded in mortar (necessarily, in plenty of mortar) but unbroken.

Nevertheless, flints can be split open fairly easily if one knows how to do it, and this was the concern of the flint knappers. Each knapper, with a pad of leather strapped to his left leg above the knee, stood, and, holding the flint on the pad, struck it with his special hammer: and this is where the skill came in, for he had to judge and control the impact, to know precisely where and how to strike. It was not just a matter of breaking the flint; this had to be done in such a way that the required shape was attained. It may have looked simple, but only those with long experience could do it properly.

It has been said that there are thirty different ways of knapping and dressing flints; yet the technique is entirely different from that required for any other kind of stone. But it was known even in Neolithic times. The Neolithic knappers had no metal hammer, yet developed great skill simply by striking one flint against another. In this way they were able to produce well-shaped spear and arrow heads, axe heads and knives. However, as was observed earlier, the flint knappers of those days do not appear to have been interested in using flint for building. In fact, knapped flints play no part in

48 Lewes, Sussex: knapped flints

49 St. Mary, Glynde, Sussex:
knapped and squared flints

English architecture before the fourteenth century. From then on, however, examples abound (**48**); one of the earliest is the barbican of Lewes Castle. The ornamental use of these flints in combination with limestone will be described in the next chapter. In Sussex knapped flints, with their glassy surfaces which sparkle in sunlight, especially after a rainstorm, have sometimes been known as 'Sussex diamonds'. In East Anglia, even today, there are still at least four firms who are marketing large flints suitable for knapping.

In the most advanced kind of flint knapping, the flints are not only split open but also squared, a lovely refinement not often found before the eighteenth century (**49**), and occurring most frequently on or near the coast of Sussex and in East Anglia. The squaring was confined to the exposed face, on which, in the best work, there is scarcely any mortar in evidence. Behind, it is very different; the flints retain their often weird shapes and a great deal of mortar is needed to hold them in position. Sizes vary somewhat, but rectangles measuring about 4 ins. by 3 ins. are the most usual. Craftsmanship as fine as this demanded not only a high degree of skill but hard labour too, and more time. So this kind of knapping was always rather expensive. But it never fails to give pleasure.

THE APPRENTICE SYSTEM

The trade guilds were in origin mediaeval, most of them being Livery Companies of the City of London. The Worshipful Company of Masons was founded in 1492. The main intention of the group of master-masons who brought it into being was to promote the best customs of the trade, including apprenticeship.

The early apprentices were bound to their masters by indentures for a period of seven years, and sometimes still longer. Premiums had to be paid to the employer, which by 1850 could be as much as £50, a sizeable sum in those days. In some areas only the sons of masons would be accepted. If they were unable to pay the premium, the employer would generally agree to accept them on condition that they served the first two years of the apprenticeship without wages. This was not as bad as it sounds, for the apprentices never received more than a pittance in cash. But if they were working away from home they very often 'lived in' with the master-mason and his family on what were known as 'bread and tankard' terms, and were usually well looked after. There are even records of apprentices in

London complaining that they were too often being fed on salmon! (Incidentally, this shows what a much cleaner river the Thames was in those days.)

The first duty of every new apprentice was to act as beer boy at the mid-morning break and at meal times. He would have to be able clearly to identify each owner's can (and there might be many) and to wash them, before setting out for the nearest inn – which might be at some distance – to collect the beer. This was a highly unpopular job, not only because it took him away for considerable periods from his proper work, but also because he had to collect the beer money from the masons, who were often very reluctant payers, as they were nearly always hard up. In some places this practice was known as 'drumming up', and the young apprentices responsible were called 'monkeys'. That is why at least one public house patronised by quarrymen and stonemasons is known as 'The Drum and Monkey'. Today's young apprentices apply the same term, 'drumming-up', to the brewing of the ubiquitous tea.

There are now plenty of young men and some young women coming forward for apprenticeship in the stone industry: rather more, in fact, than it can absorb. The period of apprenticeship has been reduced to four years, with proper indentures as before, and there are obligations to attend suitable training courses. These are conducted at some of the Polytechnics and Colleges in the stone areas, and by the Orton Trust. They may be on a basis of one day a week for a period of years, or 'block release' courses from their employment for the period necessary. At the conclusion of this training and of their apprenticeship these young people can sit for a City and Guilds craft examination, which, if passed, will help them to obtain regular employment and future advancement. Premiums are now seldom required.

At modern masonry yards there are canteens or mess rooms where the men can have their meals in cleanliness and comfort. How different from the old days when the men had to eat 'on the job' with nothing but large round up-ended wooden mallets to serve as stools.

JOURNEYMAN MASONS AND OTHERS

At the end of their time, the general custom was for the apprentices to take to the road and find good work and experience elsewhere. Moving about the country from one job to another, they became known as journeyman masons, a term that was still in use up to the beginning of the present century. Several more years would pass before they were regarded as fully trained and experienced men, entitled to claim the full rates of pay. Only those who distinguished themselves by their skill and integrity could finally qualify as Master-Masons and Liverymen of the Worshipful Company. It is said that some of the better and more fortunate ones came back after their long travels to marry their former masters' daughters. Stone was in their blood.

There was a fine *camaraderie* in this trade. Because they could afford no other way, the journeyman masons, carrying their heavy tools, usually travelled on foot, even when the distance between one building and another was considerable. So, inevitably, money would often run out. When such a man arrived on a job in search of work but entirely without resources, it was at one time an established custom that, even if his services were not really needed, he would be engaged and paid for two weeks' work in order to help him on his way. Or, if there was no work at all for the new arrival, there would sometimes be a 'whip round' amongst the masons already on the job to collect a sum averaging one week's wages, which was presented to him.

In times when wages were very low and there was no such thing as a welfare state, a similarly humane collection would be made for the benefit of a man stricken down by illness or some other misfortune. And when an old mason retired or became unable any longer to work, his mates would make payments for his tools which far exceeded their real value.

Many of the old masons belonged to very inward-looking communities. Often they were totally uneducated, and in isolated places like Portland they had little contact with the outside world. It is on record that the time came when a parson from Dorchester felt that these men should be taught something about the Christian religion. They were not unwilling to listen to him. In due course he decided to hold a Holy Communion service. So into the church they filed, and at the appropriate moment the minister poured out some wine and handed it to the first communicant. Supposing that it was all for him, he lifted the cup, called out 'Your very good health, Vicar, coupled with the name of your good friend Mr. Jesus Christ!' – and drained it.

50 Tools for Banker Masons, Sculptors and Carvers

1 Large set square
2 Large beech mallet and smaller lignum vitae mallet
3 Pitching hammer
4 Lump hammer
5 Dummy
6 Dividers
7 French Drag
8 Applewood mallet
9 Small beech carver's mallet
10 & 11 Carvers' soft malleable iron hammers
12 Letter cutter's aluminium alloy dummy
13 Small set square
14 Pair of line pins with line attached
15 Tingle to work with last
16 Sculptor's and carver's chisels with mallet heads
17 Saw-toothed scriber
18 Coxcombs (small shaped drags)
19 Combined gauge and trammel
20 Scriber
21 Paring tool
22 Wide boaster with mallet head
23 Boaster with mallet head
24 & 25 Chisels with mallet heads
26 Claw tool with mallet head
27 Punch with hammer head
28 & 29 Wide and narrow pitching tools
30 Coping tool
31 Chisels and gouges with wooden handles
32 Drag
33 Three-legged Lewis
34 Pointing trowel
35 Jointing tool
36 Banker mason's pneumatic hammer with chisels
37 Set of shift stocks
38 Set of carving and lettering chisels with tungsten carbide tips
39 Set of Italian rifflers
40 Calipers
41 Fillet saw
42 Banker mason's handsaw
43 Flat and half round rasps

THE STONEMASON'S TOOLS

Every mason has a collection, and often a large collection, of tools (**50**), and an attempt will now be made to describe briefly what they are and how each tool is used. Every one has its function; that there are so many is indicative of the great variety of purposes which they have to serve.

The story starts with the introduction of iron into this country about the sixth century B.C. The first people to quarry and smelt English ironstone were the Romans, and remains of their simple furnaces have been found near Colsterworth in Lincolnshire. By heating and reheating it in charcoal fires, and repeatedly hammering it to drive out impurities, it was possible to turn it into 'tool steel', which is of a special grade. This is the material of which all the tools with cutting edges were made; the work of the

86

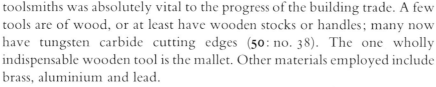

Pitcher
Mainly used for pitching off surplus stone round the edges of a rough block when hand preparing a worked surface on the block. The first tool to be used in the process. Also used for a similar purpose when trimming and straightening the edges of slabs, such as pavings.

Narrow Chisel
The second tool in the dressing process, used to work a true and narrow margin all round the face of the block. Also used for dressing narrow work.

Punch
Used for spalling off surplus stone when working down to a finished surface. The third tool in the process.

toolsmiths was absolutely vital to the progress of the building trade. A few tools are of wood, or at least have wooden stocks or handles; many now have tungsten carbide cutting edges (**50**: no. 38). The one wholly indispensable wooden tool is the mallet. Other materials employed include brass, aluminium and lead.

The commonest name for a stonemason's tool is a *chisel*, but it should be said that this is a generic term used to describe a whole range of edged tools. It should properly be employed only when the cutting edge is less than an inch. Tools are made in a great variety of sizes, edge widths, lengths and diameters; with curved cutting edges they are called gouges. For working the softer, finer-grained stones, many masons prefer a wooden handle because the softer material allows for a softer impact.

Let us first examine the old hand process of preparing a smooth ashlar face on a quite rough and irregular quarry block. Although now obsolete, thanks to the modern machine saws, most of what is finest in our heritage of stone buildings came into being in this way.

The first tools in the sequence were the *hammer* and the *pitcher*. They were used round the edges of the block to pitch off fairly large spalls of stone with the intention of achieving a nearly straight face-line. The pitcher has a blunt, almost square working edge and is not sharpened in the manner normally applicable to other cutting tools.

The mason then took a *mallet* and a *chisel*, with a steel cutting edge of perhaps $\frac{5}{8}$ in., and with these he worked a marginal draft all round the edges of the block. The handles of these chisels usually have a domed mallet head and are some seven or eight inches long.

Next came the *punch*, driven again by a hammer. A punch is a hammer-headed tool about six inches long with a cutting edge of no more than $\frac{1}{4}$ in.: sometimes only $\frac{1}{8}$ in. With this the mason would be able, quite quickly, to work off the surface stone, down to within about $\frac{3}{16}$ in. of the finished face. This was usually done diagonally. A similar tool much used by sculptors and carvers is known as a *point*.

Claw Tool
This is a Faulds Patent Claw Tool with a renewable and reversible bit. Earlier tools of this kind had the claws filed into the cutting edge of the tool before tempering.

Wide Chisel
The fifth tool in the process of dressing a stone face by hand. If chisels are over one inch in width they are called boasters.

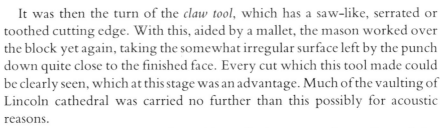

Sculptor's Point
Similar to a punch but has a sharp cutting point as its name implies. Mainly used by sculptors for roughing out irregular surfaces.

It was then the turn of the *claw tool*, which has a saw–like, serrated or toothed cutting edge. With this, aided by a mallet, the mason worked over the block yet again, taking the somewhat irregular surface left by the punch down quite close to the finished face. Every cut which this tool made could be clearly seen, which at this stage was an advantage. Much of the vaulting of Lincoln cathedral was carried no further than this possibly for acoustic reasons.

The final tools to be used would usually be, again, the mallet and the *boaster*, with which the mason worked over the surface left by the claw. A boaster is a special kind of chisel, which may be up to $2\frac{1}{2}$ ins. wide according to what is required in the finished work, and with boasters skilled craftsmen can produce a wide range of hand-tooled textures. An excellent nineteenth century instance, certainly introduced to give variety, can be seen on the ashlar bats at the Burghley Estate Office in Stamford (**65**). A much earlier example (late seventeenth century) occurs to either side of the window at Petworth (**157**). A good deal of masonry was left at this stage, especially when the stone was hard, and to get a smoother finish would have taken considerably more time. The intention was seldom purely decorative, but the outcome can be attractive. The wide tool marks are not arranged too regularly, and certainly with no mathematical precision.

Where an entirely smooth face was required, free from tool marks, the process differed in accordance with the hardness of the stone. On stones in the medium range of hardness, the mason used, and still uses, a *drag*. This is a steel plate, usually about 6 ins. wide, which has been provided with a

French Drag
Often described in the trade as a 'Frenchman'. Used on some of the French stones, as the name implies, and on some of the fine grained and softer English stones for working up to a smooth surface from rough tooling. Also made with much finer teeth at about twelve per inch, and with no teeth at all for a final smooth finish. Average length 9 to 12 inches.

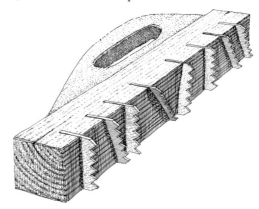

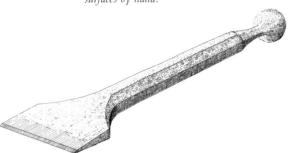

Boaster
Used for broader surfaces than the wide chisel, and for producing various textured surfaces by hand.

Coping Saw
Used at the mason's banker (bench) when hand working freestones and for sawing out small sections and profiles as may be required. Average length 10 to 12 inches, excluding the handle.

straight saw-like working edge with anything from four to eight teeth to the inch. Applied with a semi-circular combing motion, this is able quickly to remove the tool-marks left by the boaster. But for really hard stones the drag is not effective; on them abrasive rubstones, obtainable in a number of different materials and grades, had to be used. For the softer stones, on the other hand, the tool employed was, and still is, a *French drag*. This has a number of toothless steel blades set at angles in a wooden block-like handle, and on stones of fine grain will produce an absolutely smooth finish.

Many of these tools, in comparable sequence, are also used by the banker masons in the course of shaping or moulding, and to some extent by carvers and sculptors too.

Reference was made earlier (p. 65) to the *jadd* or racer (**41**), which was used both by the Romans and Normans in their quarries. The Normans also employed this tool for much of the initial dressing of their stone, before it went to the banker masons. If only the jadd were used, the profiles had to be very bold and simple – as of course in Norman buildings they generally are. For carvings and mouldings the Normans would have used chisels.

It goes without saying that these cutting tools all required continual sharpening. When a large number of masons were working together, whether at a quarry, in a workshop or on a site, it was once the usual practice to have on the staff a toolmaker, to service all the men's tools and keep them in first class working order. 'Fire-sharpened' tools were regarded as the best. For if, in order to sharpen them, edged tools continue to be rubbed on whetstones, their hardness and temper will gradually fade. It is said that in olden days some of the best chisels were made from broken swords.

But because of the frequent difficulty in finding a good toolsmith, some masons and stone-carvers still prefer to fire sharpen and temper their own tools. This is always true of the smaller yards. Any suitable steel that happened to be available could be used for making tools: old files, for example, or the tines of garden forks and pitchforks, or even old car and lorry springs.

Seamus Murphy, the Irish carver, had this to say in 1950 about the tempering of steel tools:

It is a curious thing, but I have never met a smith who could temper chisels as well as a stonie. They never get to know the steel like a man who is using it. They redden it too much and then plunge it into cold water, so that with the first bit of hardship it gets it snaps like glass, and you can see the water-break in it. When I am tempering tools I wait until they are cool after the fire sharpening and then take each chisel separately and get a blood heat on it. Next I dip each one slowly in rain-water, which is soft, hold it for a second and take it out. Then I rub it with a bit of sandstone and watch the colour coming down. With hard steel I leave it to come as far as the purple, and with some other steels as far as the straw colour. After that I plunge it and take it out to cool off. Then, after rubbing it with a bit of Yorkshire flag, you're away. It took me years to find out that it is best not to temper chisels on a frosty morning.

In recent years the problem of keeping tools sharp has been very much eased by the introduction of tungsten carbide, with which many of the mason's tools can now be tipped. Tungsten carbide is a very hard alloy which will retain a sharp edge for much longer than tempered steel. It is therefore specially valuable when work is needed on hard materials like granite.

For these hard stones, the masons now have the benefit of another useful tool: the small, power-driven pneumatic hammer. For the limestones and sandstones there are also planing machines, a boon for the cutting of straight mouldings, with the aid of a zinc end-mould or template. More elaborate cutting must still be done by hand, but here too the mason now has a wonderful tool to help him: the pneumatic chisel. The range of chisels is similar to those used by hand, except that each has a shank made to fit into a socket in the pneumatic hammer. The power is supplied by a compressor, through a specially reinforced rubber hose, usually driven by an electric motor; but if a portable compressor is required, it can be driven by a petrol or a diesel engine.

Reference has already been made to wooden *mallets*, which are among the most ancient of the stonemasons' tools. For these, various woods have been used; among the most favoured are hickory, apple wood, beech and lignum vitae. One of their advantages is that they do not harm the tops of the chisels as metal hammers would. In order not to impose excessive wear on the mallets the chisels usually have domed or mushroom-shaped heads. The weight of these mallets and hammers is dictated and regulated by the power of the impact required from each one of them. Some of the mallets weigh as much as 3 lbs, which is quite a lot to be swinging all day. Large ones average about seven inches in diameter. Smaller ones, used by sculptors and carvers, average about four inches. Some masons are now using plastic composition mallets, which are hardwearing and seem to stand up to the heavy service very well.

Some of the hammers are still heavier; the *pitching-hammer* of the banker masons, which may be of soft malleable steel, weighs, on average, about $4\frac{1}{2}$ lbs. Its main use was for driving the pitcher and the punch (see p. 87). This hammer was essential to the working of the harder stones such as granite, where a sharp impact was required. For cutting out old work during restorations, the *lump-hammer* is more suitable; this is a little lighter and of a more compact shape. Today, however, a lot of the cutting out would be done by electrically driven hammers. Small hammers, intended for sculptors, carvers and letter cutters are best made of soft, malleable iron, but hardened steel hammers are also much used.

Another favourite tool among masons working the softer stones is the *dummy*: this is like a small mallet, but usually made of a lead alloy, which is almost always used to drive wooden handled chisels. Dummies may also be made of an aluminium alloy; these are employed for carving and lettering.

But the masons needed many wooden implements too: plumb rules, levels, large squares, straight-edges, mortar-boards, hand hawks, carrying hods, floats and moulds – these were only some of them. They were all made in the builders' yards by bench joiners; and, working on woods in their dry, warm, almost dust-free workshops, these men came to regard themselves as the cream of the building trade, akin to white-collar workers, and of a status very superior to that of the stonemasons, forced to work in their own dust, often outdoors and in all weathers, who had for obvious reasons to dress in any old clothes. Time has had its revenge. The masons, as we have seen, now make their own moulds from zinc sheeting (or have their draughtsmen to do it for them), while their plumb rules, levels, hawks, hods and so on are machine-produced in metal or in plastics; and, while the joiners or carpenters do still make the mortar-boards and the straight-edges, other items are made by less skilled labour in factories, not specifically for the use of masons at all. So, while the banker masons are still in great demand, most of the bench joiners' work has entirely disappeared.

These masons' marks are a small
selection drawn from *Masons' Marks on
Wells Cathedral Church*, published by
the Friends of Wells Cathedral, 2nd
edition 1971.

MASONS' MARKS

Interest has always been aroused in the masons' practice, a very old one, of
cutting personal marks on the stones that they have worked at the banker,
and in the purposes which they served. Several questions still remain
unanswered.

The earliest recorded examples appear to date from the twelfth century,
and we have to think of very large buildings, mainly of worked stone,
where many banker masons were employed together. Wells Cathedral
provides a specially good example, for a great number have been found
there and recorded. Why, it will be asked, did the masons use these marks
rather than their own initials? The answer must be that in the Middle Ages
few craftsmen were literate; moreover, surnames were at that time by no
means general. Masons were free to devise their own marks, and this was
often done by slightly 'differencing' those used by their father and
grandfather. If by any chance two men on the same project were found to
be using the same mark, similar small changes or additions would be made.

Masons' marks must not be confused with merchants' or quarry marks,
which indicate the quarry of origin, the cubic content of the block and
sometimes the natural bedding planes. These often incorporate a personal
mark of some kind as well, as of the quarry master or merchant. There were
selection marks too, put on at the quarry by the architect, master-mason or
their assistants; they usually indicated the building or firm to which the
blocks were to be sent. All these are basically quarry marks, but a few of
them do occur from time to time on the backs of stones or on other
unworked surfaces. Sir Christopher Wren's 'wineglass' mark is widely
known.

Reference has already been made (see p. 76) to the code marks of the
fixer masons, but these are not normally regarded as masons' marks.

By checking the number of different masons' marks on a building the
number of masons who worked on it can be roughly estimated; but it is
very seldom possible to associate one individual with a particular mark.
Even when the man in question is known to have worked on the building,
this was never recorded. More research may help, but the lapse of time is
usually so great that reliable information is not likely to be forthcoming.

Masons' marks do not usually appear on the exposed surface of a
building, and when they do there is some uncertainty about the reason.
There are several possible explanations. One is that it was the established
practice in that particular region, as we know it was in parts of Scotland. Or

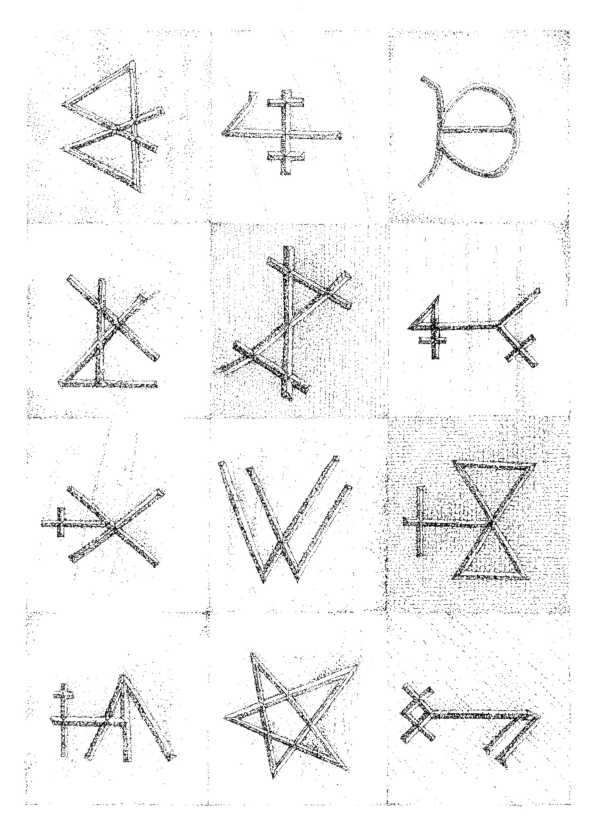

it could be simply from inadvertence. The usual place was the top bed (i.e. surface) of the stone; but if the width and height of a block were the same, the fixer mason might not be sure which way round to lay it. The mark would tell him. Or again, the intention might sometimes have been to add a final coat of stucco, so that the marks would be concealed. Or – and this is perhaps the most likely explanation – the surface marks might have been added by the fixer masons to denote the extent of one man's work, in order to enable measurements to be taken for assessment of output and remuneration. For what is certain is that masons' marks had a working connotation.

They served two main purposes. The first was positively to associate each stone with the mason who worked it, since if there was a mistake it was always the mason responsible who had to correct it. In the preparation of a piece of stone there was plenty of scope for errors, which might not be detected until the block had been hoisted into position; the personal mark would then immediately identify the man to whom it had to be returned.

The second purpose was concerned with what would now be termed bonus payments to any craftsman who in the time stipulated did more than the agreed amount of work. The master-mason or his assistant, with the aid of the marks, could quickly measure the amount of work accomplished by each man, without any grounds for dispute. This second purpose is closely related to the first, because the time spent on correcting errors would automatically reduce a craftsman's output and remuneration. From the fifteenth century there is documentary evidence for this use of masons' marks.

On the rare occasions when masons had to sign a legal document, those who were illiterate would do so by appending their marks; their names would have to be written by a scribe. This is probably the only way of bringing a name and a mark together, and unfortunately very few examples of such evidence survive.

In former times the use of masons' marks in the stone trade was widespread; they were in fact a part of general practice. But production methods in the new masonry works, combined with the growth of literacy, rendered the personal marks unnecessary, and today these are a rarity. Code and quarry marks are, however, still in use; the former are chiselled, but quarry marks may now only be painted or applied with a black crayon.

4

TYPES OF MASONRY

DRY-STONE WALLING

In many parts of England the fields are bounded by hedges. In some counties, notably Devon and Dorset, there are still too many for the comfort of the visitor, who is often compelled to drive or walk through lanes commanding beautiful views of which he sees practically nothing. Elsewhere, and particularly in East Anglia, the removal of hedges has been visually far too ruthless, and ecologically disastrous.

But our concern is with those other English counties, happily still numerous, in which the boundaries of the fields are often not hedges but stone walls. These vary tremendously according to the nature of the local stone, so much so, in fact, that with no other evidence than the field walls a discerning traveller, dropped from the sky, would often have a very good idea in what part of the country he had landed. Some of the walls are ancient: in parts of the South-East and South-West, and almost everywhere in the vicinity of villages. But north of the Thames the great majority date from between about 1760 and 1850, in association with the Enclosures. These walls were extremely well built, for the Enclosure Commissioners exercised strict supervision.

For field walls, if the stone is right, there is no need of mortar. Indeed, a well-built dry wall may last a good deal longer than a mortared wall built with the same kind of stone. Some of the less durable stones will fail in a mortared boundary wall but if used dry will last reasonably well. This is because after exposure to heavy rain the wind can blow freely through their open joints and quickly dry the stone again, which reduces the risk of frost damage. With very hard stones this is equally true, as was strikingly proved at St. Kilda. In 1930, because of its loneliness, inaccessibility and harsh climate, this remote island, which is 40 miles west of North Uist, in the Outer Hebrides, was evacuated. Twenty-eight years later, when a party of

95

scientists returned, they found the dry walls in immaculate order, whereas the mortared walls of the cottages were decaying fast.

Dry walls have been built of many different kinds of stone; in some areas the waller starts by making a foundation trench about 6 ins. deep, but elsewhere walls have been laid directly on to the turf or the surface soil. Construction took time. First the stones had to be collected off the land, the big ones by rolling or sledding. Lifting them was also very laborious; the heaviest, of course, were used at the lowest levels. So a length of 20 feet would be regarded as a good day's work: in granite districts it would be a little less than that. But although slower to build, these walls, when finished, not only look better than any others but last much longer.

Probably the most numerous are of Carboniferous limestone (**51**). Countless miles of dry walling in the Northern Pennines, in much of Northumberland, in the Peak District and the Mendips are constructed of this stone, and they are an essential component of the splendid scenery of those regions. It is a light grey stone, attractive to lichen, and weathers beautifully. Where in the northern counties dry walls are not grey but dun-coloured or brown, the stone is likely to be Millstone Grit, of which there is also an abundance in this part of England.

There is plenty of dry walling, too, along the Jurassic limestone belt, all the way from the Cleveland hills to Portland Bill. Lincolnshire and Rutland, Northamptonshire, Oxfordshire and the Cotswolds, Wiltshire,

51 (left) Dry-stone walling, near Hepple, Northumberland

52 (right) Dry-stone walling, Exford, Exmoor, Somerset

53 (below) Granite wall, Moortown, Dartmoor, Devon

Somerset and Dorset: all these counties have innumerable field walls built of hammer-dressed rubblestone. Some of these walls, it is true, are mortared, but the majority are not.

Slate, as mentioned earlier (see p. 44), has always been extensively used for dry walling in its own areas. A Devonian slate wall near Exford, on the eastern fringe of Dartmoor, is all the more attractive for harbouring many little ferns (52). Granite does not lend itself quite so well to dry-stone work as the other varieties mentioned, because it is not naturally flat-bedded and cannot easily be dressed to make it so (53). The facing of such granite walls is called 'polygonal work', and its jointing follows a wholly irregular, random pattern.

What are the secrets of dry-stone walls? What in their construction distinguishes them from mere piles of stones set up in a more or less straight line? What art or artifice keeps them erect for centuries, still thousands of miles of them, striding over hills and dales however adverse the weather? There are several factors that are important: some not apparent to the observer.

It goes without saying that the stone must itself be of good, durable quality. Not all stone is 'weather stone'. Next, in order to increase its stability, the wall should be built with both sides or faces 'battered' inwards from the vertical. A five foot wall – and this is a favourite height – will taper from about two feet at the base to a foot at the top, immediately below the coping.

The two sides of a dry-stone wall are usually constructed separately; and wherever possible every stone should be set so that its top surface slopes slightly downwards towards the outer face; as the old walling masons used to say, 'Keep their tails up, boy'. To help this process, small flakes of stone will often be wedged in under the big ones. The purpose, of course, is to run off from the centre of the wall as much as possible of the penetrating rain-water. In the Cotswolds, however, where most of the stones are fairly small and flat, and much more easily dressed than in the North, they can be packed so tightly that the interstitial stones are often unnecessary, and indeed disapproved of.

Since dry walls are specially characteristic of hilly districts, they frequently run up and down the hills. The essential point here is that the stones should be laid horizontally, and not parallel to the slope. And the coping stones, if not 'set on edge', must always slope towards the hill – be laid 'against the hill', as the old wallers put it.

Reference was made earlier (page 80) to throughs, which are a characteristic feature of the dry walls of Pennine Yorkshire and Lancashire. These are in effect bonding stones, employed to bind the two faces of the wall together at intervals and thereby to strengthen them. They must be well bedded. They are often left projecting, sometimes on both faces of the wall in regular courses, as in the Upper Swaledale example here illustrated (**54**), but often only on the side facing the farm animals, and not in courses as here.

The infilling is very important. Between the two faces there remains an irregular but continuous space, which unskilled people sometimes fill with small stones. This is a mistake, for there is no strength in unmortared small stones. Whether or not through stones are employed, what is required are the largest stones that can be fitted into the centre of the wall at every point; only after these have been introduced should the remaining, much smaller cavities be filled with little stones. In the absence of throughs, these large stones at the centre of the wall, interlocked with the facing stones throughout the width, length and height of the wall, are the only way in which bonding between the two faces can be achieved. A good walling mason always lays his big stones at right angles to the direction of the wall: never lengthwise.

No wall is complete without a coping, which is important both functionally and aesthetically. Coping-stones, which are also known as capstones, and in some areas, more colloquially, as bucks and does, cocks and hens, or cock-ups, are often somewhat larger than most of the other stones of which the dry wall is composed, and laid differently. A favourite practice in mountain areas is to place them vertically, with a sharply serrated edge (**52**). The primary intention here is to provide a deterrent for jumping sheep, but sometimes, especially where projecting through-stones on the public face of a wall offer a temptation to hikers, they may serve to discourage human intruders too. Other copings are more regular in

54 Dry-stone wall with triple layers of through stones, Swaledale, Yorkshire

appearance, often of a roughly dressed square or half-rounded section, as in Swaledale (**54**). But this Yorkshire dale can also show at least one wall with hammer-dressed capstones of triangular form (**55**). These are not common, but give to a rough field wall an air of great distinction, delightful to contemplate.

RUBBLESTONE

Far and away the commonest type of masonry for our old stone buildings is rubblestone, bedded in mortar. This was not only the least expensive way of using stone, but with many varieties it was the only way. All that could be done with stone of the harder, more intractable kinds was, after quarrying, to break it up into the sizes required, and start building. Sometimes there could be no question of regular coursing, and with the humbler buildings this is of no importance (**56**), for even when random coursed, this kind of masonry can look extremely crude (**176**). Where it was possible to square the blocks, even very roughly, this was usually done. If the stone could be quarried – and it frequently could – from close-bedded strata, say between two and five inches thick, that would help to reduce the amount of labour involved. It is for this reason that the majority of stones comprising a rubblestone wall are often rather small, as at Low Hall, Corbridge, with its pele tower (**57**).

55 Dry-stone wall, Swaledale,
Yorkshire

56 St. Anne's Hospital, Appleby,
Westmorland (now Cumbria)

57 Low Hall, Corbridge,
Northumberland

58 St. Cuthbert's Chapel, Oborne, Dorset

59 Hovingham, Yorkshire: coursed rubblestone

60 (right) Poulton Manor, near Fairford, Gloucestershire

For churches, however, uncoursed rubblestone was less acceptable; The House of God merited something less uncouth. So in regions where no better stone was available, a thin coat of rendering would always be applied internally and sometimes outside too. Whether or not the exterior were rendered, the rubblestone would invariably have been concealed under a coat of whitewash.

Wherever feasible, these irregularly coursed stones would be levelled up (58); for window-sills and at the eaves this was essential. But sometimes the builders could improve on that. In the type of masonry known as coursed

rubblestone there may still be a good deal of variation in the size and shape of the individual stones; often, as at Collyweston in Northamptonshire (**167**), they are small. Where some are larger, the courses may well differ a good deal in height, but each course is more or less level, and such buildings, unlike those described above, are no longer country bumpkins (**59**). As, however, the shapes of many of the stones may yet be far from regular, considerable quantities of mortar are still essential.

In the most refined type of rubblestone, the stones are squared and hammer-dressed, even though the course heights remain irregular, as in the Cloister Quadrangle at New College, Oxford (1360–86). Where, as here, the beds have been made flat, much closer joints become possible. Unlike much more recent stonework at Oxford, this, chosen and laid just six hundred years ago, has never required much restoration.

Now and again, in high quality rubblestone walling, it will be found that the level coursing has been deliberately interrupted by the insertion here and there of a specially large squared stone to provide variation. This, jumper work or snecking (cf. p. 81), is now admissible, and by some architects even felt to be desirable, in the most refined masonry, but in Stuart and Georgian buildings of the finest type it would never have been allowed.

In and around Oxford, this high quality rubblestone is commonly described as hardstone. It generally comes from the lowest level of the quarries. A fine illustration is provided by Poulton Manor, between Fairford and Cirencester (**60**). Here the side wall is of ordinary uncoursed

Cotswold rubblestone, but the front is of carefully hammer-dressed hard rubble with freestone dressings. The wall abutting on to the road exhibits similar contrasts. This charming example of a small late-seventeenth century Cotswold manor house will be referred to again more than once in later chapters.

Where a thick wall was required, the rough backs of the facing stones would project into a cavity space, which would then have to be filled up with a core of rubble. At all periods, the quality of the infilling has varied considerably. To make a strong wall, the cavity should be packed as far as possible with large stones, and each piece should be carefully bedded in with plenty of mortar, (while leaving spaces here and there for aeration). Sometimes, however, only small stones were available and lime for mortar was in short supply, or perhaps the work was, quite simply, skimped. Some Norman work was excellent, but by no means all. Many of the Norman towers later collapsed, usually because of building failures. Some years ago the cores of the Norman piers in Winchester Cathedral were found to be hazardously defective. Nowadays, all too often a short cut is taken by pouring in weak concrete, in which there is very little intrinsic strength.

But the infilling was often of quite a different material from the facing. At Ely Cathedral, where the axe-dressed freestone facing is of Barnack rag, a hard brown stone, as yet unidentified but probably a carstone, was employed for the core. Rubble-faced walls tend to get thinner towards the top. At the lower levels the mediaeval castles often had passages running along within the thickness of the walls. These might be, as at Barnwell in Northamptonshire (where the Castle was probably built in 1266), 9 ft. thick at the base with an infilling occupying about 7 ft.

ASHLAR

Ashlar is the name given to masonry that has been carefully cut, dressed and squared, to be employed as a facing stone in finely jointed level courses. The word derives from the Latin *axis* or *assis*, meaning originally a little plank or board: an example, not unique, of a masonry term originating in the practice of timber building, since the use of wood preceded that of stone. It is never applied to moulded work; it is just the plain facing.

Ashlar masonry can be achieved, although until recently only with a great deal of labour, in granite, but nearly all our ashlar is limestone or sandstone, and the

61 Athelhampton Hall, Tolpuddle, Dorset

stone has to be of sufficiently fine grain and homogeneous enough in structure to qualify as freestone. This is stone that can be cut 'freely', in any direction, either, until recently, with a hand-saw or with a mallet and chisel. In some areas the final stage would be to rub down with lumps of some other hard, close-grained stone, employed as an abrasive, if these were available. From early in the present century carborundum was used. The introduction, within the last generation, of new power-driven stone-cutting machinery has radically changed the circumstances under which ashlar is produced, as will be described in our final chapter; but until comparatively recently ashlar, because of the work involved and the high quality of the stone required, was always the most expensive kind of masonry, and before the Tudor period was hardly ever employed except for buildings of major importance. Even on the limestone belt there were many localities with no freestone for making ashlar. For the dressings, therefore, a certain amount of freestone would have to be brought, perhaps from some distance, by wagon or by water. The mediaeval church which was completely ashlared was rare. But the immensely greater refinement of ashlar masonry captivated the eye of every client who could afford it, as is well seen in the picture of part of the Elizabethan wing of Athelhampton Hall in Dorset (61), where the exquisite Portesham stone ashlar leaves the coursed rubblestone buttress looking very crude by comparison.★

In order to reduce the weight of the stone to be carried to the masonry works or to the building site, every block used to be roughly shaped at the

★The dressings here, seen in the window, plinth and string-course, are of Ham Hill stone, perhaps because it could be quarried in larger sections.

62 No. 55 Boroughgate, Appleby, Westmorland (now Cumbria)

quarry. Today this is no longer so necessary. Ashlared blocks are smooth on the face and at the sides, but the back, bonded into the wall, which will have been of rubblestone or brick and today may well be of concrete, used to be left rough. Ashlared facing blocks were formerly never less than 4 ins. thick, but nowadays the blocks may also be quite thin: indeed, when used to clad ferro-concrete frames, the thinner the better, again because of the reduction in weight. A thickness of only 2 ins. is now normal. But broad (or, as masons say, deep) courses, 7 ins. at least, and usually from 12 to 15 ins., have always been a requirement for true ashlar. Narrow courses, even when the finish is absolutely smooth, have not quite the same dignity, although perfectly acceptable for a modest house like the one at Appleby (**62**). This house, faced with Penrith sandstone ashlar, has courses of varying breadth. Where all the courses are narrow (under 7 ins.) the term used in some localities to describe this type of masonry is 'range walling'. No builder liked to waste his large offcuts, so at slack periods the men might well be employed in cutting up and trimming these, which were often known as ashlar bats (in the same way that broken bricks are called brickbats).

From the seventeenth century onwards, except when variations of texture were a conscious aim, an ashlared surface was nearly always regarded as the ideal, and for public buildings this finish was almost taken for granted. The gatehouse at Stanway (c. 1630) (**156**) is a beautiful example. Only its higher cost sometimes stood in the way. In the eighteenth and nineteenth centuries, both technically and aesthetically, the quality of the ashlar was frequently superb (**46, 133**). The most favoured limestones were those, like Portland Whitbed, in which the fossils are very small and not very much in evidence, or Hardwhite Ancaster and Ketton, in which they are almost wholly absent; the most desirable sandstones were those in which the grains of quartz and other minerals and the cementing material or matrix were most firmly consolidated.

It is nevertheless undeniable that ashlared surfaces in such stones as these, with their close grain and unvarying texture, can, when the building is a large one, look bland, and even, over big areas of walling, somewhat monotonous. Within the present century, therefore, there has been a decided reaction against the employment of the smoothest ashlar, except for very big buildings, on the ground that large, square-edged blocks and very close joints make a wall look too monolithic.

The simplest departure from a too monolithic appearance can be achieved, and sometimes was, by lightly bevelling the edges of each block. Proceeding further than this, the reaction has taken two forms.

First, there has been a swing in the pendulum of taste towards the use of more highly textured kinds of stone. A prime example is the changing attitude towards the employment of Portland stone from the Roach bed. The three principal beds of Portland stone are the Roach, the Whitbed and the Basebed. The two latter are closely compacted and very even in texture. Not so the Roach, which has plenty of texture, due not only to a profusion of fossil shells but also to an abundance of small voids which are natural to it. This is exactly what the Georgian builders disliked; it was not nearly smooth enough for them, so they threw it out. Nor was it always white.

It is fair to add that, until the invention of saws that could deal with it, the Roach stone was always very difficult to work, and with plenty of the other kinds to hand, the Georgian builders had no incentive to bother with it. Today it is much liked, especially for cladding. Sometimes the little interstices are carefully filled with cement, but this is a mistake: these small holes add an interest and are not a source of weakness. On the contrary, this is the best wearing Portland stone of any, and so strong that it can even be used as an alternative to granite for underwater work like quays and breakwaters, as can be seen at Lyme Regis (**132**). But, even with the fine modern saws, because it is so hard it takes longer to cut than Whitbed and is harsher on the blades, so costs up to twenty-five per cent more.

The other reaction from what in some quarters has been regarded as the over-bland effect of some smooth ashlar carried over large areas has been in the direction of tooled finishes. These have long been in favour in the North-East, where the application of a textured surface to the Carboniferous sandstone ashlar was already quite a common practice in the eighteenth century. The usual tool was a *boaster*: others sometimes employed were a *punch* and a narrow chisel known as a *broach*. Many different patterns were adopted, as can be well seen at Alnwick and at Berwick-upon-Tweed, where tooled surfaces became something of a local speciality. The most pleasing treatment is the simplest: an all-over pattern of reeds separated by grooves. This is seen to perfection at a National Trust property in that part of County Durham now known as Tyne and Wear: Gibside Chapel (**63**), built soon after 1760, with James Paine as the architect. The entire surface of

63 and 64 Gibside Chapel, County Durham (now Tyne and Wear); with (right) close-up of reeding and corduroy work

65 Burghley Estate Office,
Stamford, Lincolnshire: narrow
fluting

the ashlared sandstone was reeded (**64**), no doubt while the stone was still
'green' (see p. 26). Some of the reeding here is cut horizontally, which is
unusual; nearly always, as in nature, it runs vertically. The scale varies;
when the grooves are very close together (four or five to the inch), as can be
seen on the right of the photograph, this is termed corduroy work. Reeded
and corduroy surfaces were specially liked in some stone districts in the
nineteenth century. These finishes can now be produced by machinery, and
although, inevitably, they look more mechanical when this method is
adopted, they are still quite acceptable.

Fluting differs from reeding and corduroy in that the flutes are concave,
whereas the others are convex. Usually employed to enrich columns and
pilasters, flutes can be very bold, and crisply cut. Narrow fluting can be
seen on the Burghley Estate Office (**65**), a Victorian building in St. Martin's
at Stamford.★

★For the plinth, for some reason, stone was brought in from elsewhere, and has weathered
badly.

66 Pump House, High Peak Junction, Derbyshire: detail of rock-faced walling

ROCK FACING

Rock facing is visually at the opposite pole from ashlar, but in the right place and with the right stone can look most impressive. The stone must be hard and the tool required was a *pitcher*, which was struck with a special *pitching hammer*. For this purpose the pitcher could be up to 3 ins. wide, and was sharpened at an acute angle, quite differently from all other tools. Today a hydraulic splitting machine is sometimes used, and the process is not difficult. But rock facing has a long history.

The Pump House at High Peak Junction near Cromford in Derbyshire (**66, 67**), which was built about 1792 for pumping water from the River Derwent into the Cromford Canal, is a splendid example, because it demonstrates how the same stone, Millstone Grit, can be fashioned in two entirely different ways. The main walling, as can also be seen on a fine railway viaduct near Penistone (**128, 129**) is rock-faced but not at all crude; the blocks are brought to the same height throughout and are meticulously coursed. But the dressings are of ashlar, providing a beautiful smooth foil to the intense vigour of the rock facing. At the foot of the chimney the stone is not only ashlared but moulded, to emphasise the transition from the octagon of the shaft to the square of the base, with its *drafted* vertical margins at the angles. Around the window the natural bedding planes of the gritstone can be detected, especially round the arch, where they are also tooled. Here the bedding planes are kept under compression in accordance with the rules of the best building practice. These smooth stones are also boldly rusticated.

7 Pump House, High Peak
unction, Derbyshire

DECORATIVE FINISHES

High quality stonework is visually so profoundly satisfying that it can
frequently be left to speak for itself; there will be the dressings, moulded
and carved, but the walling itself can, and often should, be left absolutely
plain, for it is from the inherent quality of the stone, with its closely
matching range of tints, and the interesting ways in which it ages and
weathers, that much of its appeal derives. But, as we have said, there are
varieties of stone with little natural texture, the surface of which can be
made more interesting by the application of tooling, and there are others
which for reasons of design require the addition of tooled finishes to their
lower parts to obtain, here, a semblance of strength. Many different finishes
have been evolved, some long established, others quite recent, to meet the
requirements of architects and their clients. The intention was always an
aesthetic one, and until the present century these finishes were all hand-
wrought. Now most of them can be achieved, at a great saving of labour,
with pneumatic tools or other machines, which are, however, seldom
applied to the softer stones.

When, as is frequently the case with the grander houses in the classical
style, the principal rooms are on the first floor, architects are presented with
a problem, which is how to give sufficient weight to the ground floor, or
base storey, to save it from appearing insignificant or unworthy of
supporting the splendours of the *piano nobile*, as it is known in Italy.

The simplest method was to provide the base storey or plinth with a rock
face, since this always conveys sensations of vigour and strength. But the
stonemasons had many subtler variations in their repertoire. The
commonest, and perhaps also the best, was the device known as *rustication*,
which could be used in combination with rock facing. The essential
characteristic of rustication is the apparent recessing of the joints between
the blocks of stone. The joints themselves (that is to say, the mortar beds)
are in fact nearly always very thin and close. On the face of the wall the
effect of a wide joint is obtained either by chamfering all the edges of every
block (except at the angles) or by square sinkings: by this is meant cutting
round the face edges of each block of stone a square-angled recess called a
sinking, between 1 in. and 2 ins. high (according to the scale of the
building) and about $\frac{1}{2}$–1 in. deep. These recesses attract shadows, and
thereby the outline of each block is emphasized. A very beautiful example of
the aesthetic value of rustication is offered by the Palladian Bridge in the
grounds of Wilton House (**130**) (see p. 176). A rusticated plinth can be seen at

113

Attingham Park in Shropshire (**134**). Another favourite use of rustication was to emphasize the quoins of buildings whose walling is otherwise plain, as at Poulton Manor (**60**) and at the London church of St. George, Hanover Square (**5**). When, as at Petworth House, only the horizontal joints are treated in the manner described, the term used is *banded rustication* (**68**). These are square sinkings.

Another textural device employed quite frequently in classical architecture is that known as *vermiculation*: the cutting of the surface of the block of stone to suggest the winding tracks of worms. The gate-piers at Fonthill Gifford are excellent examples (**69**, **70**). Sometimes, as at Studley Royal (**71**) and as at Somerset House, London (**120**), this is also combined with rustication. The usual method of 'vermiculating' was to draw a pattern freehand on the ashlared block with charcoal; in the best examples, as in both these, no two patterns are exactly alike. Sometimes, however, when a lot of vermiculated stones were required, a pattern would be cut through a piece of zinc and traced on from this, prior to chiselling. Often, too, especially in the non-stone areas, blocks were impressed from moulds in artificial stone. In Bedford Square, London, for example, or in predominantly brick towns like Exeter, many later Georgian examples can

69 and 70 Fonthill Gifford,
Wiltshire: vermiculation; and
detail

68 (top left) Petworth House,
Sussex: banded rustication

71 Studley Royal, Yorkshire:
vermiculated rustication

72 and 73 Gateway, Fonthill Park, Wiltshire; and close-up of intermittent rock-faced ornamentation

be seen in Coade stone (**184**), of which more will be said in a later chapter. Here, being mould-made, the vermiculation on every stone of similar size is identical.

The Fonthill estate has another, much more spectacular gateway at Bishop's Fonthill, the northern entrance to the park (**72**, **73**). Here there is a dramatic contrast between the smooth accomplishment of the architecture, once attributed to Inigo Jones but now believed to be mid-Georgian, and the highly sophisticated rusticity of the decorative blocks. This is vermiculation with a difference, for the rock-faced stones are all bossed – that is to say, they project – and are intermittent. The impact is unforgettable.

In 1746, on the facade of his little Temple in the park of Euston Hall, Suffolk, William Kent achieved a comparable effect in the local white brick and flint. The principal accents, including the quoins, are carried out in grey and white flint, used here, and very effectively, to simulate vermiculated stone.

There are other variants not often seen. One is the finish known as *reticulation*, which differs from vermiculation in that the face of each block is covered not with wandering tracks but with straight lines suggestive of a net: that is to say it is geometrical, not random. Another is *sparrow-pecking*, achieved by incising numerous small holes at random with a punch or point, sometimes at the base of a sinking to make it appear darker. With both these finishes a plain margin about an inch wide is often left round the edge of each block.

Punching is about the only ornamental surface which can be given to granite: at the Moretonhampstead Almshouses (**89**) even the mouldings and carvings are punched, as so often in Devon and Cornwall. But with granite, because the material was so hard that a smooth surface would have entailed labour entirely disproportionate to the value of the result, the punched surface was primarily practical rather than decorative; applied to

116

kerbstones, the effect was to render them less slippery to walk on when wet. For granite it is essentially a rustic finish, since the intention is to produce a deliberately rough texture.

Far from rustic, on the other hand, is the finish known as *frost-work*. The idea here was to cut the surface of the stone to simulate stalactites or icicles: a treatment confined, we believe, to the eighteenth century. The illustration shows a key-stone at Bath (**74**).

Although its intention was by no means always merely decorative, this is perhaps the best place to speak of *herringbone masonry*. This has never been very common in England, but it has been produced occasionally for many centuries and in various parts of the country. Two entirely different methods have been employed.

Punched herringbone work was a speciality of the North-East. Patterns were produced by cutting punched strokes diagonally from both long edges of the block, to form a 'V' shape. An early example can be seen at Raby Castle (**75**). Here the intention was not primarily decorative: it was to reduce the time needed to dress each block.

But there is also herringbone walling proper, which goes back even to Roman times. There was something of a vogue for it in the early Norman period: sections of herringbone masonry of the late eleventh century can be seen, for example, in the east curtain wall of the Castle at Richmond in North Yorkshire. The courses are not specially regular, but each stone is laid at an angle of approximately 120°; the succeeding rows of stones are set at opposing angles and interlocked with the upstanding ends of the

74 Grosvenor Place, Bath: frost-
work keystone

75 Joan's Tower, Raby Castle,
County Durham: early
herringbone finish

76 Queen Anne's Walk, Barnstaple,
Devon: herringbone retaining wall

previous row. For reasons which are not readily apparent, this type of masonry was sometimes favoured for retaining walls. There is a notable example on the old quay adjoining the early eighteenth century Exchange known as Queen Anne's Walk at Barnstaple in Devon (76). The wall here is built of thin-bedded rubblestone from the nearby Culm Measures.

In mediaeval buildings herringbone stonework can be seen from time to time in the backs of large open-hearth fireplaces; used thus, it is the equivalent in stone of herringbone brickwork, which was also employed, and much more frequently, for fireplace backs.

BANDS, CHEQUERS AND FLUSHWORK

Many buildings display two different kinds of stone. Far and away the commonest reason for this is when the main walling stone cannot be ashlared and is therefore unsuitable for the dressings. This can cause problems, for limestones and sandstones differ chemically and the interaction of the two has been a constant source of decay. Such troubles do not arise when the different kinds are both limestones or both sandstones. In all these cases, however, the intention was functional and not decorative.

77 Lord Burghley's Almshouses, Stamford, Lincolnshire

78 (right) East Farm, Piddlehinton, Dorset

But when a wall combines two kinds of stone in determined patterns, an ornamental intention may be inferred. Even then another, non-decorative factor may also operate: the desire to economize by eking out the use of the more expensive stone. The easiest way of doing this was by laying the two stones in alternate courses.

On the limestone belt many examples can be seen, especially in Northamptonshire, of the use of alternating *bands* of oolite and lias. The oolite is generally lighter in tone: grey, cream or buff. In the Midlands the Middle Lias contains a bed known as the marlstone which is often heavily impregnated with iron, and of a tawny brown hue. A well-known example is Sir Thomas Tresham's Triangular Lodge at Rushton, a strange little building replete with symbolism, completed in 1597. Less eccentric buildings showing banded masonry can be seen in many of the villages between Towcester and Banbury. In that area they were something of a local fashion.

Farther north, in the Stamford region, bands, dating mainly from the Regency and early Victorian periods, were produced from two kinds of local stone. The oolitic freestone, up to 9 ins. thick, is interleaved with several courses of brown Wittering pendle. This is a hard fissile stone occurring in very narrow beds, ranging from $1\frac{1}{2}$ to $3\frac{1}{2}$ ins. Collyweston slates, of which there will be more to say presently, came from the same geological formation. Pendle was useful structurally because it is both flat-bedded and very durable★; it could also be employed decoratively, as can be seen on the end-gable of Lord Burghley's Almshouses at Stamford (**77**) and on the former toll-house across the bridge, both dating from 1849.

★Wittering pendle is so impermeable that in the first part of the nineteenth century it was sometimes used for the foundations of buildings mainly constructed of some other stone, serving therefore in effect as a precursor of the damp course.

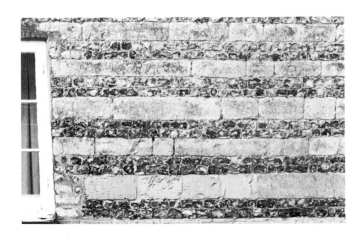

79 East Farm, Piddlehinton, Dorset: detail of banded flint and chalk freestone

When ashlared stone is used in conjunction with flint, the colour contrasts are more positive and there are stronger contrasts of texture too. This combination is specially well seen in parts of Wiltshire and Dorset, but it also occurs along the Kentish side of the Thames estuary, where in the fourteenth century there was a vogue for bands among the church builders. Here Kentish ragstone, which is almost white, was combined with knapped flints, which are often nearly black: the effect can be strident. At the church of Cliffe-at-Hoo the stripes would look better on a zebra.

The Dorset banding is gentler and more pleasing. The further part of East Farm at Piddlehinton, north-east of Dorchester (**78**), is dated 1622. To every course of chalk freestone (and they vary somewhat in breadth) there are two courses of flints, which have been knapped and roughly squared (**79**). On the other part of the house the bands are fewer and more tentative. It should be emphasized that the purpose of these bands was not primarily decorative. The main function of the limestone is to make the wall stronger. The flints are bedded into mortar and behind these there could be anything: here, probably chalk rubble. The blocks of stone go back much farther into the wall. It is on them that the wall mainly depends for its stability. The surface of the stone here was not chiselled; the tool employed was either a stone-axe or a jadd pick.

On the front of the late-Elizabethan Stockton House in the Wylye valley of Wiltshire (**80**), there is, as befits a much grander building, a higher proportion of limestone (here it is Chilmark); the flints have been reduced to a single course, and from the central feature have disappeared altogether. Adjoining the house, on the left, is a wing added, it is said, under the Commonwealth to accommodate a chapel. Here the facing is not in bands but in *chequers*, which may be felt to be aesthetically preferable. There is no regularity in the sizes of the squares, which is all to the good (**81**). The flints are all knapped but laid random, not shaped; there may be as many as twenty in a single square. Wiltshire buildings of the late-sixteenth and seventeenth centuries provide many examples of chequer-work, using

80 Stockton House, Wiltshire

81 Stockton House Chapel: detail
of chequer-work

82 Holy Trinity, Long Melford, Suffolk: flushwork

83 St. Mary, Stratford St. Mary, Suffolk: flushwork

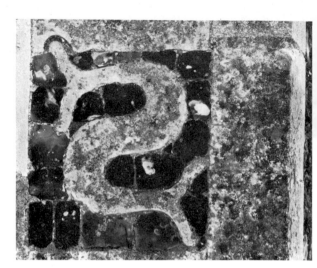

flints; the stone may be chalk, oolite, or greensand, as at Tollard Royal (which is just over the border with Dorset). But, unlike banding, chequers also occur frequently in East Anglia. A favourite place was the parapet of a church wall. At Woolpit in Suffolk there are chequers on the side-walls of the handsome south porch. On the Guildhall at Norwich, they are set diagonally.

The counties of Norfolk, Suffolk and Essex were, however, the home of a far more spectacular development of flint and stone used in combination: the process known as *flushwork*, the decorative use of knapped flints in conjunction with dressed stone. Either the designs were outlined on the blocks and left to stand flush after the intervening spaces had been hollowed out, or the blocks were sawn into thin slabs, out of which were cut ornamental pieces of many different kinds. Since the principal user of flushwork was the Church, cusped Gothic arches, pierced tracery and crocketed pinnacles often figure prominently, as in great profusion at Long Melford (**82**). But other motifs which occur frequently include shields of arms, crowns and monograms, and at Stratford St. Mary there is even a complete alphabet offered, it is said, in place of the many prayers which could be constructed out of it. Both these Suffolk churches, Long Melford and Stratford St. Mary, also display long inscriptions, recording the names

84 Butley Priory, near Orford,
Suffolk: flushwork

of the benefactors and inviting prayers for their souls. At Long Melford
these are high up, above the clerestory windows, whereas at Stratford St.
Mary they are on the plinth and buttresses of the north aisle. The date here
is 1494. The letters, Gothic and extremely decorative, are boldly cut in
white limestone, for which the dark grey tone of the knapped flints
provides the perfect foil. The S reversed (**83**), on the north-west corner
buttress, stands for *Salutem* (salvation).★

   In all these East Anglian buildings, the main body of the wall was
probably flint rubble. On to its surface the flushwork face was carefully
mortared. Where the stone was cut out to form patterns, the knapped flints
that fill the interstices were fitted in with great care, so as to expose as little
mortar as possible. The effect, carried over an entire wall surface, can be
spectacular. The earliest example, dating from the 1320s, is on the former
gatehouse of Butley Priory near Orford, now a private house; here there is
a considerable quantity of flushwork but no overall design (**84**). This defect
was remedied when the process became widespread in East Anglia in the
second half of the fifteenth century. The grand church of Long Melford
furnishes but one of many excellent examples; a favourite place for
flushwork was the tower, as can be seen to striking effect at Eye, Redenhall,
Laxfield and elsewhere. The finest achievement of all dates from 1481,
when at St Osyth's Priory in Essex, not far from Clacton, a magnificent
gatehouse was erected, to contain guest rooms and private apartments for
the Prior, away from the main buildings. This, after five centuries, is still
well preserved, and displays the technique of flushwork to perfection.

★We are indebted to the Rev. Leonard Rowe, Rector of Stratford St. Mary, for kind help
with the interpretation of this flushwork alphabet and inscription.

5

MORTARS AND POINTING

MORTAR

The earliest walls, as was noted in Chapter 4, were laid dry. When it was desired to fill in the interstices between the stones, this was at first done simply with earth or mud; sometimes the dung of cows or horses and chopped straw were added to make it more cohesive. If the mud was chalky, that was all to the good, for lime is a valuable binder. In antiquity, other mixtures were also used. Some of the early Egyptian buildings, for example, are jointed with natural bitumen. But the Greeks usually dispensed with mortar altogether; in some of their finest buildings the blocks of marble were rubbed with an abrasive sand of natural emery and water to ensure close-fitting joints, and, as already observed, the drums of the columns, when not monolithic, were held in position by metal dowels inserted into sockets at the centre of each.

The first hard-setting mortar was the cement evolved by the Romans. For internal work marble masons long relied for their jointing on plaster of Paris, which is obtained by burning gypsum. In the Middle Ages, ox-blood might be added to the sand and lime mixes to make them harder, and there are even recorded instances of hundreds of eggs being used for the same purpose! Other ingredients of mortar, introduced from time to time, were wood ash and, in areas deficient in natural sand, road mortar. This was the silt-like mud of ground-up stones made on the primitive roads by the wheels of wagons, and later of coaches, to which a little lime would be added. And dust from the sawing and working of the stone, again with the addition of some lime, made a most useful mortar. In short, the early builders improvised, making their bedding and jointing material out of whatever came conveniently to hand. Some of these improvisations, inevitably, proved far more durable than others.

The two basic constituents of good mortar are sand and slaked lime, and from early times until well into the nineteenth century the preparation of the lime was no easy matter. It can be obtained from any of the limestones, including chalk, which today provides about a third of the total quantity of lime used in the building trade; but the general belief is that 'stone lime' is superior to 'chalk lime'. Some of the best is made from Blue Lias limestone. The first step was to convert the lime into quicklime, and to do this it was necessary to burn it. The old kilns were little more than large circular holes in the ground, fired by timber and brushwood covered, wherever it was available, with a layer of coke. Over this was placed a layer of broken-up limestone, and then more coke and so on in alternation; the kilns were about ten feet deep. The fire was then lit, and as the layers of coke were consumed the burnt lime dropped to the bottom. The situation is very different today; the process is now carried out under scientific control in enormous steel kilns lined with firebricks, coke, oil or gas fired, and continuously burning.

The burnt lime removed from the kiln, quicklime, or lump-lime as it was called in some areas, was now in a volatile state. This incidentally rendered transportation very difficult. Before the Industrial Revolution heavy materials could only be carried over long distances by water. But quicklime could not be put into barges, because with the slightest dampness it would start to heat and slake, and that might mean serious damage, even the burning and sinking of the vessel. So the limestone had always to be shipped unburnt, and the kilns erected close to the building site or, if that proved difficult, at least on the quayside at the point of disembarkation. When quicklime was loaded on to carts or wagons, and later on to railway trucks, these risks still had to be countered. Only with the development of hydrated lime was this difficulty overcome.

There were two main processes for slaking lime: the liquid and the semi-dry methods. In the former, lumps of burnt lime were carefully placed in a large, generally circular, tub or tank half-filled with water and stirred. In a short time, as it absorbed the water, the lime became hotter, and with more stirring it would boil from its own nature, without the application of any other heat. In this state it could be dangerous; above all the eyes needed protection from this bubbling white liquid. More lime would now be added until, with yet more stirring, the liquid became thicker and acquired a creamy consistency. It was then ladled out and poured through a fine sieve into what was called a pan. This would be either a shallow hole in the ground or a container on the ground built up with sand to a height of perhaps eighteen inches and lined with sand at the bottom. In this the liquid had to be left to cool for a week or two. During this period the water would gradually evaporate. When it had reached about the consistency of butter, it was known as 'putty-lime', and was now ready for making into mortar. Some people, however, were in no hurry to do this, believing that the longer it was kept in stock the better would be its quality since any fragments of lime that had passed through the sieve inadvertently would have time to 'blow'. If this only occurred when the work was finished it could be serious; in bad cases, indeed, 'blowing' might cause a mortar bed to 'lift' or swell even to the point of dislodging a block of stone. So the putty-lime might be left to stand for a year or even more. All that was needed at this stage was to mix it with sand.

In some parts of the country the semi-dry process was preferred. The first move here was to spread out a layer of sand, on to which were placed alternate layers of quicklime and sand; each layer of lime was then watered, but sparingly, because what was required at the end was a dry powder. Gradually a conical heap was formed, which might be five feet high and six or seven across at the base. After the final watering, the whole was covered with a layer of sand and left to heat up of its own accord, expand and blow. After being thrown through a fine screen, it was ready, by the addition of more water and sand, to be converted into mortar as required.

Most limestones are not naturally hydraulic: that is to say, they will not harden when wet. Indeed, the purer the limestone the less hydraulic is the mortar derived from it. This explains the strange additions of early times, and accounts for the frequent introduction nowadays of a little Portland cement to temper the mortar and harden it.

But there are varieties of lime in Sussex, Cambridgeshire, Leicestershire and elsewhere which are hydraulic, and have a reasonable tensile strength; and these are the best for the production of mortar, not only because they set more firmly and have the colour of natural stone but also because they are free from those sulphates and other substances which can cause surface staining or other defects.

The Collyweston stone slaters (see Chapter 8), who bed their slates on the roof, used to make their mortar with limestone from their own pits. This was mildly hydraulic, so when they added the sand, very little water was needed. To obtain a workable consistency they used to beat the mixture with flails, not unlike those formerly used for threshing corn.

After the First World War the situation was very much eased for the stone builder by the introduction of manufactured hydrated lime. Mixed with specified quantities of sand or stone-dust, this lime can be used straight from the bag without any need for slaking. It has already been reduced to a fine powder, which is inert and, so long as it is stored in a dry place, will neither heat, expand nor blow. All that is required, for blending this powder with the sand or stone-dust and water, is the ubiquitous concrete mixer. A great deal of time, as well as labour, has been saved. (But after a while hydrated lime does tend to go stale and lose strength.)

So all the old skills required for the manufacture of mortar have now become obsolete; this is but one more example of the great difference that modern science has made to the craft of a builder. One precept, however, remains and still requires personal judgment to apply: whatever mortar is used, it should never be stronger nor harder than the stone that it is bonding, and is best when slightly softer.

Interior plasterers have been just as fortunate. In the past they also needed a fibrous mortar. For decorative work on walls or ceilings they used to add cow hair obtained from the tanneries, which they beat and 'larried' into the putty-lime before any fine sand was added. They then had to blend their lime mortar with plaster of Paris (burnt gypsum) to harden it and give it tensile strength, particularly for the final or 'setting' coat, as well as for moulded cornices and all the decorative plasterwork. Today there are at their disposal, and much less trouble to use, patent plasters manufactured from gypsum.

POINTING

The purpose of mortar is to add stability to a wall or building, and make it weatherproof. Most of it is of course concealed, but on the surface of a wall it is exposed, and requires to be carefully finished. This is what is called pointing. If carried out correctly it can contribute to a wall's ability to resist the weather; it is also of vital importance aesthetically. There are many different methods of pointing; some are so good that they actually enhance a building's appearance, while others can do appalling damage.

The mortar exposed to the surface may be that which has been used throughout; on the other hand it is not unusual to point with mortar of somewhat finer quality, more carefully mixed. The first consideration is to ensure that the mortar is of the right strength and of the right colour for the wall. In both hardness and porosity it needs to be similar in nature to the stone itself.

The besetting sin of much modern pointing is to mix too much Portland

**85 Craster Tower,
Northumberland: boundary wall**

cement into the mortar. All stone absorbs a certain amount of moisture in
wet weather, and in order to dry out again it must be able to 'breathe' freely
through the mass in every direction. Unless this can happen some kinds of
stone will fail, and all can be adversely affected. Very hard non-porous
joints impede this aeration and are therefore wrong.

The aesthetic effect of too much cement in the mixture is also invariably
bad. A good working mixture for most purposes is ten parts of clean sand
to two or three of lime, beaten up with water, with the addition of no more
than one part of ordinary Portland cement; the object of adding cement is
to help the mortar to harden, and no more should be introduced than is
sufficient to make sure of that, nor should any be added until just before the
mix is going to be used. On exposed sites and with the harder stones a
slightly higher proportion of cement is sometimes acceptable. For historic
buildings, on the other hand, Portland cement is never right and is no
longer used at all by the Department of the Environment. In Bath
repointing is usually done with a mortar consisting of two parts of lime to
six of sand, with the addition of just a little white cement as a strengthener.

No less important is it that the pointing mortar should be of the correct
colour; here bad mistakes constantly occur. The determining factor is the
colour of the sand, remembering that this will be somewhat lightened by
being mixed with lime. The utmost care should be taken to obtain the right
sand, and, for repointing, to secure a good match with the existing mortar.
As a general rule the pointing mortar should be the same colour as the stone
or slightly lighter in tone: never darker. The bad effect of too dark a mortar
can be seen in plate **143**. But using too light a mix can be equally
unfortunate, as shown in the repointing of the estate wall at Craster Tower,
Northumberland (**85**). (The section of unrestored wall on the right of the
picture is as it should be.) Another unfortunate example is Castle Drogo
(**86**), where the flat roofs and the driving Dartmoor rain bring penetrations
of damp which are a chronic problem for the National Trust. The record of
Lutyens's original mortar was unfortunately lost, and some of the worst

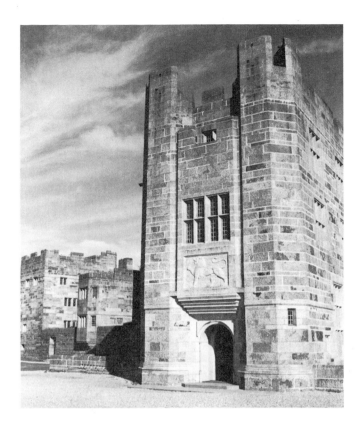

86 Castle Drogo, Drewsteignton, Devon

repointing occurred before the Trust acquired the property. The Trust, with advice from the Society for the Protection of Ancient Buildings and the Buildings Research Centre, sought to do better, but the early experiments were not successful. Then contact was made with an old man in the neighbouring village who had worked for the last owner as a handyman; he was able to recall what the old mason who built the house had told him. Lutyens, he said, had made his mortar with sand extracted from the bed of the Teign, which flows immediately below the rocky eminence upon which the house is sited. To the river bed they now went, and did produce a better mortar, both as regards colour and texture. Meanwhile, alas, a great deal of damage had been done, and at present remains. As can be seen, the excessively light-toned mortar has the effect of putting a ring round each block of stone and thus isolating it from its neighbours, resulting in a 'box of bricks' effect which is quite alien to the monumentality that is one of this granite building's leading characteristics.★

The amount of pointing that a building requires depends very much

★In fairness to the National Trust it should be added that since 1980 strenuous efforts have been made, in consultation with the Department of the Environment, to find the best possible mortar for Castle Drogo.

upon the character of the masonry. Mortar usually looks best when it is inconspicuous. The late seventeenth century Manor House at Great Weldon in Northamptonshire (**171**) is faced with freestone, brought, needless to say, from the quarry close by. In so far as the stonework can be seen to either side of the destructive ivy that half-smothers it, the courses will be found to be narrow and the blocks not large. Over-prominent pointing would therefore at once impinge on the scale.

Ashlar needs very little pointing; because the shaping of the blocks has to be very true, the joints, as noted earlier, rarely exceed $\frac{1}{8}$ in., and may be even less. All that is therefore necessary is for the mortar to be the same colour as the stone and for the joints to be filled flush with the wall-face. They should be left smooth without any smears on the surface of the stone. Easton House near Corsham (**87**) is such a perfect example that it deserves better than to be blurred by wisteria. At Athelhampton Hall (**61**) the delicate pointing of the main wall, with its exquisite masonry, is in vivid contrast to the much cruder construction, with obtrusive pointing, of the buttress. If the stone is red, as in the house at Appleby (**62**) which is faced with Penrith sandstone ashlar, the

87 Easton House, near Corsham, Wiltshire

88 High House, Uley, Gloucestershire

sand for the mortar must also be reddish, as indeed it is.

When ashlar needs repointing it will sometimes be found that the arrises of the blocks of stone have become worn. There is then a temptation to carry over the new mortar on to the wall-face. This is always wrong and can be an aesthetic disaster. The right way is to recess slightly the face of the new mortar.

The differences between the pointing of ashlar and of rubblestone are well illustrated by two adjacent houses, both late Georgian, at Uley in the Cotswolds (**88**). High House has a beautifully smooth front, with the minimum of pointing, below a moulded cornice. At Uley Cottage, next door, the proportion of mortar is greatly increased, because the stones are much smaller and the bedding surfaces are no longer smooth; furthermore, stone of this kind often has rounded edges, which cause the joints to appear to be still larger than they actually are. In this type of masonry the mortar joints are seldom less than $\frac{3}{8}$ in., and, depending on the nature of the stone itself, can be a good deal more. It is for the pointing of joints such as these – or for courses still more closely spaced, between stones still smaller and more irregular, as at Collyweston (**167**) – that a number of different finishes have been devised.

One of the best, and popular today, is to recess the joint a little with a tool of wood or steel known as a former; then, when the mortar has dried, it is rubbed over with a soft dry brush or a piece of dry hessian sacking. With this method the whole face of the stone is revealed; nothing is obscured, and it is very durable. The best texture is obtained by using a fairly coarse sand, and for repointing old stonework of this kind, which often has very wide joints, the texture of the mortar is sometimes still further improved by the addition of fine shingle.

Another method is known as weather pointing. Here the joints are kept smooth but slightly recessed at the top and brought flush with the wall at the bottom. Although this can be acceptable, it often has a somewhat overworked appearance, and is expensive to do. Generally speaking, in pointing, a smooth trowelled surface should be avoided.

Often on old buildings the joints will be seen to have been brought flush with the face of the stone, and in favourable conditions it is remarkable how well some of this old pointing has lasted; generally, one must suppose, it was done with hydraulic lime. But with very wide joints the effect is sometimes relieved by the addition of straight lines lightly incised with a steel former into the mortar before it dries. This is the way the punched granite blocks of the Almshouses at Moretonhampstead (**89**) would originally have been pointed. But in renewing the pointing two bad mistakes have been made. The new mortar is not in tune with the stone: it is too dark. And in some places, ribbon pointing has been introduced. This form of pointing, which was never employed by the old builders, involves the use of a hard-looking cement mortar which often projects a little and is trimmed along both top and bottom. Thereby a mechanical-looking effect is produced which is also, as here, over-assertive.

Ribbon pointing never fails to detract from the natural beauty of stone; and where the rubblestone is uncoursed it can look even worse. There are quite a number of English churches built of uncoursed stone with walls that exhibit this technique. Broad bands of cement mortar have been trowelled on to the surface of the joints and kept forward about $\frac{1}{8}$ in.; this has then been trimmed in such a manner that every stone emerges surrounded by a heavy ribbon of hard-looking mortar, which may sometimes be nearly an inch wide. Only a very insensitive eye could perpetrate such a method of pointing as this, which is a sure sign of unskilled workmanship or lack of

89 Almshouses,
Moretonhampstead, Devon

90 and 91 (above right and
right) Cosy Cottage, Askrigg,
Yorkshire; ribbon pointing

adequate supervision. In some areas domestic examples also abound (90, 91).★ The aesthetic effect is absolutely disastrous, and employed externally it is also technically very unsound, because the ledges formed by the projecting mortar arrest the flow of rain water down the wall and lead it instead into the joints behind this hard pointing; this may ultimately cause the stones to perish.

★This little building also suffers from grotesquely unsuitable fenestration and a poor little door, all the worse for being white. Visually, in fact, an anything but cosy cottage.

92 Stokesay Castle, Shropshire

93 Ironstone Cottage, Fittleworth, Sussex

Even without ribbons uncoursed rubblestone is frequently pointed to excess, producing a kind of vertical crazy-paving effect which is most unsightly. The proper way to point rubblestone which is uncoursed or only very roughly coursed can be seen at the Archbishop's Palace in Maidstone (**13**) and at Stokesay Castle (**92**), where the rough Silurian limestone, going back to the thirteenth century, is still remarkably well preserved.

The appropriately named Ironstone Cottage at Fittleworth in West Sussex (**93**) provides an object lesson in both good and very bad pointing. The stones being small, the original pointing erred on the side of being over-emphatic. But the recent pointing seen below the central window downstairs and to the right of the middle window upstairs, is a disgrace. The delicate texture of the original building has been insulted.

Where the stone is not sedimentary in origin but igneous or metamorphic, and often of great antiquity, the pointing problems are different. Such an area is the Charnwood Forest of Leicestershire. Fountain Cottage at Woodhouse Eaves (**25**) is built of slatestone, all four walls and roof alike, probably brought from Swithland, which is quite near. Since the walls are chunkily shaped and dark in tone, there is much to be said for using a light-toned mortar here and over most of the house this thread-like mesh of pointing is not unattractive. But on the extension to the right and on the wall adjacent to it, the craftsmanship was far less skilful, and a great deal too much mortar was used. Silken threads have given place to ropes, and the result is sadly ham-fisted.

The stone which, on account of its amorphous shape, requires more mortar than any other kind is flint (**48**). Because the effect of a wall of flints can be rather shrill, the colour of the mortar should always be subdued, and, although for practical reasons the pointing should be carefully done, no refinements are called for.

GALLETING

In days when the transporting of heavy materials could easily cost more than the materials themselves or the wages of the men who worked them, by no means all English builders were fortunate enough to have at their disposal fine-grained limestone or sandstone that could be shaped fairly easily into smooth manageable blocks. Many had to make do with rougher, more intractable stones which were so irregular on their beds that it was often difficult to place one block upon another without rocking. To counteract this required a great deal of mortar, and even then the result might not be satisfactory, especially as the lime mortar would certainly be less durable than the stone. Moreover, some stones – sarsens, for example, and all the granites – are non-absorbent: they lack suction, as the masons say. With them mortar adheres only with difficulty.

This difficulty was, if not overcome, at least lightened by the introduction into the mortar of little stone wedges to help stabilize the large stones and counteract the rocking. These wedges might consist of chippings picked up in the quarry or in the masons' workshop, or the flakes of flint produced in flint-knapping, or just pebbles. The process became known as galleting (sometimes spelt galletting), from the French *galet*, which is the word for those little water-worn pebbles found on the sea-shore and in the beds of streams. The introduction of gallets into broad courses of mortar is a practice which goes back to mediaeval times, and there can be no doubt that the intention was originally structural.

Around Aberdeen this practice continued until the introduction of new diamond-toothed saws in quite recent times. Faced as they were with huge lumps of intractable granite which had to be converted into usable sizes, the masons could reduce their labour considerably if the intervening spaces between only very roughly shaped blocks could be filled with mortar, strengthened with smaller pieces of stone performing the structural role of gallets (although much larger here than in the English examples).

But, as so often in the history of architecture, what started from practical necessity developed in the course of time into something whose principal, if not sole, *raison d'être* was decorative. Most of the galleting to be found today is of this kind.

Many people will never have heard this term, for in large parts of the country there is no galleting at all. Quite apart from the areas more or less devoid of stone altogether, gallets were never needed where there was freestone; they have no place at all in ashlar masonry. Ornamental galleting only occurs in England, in fact, in combination with a few of the coarse, gritty Cretaceous sandstones and with flint, and is virtually confined to two areas. One is Norfolk. Flint gallets can be seen on the Guildhall at Norwich, but most of it is not in flint but in carstone, and occurs in the area of the so-called 'gingerbread stone' to the north of King's Lynn, including the Sandringham estate.

The other and more important area is in the South-East, in and around the Weald. In all those parts of the counties of Surrey, Sussex and Kent lying between the North and South Downs, together with the corner of

East Hampshire that contains Selborne, galleting with pellets of ironstone (sandstone from the Greensand) long remained a local fashion. It is well seen on the church walls at Dunsfold (**94**), one of a group of buildings around Godalming constructed of Bargate sandstone, so chunky that even rough, irregular coursing, as here, was a considerable labour. These walls date back to about 1270; needless to say, the present pointing and galleting are much more recent, but it seems not unlikely that the gallets – which, as usual in the Weald, are of carstone (ironstone) – were reused. Not far away is Tigbourne Court, one of Lutyens's most original houses: this too is of Bargate stone, and galleted throughout. As for galleting with flint, the most remarkable examples in England are to be found in Chichester. All date from the early part of the nineteenth century, when the houses were

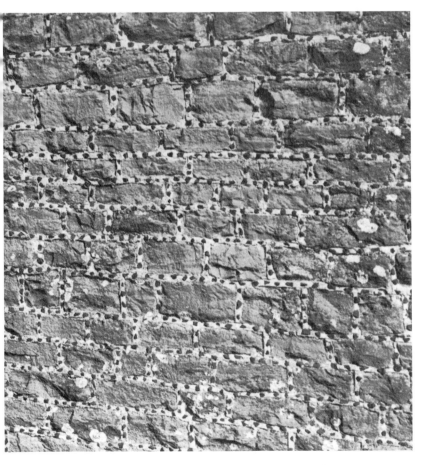

94 St. Mary and All Saints, Dunsfold, Surrey: galleting

erected. At 44 South Street (**95**) the builders deliberately chose to use flints, probably gathered from a nearby beach, that were all of about the same size, so the coursing is, for this stone, unusually regular; nevertheless the galleting is abundant. For 40 North Street (**96**) most of the flints were knapped, but the shapes are so amorphous that a great deal of mortar was unavoidable. This mortar was masked, and perhaps strengthened too, by having literally thousands of flint slivers pressed into it while it was still wet. There are, we believe, no other instances of ornamental galleting carried out with such lavish profusion.★

★Mr. E. W. O'Shea of Lewes argues that chips, flakes and slivers of flint or other stone are not, strictly speaking, gallets, which were originally only ornamental pebbles, and that the extension of the term to embrace them is a later aberration. (See *Lewes Archaeological Group*, Newsletters 60 (Feb. 1982) and 64 (Jan. 1983).)

6

THEMES AND VARIATIONS:
Stone in many Guises

At this point in the book we are inviting you to pause and take stock of some of the more distinctive and conspicuous undertakings of the English stone builders.

Their supreme achievements were certainly the cathedrals. At a time when roads were mostly very bad, the means of transport primitive, the range of tools much more limited than today and power-operated aids almost non-existent (for wind and water were not much help here), the erection of these vast buildings was an astonishing venture. The English vaults, it is true, did not soar nearly as high as the French, but even France cannot, we believe, show a single major stone vault that has stood for over eight and a half centuries without requiring considerable restoration, if not, as at Vézelay, complete rebuilding. Yet that is what was attained at Durham – not, admittedly, over the choir, the vault of which had to be reconstructed in the thirteenth century, but over the transepts, vaulted by about 1110 and over the nave, complete by 1132. Some of the Gothic vaults were both technically and artistically still more remarkable: to this day the vaults of Exeter, Norwich, Gloucester choir, Canterbury nave, Winchester nave and Wells chapter house (**144**) stand as achievements in the very highest class. As for the towers and spires, words fail. That before the middle of the fourteenth century the stonemasons should have dared to carry the spire of Salisbury up to the vertiginous height of 404 ft. is frankly stupefying.

We take the view that religious fervour had very little to do with all this. These were men in love with stone and all its potentialities, and, like all such people at every period of history, their sole concern was to find a patron who would commission them to build. At that time there was only one: the Church. But here was a magnificent patron. Churchmen had the faith to commission these buildings to the glory of God (and sometimes, no doubt, in order to surpass the work of their neighbours) and the masons were only too willing to go along with them. There were misfortunes, of course; vaults cracked and towers foundered. But wherever the design was sound and the stone good – and for about two-thirds of the mediaeval cathedrals excellent stone was fortunately available – the quality both of the structure and of the ornamentation was extremely high, and a great deal remains to bear witness to it.

But the cathedrals, the abbeys, the priories and the parish churches have so often been described, in books wholly devoted to them, that it is not proposed to say any more about them now, other than to point out that in the Middle Ages they had to be of stone; for buildings conceived on this scale, there was in England no other material available.

As time went on, this no longer held good. When Wolsey built Hampton Court Palace of brick, the material was still fairly unusual, and had never before been employed in this country on so large a scale; but from then on brick started slowly to become a viable alternative, and eventually, in many areas, to take over. Before the end of the eighteenth century many major buildings which appear to be of stone were in fact of brick with a stone cladding, which was surely a perfectly sensible and justifiable practice. In the present century stone is hardly ever employed in any other way; the differences are that the underlying structure is now more likely to be steel and concrete or breeze blocks and the stone cladding will be thinner.

Happily, however, stone architecture is still very much in evidence in many parts of England, and is sure to remain so. Let us now look at certain aspects of this achievement in a little more detail.

CHIMNEYS

In countries with a climate as cool as our own chimneys were, until the introduction of central heating, indispensable. The Palladian architects, looking towards Italy, where chimneys are less essential, disliked them and sometimes strove to reduce their prominence, but even they did not always do so: at Holkham, for instance, there is a plethora of tall stacks, and even at Chiswick the chimneys are very noticeable. The only rational course was to accept them and if possible turn them into a pleasant feature of the overall design, and this is, for centuries, exactly what occurred: from Tudor times

97 The Chequer, Abingdon Abbey, Berkshire (now Oxfordshire)

until Lutyens the skylines of English houses are peppered with chimney-stacks, some very tall indeed.

Before the Tudors heating arrangements were not so efficient. But even in the Norman period chimneys were not unknown; one, a tall plain shaft built of Purbeck limestone, survives on the ruined keep of the late-twelfth century castle at Christchurch in Hampshire. In general, however, although the principal apartments of the Norman castles had large fireplaces, the flues were short and there were no chimneys; the rooms must sometimes have been filled with smoke. So also with the first manor houses. At Stokesay Castle (really a manor house) the fire was lit in the centre of the great hall, and the smoke found its way out as best it could, through windows not glazed but closed only by wooden shutters.

Contemporary with Stokesay (that is, of the latter part of the thirteenth century) is our earliest surviving chimney of any architectural distinction, to be found among the former monastic buildings of Abingdon Abbey (**97**). The smoke was emitted from the sturdy stone stack through tiny triplets of stepped lancets under little gables. The following century saw the

appearance of the louvre, an opening, often octagonal, to allow at least some of the smoke from a central hearth to escape. Not many of these fourteenth century louvres remain; one which has disappeared formerly crowned the roof of the great hall at Penshurst Place. A notable survivor, from the early fifteenth century, is the two-storeyed louvre at Preston Plucknett (**98**), which served not the hall but the kitchen. It is interesting to notice that, whereas both the house and the barn (**6**) are entirely roofed with stone slates, the coping of the gable carrying the louvre is of simulated slating worked in freestone.

By this time stone chimneys were beginning to be regarded as necessities for the better class of country house. At Bodiam Castle, largely built in 1386, every room of any consequence had its own fireplace and stone chimney. In the fifteenth century examples multiplied, and with the advent of the Tudors builders of chimneys had a wonderful time. Many, it is true, were of brick, for good brick, being itself kiln-burned, is more fire-resistant than stone; but stone chimneys also survive in considerable numbers from the sixteenth century. Barrington Court, dating from 1514, has a profusion of twisted chimneys in Ham Hill stone. Lacock Abbey, suppressed in 1539, was acquired by Sir William Sharrington, 'a Tudor profiteer of doubtful reputation but excellent architectural taste',* who in the course of

*Robin Fedden and Rosemary Joekes, *The National Trust Guide* (1973), p. 367

converting the monastic buildings into a fine private house added tall
slender stone chimneys of many different forms; there are not only spirals
but zigzags, and other more complex designs, chimneys with corner shafts,
for example, and even with miniature flying buttresses. Sharrington must
have had the help of an extremely gifted master-mason.

With the advent of the Renaissance, chimneys began to adopt columnar
forms, with moulded bases and cornices. On the smaller buildings, like the
terrace pavilions at Chipping Campden (**99**) which survived the
destruction of the manor house in the Civil War, only single shafts were
required; here the spirals are seen again, and the crowning finials, the
purpose of which was to prevent a down draught, are very fanciful. The
bases are also unusual in that they show strapwork in reverse: the parts that
are sunk would normally be in relief. But on the big houses, where many
chimneys were needed, the architects liked to group them, generally in
pairs or triplets, and, as at Wollaston Hall (**100**), to link them together at
cornice level. On the corner towers here (cf. also **152**) the chimneys are
treated in a most unusual manner; the flues of fired clay are gathered
together by means of ogee arches to form a central stack (not improved by

101 and 102 Burghley House,
Stamford: chimneys; and roofscape

the much more recent chimney-pots). At Burghley House, where there is a
veritable forest of chimneys, ten to twelve feet high and grouped in clusters
of two, three, four and even six, the shafts are linked not just by a shared
cornice but by a complete section of entablature: architrave, frieze and
cornice (**101**). The shafts, following the example of Longleat, are Doric
columns with the correct entasis; the Barnack freestone (not ragstone),
from a quarry on the estate, is of splendid quality. A perambulation of the
roof of Burghley House offers one of the most fantastic architectural
experiences in the country (**102**). (The castellated chimney-pots are of
course much later, and to be regretted. One would expect them to be
terracotta, but in fact some at least are of Ketton stone, meticulously hand-
carved in the estate workshop.)

On smaller houses of the Elizabethan and Jacobean periods the chimneys
were no less prominent but of simpler form, appropriate to the rest of the
design. The best examples in stone are still mostly to be found on the
Jurassic limestone belt. A favourite practice, which always gives pleasure,
was to set them diagonally to the face of the wall and to the axis of the roof,

148

104 **Thorpe Hall, Peterborough:**
chimney stack

103 **Almshouses, Chipping**
Campden, Gloucestershire

as at Owlpen Manor (**164**) and at the Sir Baptist Hicks Almshouses at
Chipping Campden (**103**), a perfect example of Cotswold stone
masoncraft, dating from 1612. But a change was now about to occur;
indeed, examples of the new, typically seventeenth century type of
chimney can also be seen on this very building. The essential difference was
that the emphasis on the individual shaft was superseded by the more
massive stack, in which several flues were concentrated. At Chipping
Campden and at Great Weldon Manor House (**171**), an excellent
Northamptonshire example, there is still a long narrow vent between the
flues. Presently even this was to disappear, giving place to a solid, generally
rectangular pier, enriched not only with a strong cornice but sunk panels on
every face, carefully moulded, as can be seen, for example, at Belton House.
At Thorpe Hall near Peterborough, where the architect was Peter Mills,
the quality of the Ketton stone masonry is outstanding (**104**). At the angles
of the four stacks are rusticated pilasters, crowned by acanthus-palmette
capitals: a most unusual feature.

Chimneys, then, grew more massive, but they did not become any less
prominent. In latitudes such as ours, a fire was and is often welcome for at
least eight months in the year, so within, the chimney-piece is not only
regarded as essential but is the dominant feature of the room, in relation to

149

which all the furniture is arranged. Externally it was the same; although the classical architects would probably have liked to dispense with chimneys, they did not do so. Chimneys had to be accepted; all that could be done, on the great houses, was to design them to look as stately as possible, and for this of course stone was much the best material available.

It is sad to see how often the artistic impact of these well-designed stacks was later compromised by the addition of chimney-pots. These were not seen in England before the reign of George III, and most of them belong to the nineteenth century. Even when, as is sometimes the case, their orange-red colour is quite rich, big chimney-pots are excrescent. Nor are they necessary; most countries, including the United States, manage perfectly well without giving them any prominence. Good chimney construction requires that the wind shall not blow across a horizontal plane but impinge against an edge, and this can be achieved with a pot projecting no more than about two inches: the rest can be, and often is, sunk within the flue, so that the pot is invisible from below. If there is also too much direct down draught, this can be checked by the simple device of tilting two thin slabs of stone against one another over the chimney aperture. This can quite often be seen on stone shafts in some areas. If it is felt that clay pots must be retained on a stone house, it is undoubtedly preferable that they should be stone-coloured, and of uniform design and height throughout. But in these days of widespread central heating and of compulsory smokeless fuel in cities, many chimney-pots could be removed, with great aesthetic advantage to the buildings concerned.

In the limestone and sandstone areas almost every chimney-stack from the seventeenth century onwards was either rectangular or square; the tapering chimneys of Lord Burghley's Almshouses at Stamford (**77**), Georgian replacements, provide a charming exception. But where the local stone is very hard – such as granite, whinstone (basalt and dolerite) or flint – round shafts were preferred; they were so much easier to build, for with stones such as these the angles are the most difficult part. Accordingly there are many round chimneys in the South-West (**105**) and also in the Lake District (**106**); it is a pity that the chimneys of the cottages near Crook, which is a little east of Windermere, have been roughcast. Some believe that in exposed positions round chimneys are better able to resist the gales.

Yet, although stone of almost every kind has been widely employed for chimneys in many parts of the country, it has to be said that, from the practical standpoint, brick is for this purpose superior. This is particularly true of limestone, which when it is wet does not like sulphur, salt or frost. In

105 Round front-chimney cottages, Bossington, Somerset

106 Round chimney cottage, near Crook, Westmorland

107 **House at Reeth, Yorkshire:**
flue discolouration

the days when domestic heating depended entirely on coal fires, the chimneys were the part of a limestone building most likely to fail, which accounts for the curious aspect of Malmesbury in Wiltshire, where all the older houses are of stone but almost every chimney is brick. If, as often, the limestone is fairly porous, the sulphurous smoke from coal and the fumes from gas fires and boilers will sometimes condense into dangerous liquids which can corrode the stonework and stain it. That is what has happened at the house illustrated at Reeth in Swaledale (**107**). The chimney here is of gritstone, but the walling material is Carboniferous limestone. The staining of both is unsightly, and cannot be eradicated; moreover, the soot-stained stonework will decay sooner than the rest.

It is hoped that this problem has at last been overcome. In new construction flue liners are now available for chimneys: these are tubes of burnt fireclay, usually about 9 ins. in diameter, although they can be larger. Even more useful are flexible aluminium liners, which are inserted from the top, and will follow all the bends of a flue right down to the fireplace. If a new chimney is being constructed of stone, especially freestone, another precaution which should be taken is to insert a damp course at the base, with the object of preventing dampness from creeping down into the lower rooms by way of the flue.

The largest chimneys, needless to say, are industrial. Generally they are of brick, but in the industrial North tall stone chimneys are by no means rare. They can be rather splendid; they have caught the imagination of a number of painters, and notably of L. S. Lowry. But if they happen also to be works of art, it is likely to be by accident and not by design.

108 Piece Hall, Halifax: setts and paving-stones

PAVING-STONES AND STEPS

Stone has always been much in demand for paving, both externally and internally. Leaving aside for the moment cobbles and setts, there are only two essential requirements: the stone must either be thin bedded or well laminated, so that it can be split into reasonably thin slabs, and it must be hard and durable without being brittle. A 'non-slip' surface is usually another great asset, while the size of the slabs may also be a factor of importance, as for example in the flooring of a cathedral.

Even before the Industrial Revolution York paving stone and granite setts were in considerable demand, particularly in London; all of course were brought by water. But in places that were less affluent or less accessible by water transport, there was seldom any choice; whatever stone was available locally had to be used, and the really unlucky people were those who had almost no stone at all, as in Essex. Thus in the Stamford area Ketton stone was used extensively for paving, a purpose for which externally it was not really very suitable. After the construction of the canals, and especially after the advent of the railways, the tougher varieties of stone were able to travel to all parts of the country.

The demand in the Victorian period was tremendous. Towns were expanding at a great rate, and now they all needed pavements for walkers. The ideal material was Carboniferous sandstone: Millstone Grit and the products of the Coal Measures, and above all what is known generically as York stone. This does not come from York but from a number of quarries to the south of Leeds and Bradford, and around Halifax and Huddersfield. Over twenty are still working. It can be quarried in very large blocks, and sawn or split comparatively easily, sometimes into slabs as little as one inch thick, but the usual thickness is between $1\frac{1}{4}$ and 3 ins. York stone retains too much moisture to be good for roofing, but for paving it is ideal (**108**), and vast quantities have travelled to London, and to many other cities and towns besides. The thin laminations of this stone often lead with use to irregular 'peeling' of the surface, which can be a help in combatting the risks of slipping in wet weather. In the West country there is a somewhat similar Carboniferous sandstone, quarried in the Forest of Dean and at various points in Gwent (Monmouthshire) and Glamorgan, which is also very well suited to paving.

Other sources of good Carboniferous sandstone for paving, mostly even-grained and all extremely hard, are in Derbyshire (Wingerworth and Grindleford), Cheshire (Kerridge near Macclesfield: this stone was also much used for roofing: see page 226), Lancashire (Appley Bridge and Howlett Hill, both near Wigan) and Northumberland (Ladycross near Hexham). Most of these quarries are still working, and this list is not exhaustive.

The Devonian and Old Red sandstones have also provided many excellent paving stones. An important source of supply among the Old Reds was Caithness. In the Victorian period 'Caithness flags' were shipped southwards in huge numbers.

The Devonian rocks of the South-West are, as observed earlier, not all sandstone: some are limestone and many are slate. It was the limestone which provided much of the paving-stone in the rebuilding of the civic centre area of Plymouth after the Second World War: stone which was later, alas, partly replaced by concrete. The Carboniferous limestone quarried at Orton Scar near Tebay in central Westmorland (now part of Cumbria) has also produced very good paving-stones. But most of the Jurassic limestones, which figure so prominently in this book in many other ways, are not sufficiently tough to be used for paving-stones, except internally, as for example for church floors. There are a few exceptions, of which Purbeck and Portland are the chief. Sawn slabs from all the three beds of Portland stone have been widely used in the south of England for paving, as also formerly, on a very large scale, from Purbeck: they have given excellent service. Internally, huge slabs of Blue Lias limestone from Street in Somerset were used to pave Wells Cathedral.

Wittering pendle, referred to in Chapter 4 (p. 120), is no longer quarried, but was at one time used extensively in the locality both for interior floors and for external paving. It occurs in such narrow beds that the smaller pieces can be set on edge; laid in this fashion it would, far better than any other local stone, resist very hard wear from the iron shoes of horses. Pendle was therefore much in demand for the floors of stables.

Although most of the choicer limestones are unable to stand up to the rough and tumble of the public thoroughfare, some of them are a great embellishment to gardens. One which is durable enough for this purpose is Blue Lias, seen in the garden path at Lytes Cary, a National Trust house in Somerset (**109**). Part of the beauty of this path resides in the manner in which the stone naturalises, allowing lichens, mosses and minute plants to live on and in it, as York stone and the other Carboniferous sandstones rarely do. With garden paths, however, it is generally preferable not to use mortar but to leave the joints open, so that rain and snow can disappear more quickly into the soil. For the same reason raised kerbs at the sides are best avoided.

Paving-stones can be either riven or sawn: these at Lytes Cary are riven. For gardens riven stones are always preferable; they have more texture and develop a patina more quickly than smoother paving. Their surface is also less slippery. But in an urban setting sawn slabs with an absolutely smooth face are generally regarded as more appropriate.

Many of the fossil-packed limestones which in England carry the courtesy title of marble have been used extensively, and often very effectively, for internal flooring: most of all Purbeck, but also Sussex 'marble', Bethersden from Kent, Stamford, Frosterley and several others.

109 Lytes Cary Manor, Somerset: stone pathway

110 Clareville Street, London, S.W.7: granite kerb

111 Stanhope Mews, London, S.W.7: setts

Now and again, as for the churchyard path at Great Chart, Kent, the next village to Bethersden, they were used externally, but even if tough enough for this, they are all seen to much better advantage inside, for in an unpolished state they lose most of their attraction. The most 'sumptuous' of these stones are from the Carboniferous limestones of Devon and Derbyshire, which are sometimes employed for cladding walls as well as for paving. They are expensive, but can be a great embellishment; the use of Ashburton marble in a side chapel at Guildford Cathedral was mentioned earlier (p. 49).

The large black ledgers which are such an adornment to many of our old churches, and for which there was a great vogue in the Georgian period, are Carboniferous limestone imported from Belgium, especially Tournai.

Slate, being fissile, is another excellent material for paving, and before the invention of fast-moving mechanical saws was almost always riven. In urban situations sawn slate may be more practical, but riven slate always looks better. There are plenty of houses in Cornwall and in Cumbria that are entirely floored with slate, which was of course specially suitable for passages, dairies and still-rooms. In the nineteenth century a great deal of slate was also imported from North Wales.

Granite, until the advent of the modern cutting techniques to be described later, could not be split into thin slabs, so old granite paving, even in Cornwall, is a rarity. The handsome pavement to be seen outside the Cathedral at Exeter, comprising huge slabs of granite with large felspar crystals, would have been an impossibility before the advent of this machinery. But long before there were machines, there was a call for kerbstones, for which blocks of granite were invaluable; for this purpose they were despatched all over the country during the Victorian period. These kerbstones look as if they will last for ever (110).

Granite was also much in demand, especially in the nineteenth century, for setts. In London these became the standard paving material for the principal streets in Victorian times. They were roughly dressed rectangular blocks of varying sizes, but usually not more than 7 ins. × 4 ins., with a

depth of at least 5 ins. The principal source of supply was Aberdeen, but other lively centres of production were Mountsorrel and Markfield in Leicestershire, the Channel Isles, Cornwall and Lundy Island. Considerable quantities were also shipped across from Norway. Besides granite, other igneous rocks also made their contribution: basalt, dolerite, syenite, diorite, gneiss. But granite setts did not reach Halifax before the closing years of the nineteenth century, and those in the courtyard of the Piece Hall (**108**) are of local sandstone from the Lower Coal Measures: probably from Elland Edge.

Sett-making was exceedingly hard work, for the men had no mechanical aids of any kind. A road paved with granite setts has a strength with which no other can compare; sometimes they were laid in interesting patterns, of which a repeating fan design was perhaps the favourite. In busy commercial areas such as docks, harbours and railway yards, the setts proved invaluable, although also very noisy, as before the invention of pneumatic tyres the iron wheels of the vehicles combined with the horses' hooves to set up a tremendous clatter. In the more affluent parts of the capital large numbers of these setts can still be seen in what were formerly mews (**111**). Elsewhere many more survive than might be supposed, for the majority came in due course to be covered with macadam or asphalt, for which they provided a splendid foundation. But often, especially in London, in order to reduce the noise and the vibration from horse-drawn vehicles, they were later replaced by tarred wooden blocks bedded on concrete.

Apart from setts the most durable road surface was supplied by cobbles, which were even noisier. The use of cobbles for paving has a much longer history, going back in fact to the Middle Ages. Many town streets were once paved with them. A few still are: Merton Street at Oxford, for example, and Elm Hill at Norwich. In the days of horses, manure often caused grass to flourish in the interstices.

Cobbles came from many different sources. In the Vale of York and parts of Lincolnshire they are likely to be igneous rocks from the Boulder Clay, transported aeons ago from the Cheviots or beyond by glacial drift; these are well seen in a much trodden tourist area at Lincoln between the Cathedral and the Castle. In the Lower Greensand region of south-western Surrey (the Guildford–Godalming–Farnham area) the cobbles are lumps of dark brown sandstone, retrieved from the much looser surrounding sand.

Hard but brittle, thus easily broken into fairly thin manageable pieces, they
were usually laid on edge: the sharp surfaces were soon rounded off by use.
Elsewhere cobbles were often oversize rejects from gravel pits. Pebbles
from beaches are not so suitable because they are likely to be impregnated
with salt, which may eventually loosen them. Cobbles can be kept clean by
spraying with fine jets of water. Wherever it is desired to discourage either
pedestrians or cars, they can be very effective. If carefully selected and
properly laid, their appearance can also be delightful. The old way of laying
them was to bed them in clay, pointing downwards, like an egg in an egg-
cup: never sideways. Nowadays they are set in cement and sand, leaving
the top third of each cobble revealed; in order to achieve a level surface a
board is laid over them and gently tapped.

In the garden of Minster Lovell Hall in Oxfordshire there is a cobbled
way which may go back to the fifteenth century (**112**). This house, mainly
built in the 1430s, was allowed three centuries later to become ruinous. The
pathway led from the great hall to the kitchen and the stables. The strips of
limestone which criss-cross it not only added visual interest but served a
practical purpose too: they provided a level surface to work up to and
helped to retain the cobbles in place. But the limestone, probably from
Taynton, has flaked (**113**), whereas the cobbles, although not all laid in the
best way, show virtually no signs of wear. Minster Lovell Hall stands beside
the Windrush, and another favourite place for gathering cobbles was the
bed of a stream or small river. Some at least of those in the courtyard of St.
Anne's Hospital at Appleby (**56**), which are also not all laid in the best way,
are likely to have come from a similar source. As observed above, they do

not provide a comfortable surface for walking, and here, thoughtfully, a flagstone path has also been introduced; but visually they are very satisfying.

A rarity in England is the pavement in front of the gatehouse at Bickleigh Castle near Tiverton (**114**). This too is mostly made of river-washed cobbles, taken from the bed of the river Exe, which flows within fifty yards. (There are also a few bits of spar – the whitish stones – which glint in the sun). It was laid in 1945–46 by Italian prisoners of war, who were working as farm labourers before being repatriated, and did this in their spare time for their own pleasure and that of their employers. Long cobbles were selected, mostly set on their sides. The design was taken from a handbag of woven wool! It is a happy coincidence that the fine wrought-iron gates, believed to date from about 1780, are also Italian.

Many of the kinds of stone best suited to paving have also been employed for steps, and some, but not all, are equally suitable for roofing. As staircases often receive very hard wear, the most durable locally available

114 Bickleigh Castle, Devon: decorated pavement

115 Castle Bolton, Yorkshire:
newel stair

116 Burghley House, Stamford:
'Roman Stair' with stone ceiling

stone which could be dressed into the necessary shapes would always be used.

Early staircases were often circular and of the newel type.★ The newel is the central pillar from which the steps of a circular stair radiate (**115**). Each step has, of course, to be wedge-shaped, and at its inner end carries a section of the newel worked as part of it. This was the traditional way of constructing newel staircases from the very earliest examples. Sometimes the steps were linked by iron dowels fixed into the centre of the newel. The problem was to adjust the height and width of each step to allow for sufficient headroom and to arrive at the correct point of egress on each of the upper floor levels. Newel staircases often have a moulded handrail inset into the outer wall, but are usually very narrow, either because space was much restricted, as in the stair-turrets of church towers, or for purposes of defence, as in nearly all mediaeval castles. In these the stairs are also believed to have been designed, wherever possible, to suit right-handed defenders when it came to swinging swords in such restricted space.

The so-called Roman staircase at Burghley House (**116**) still went up round a solid core of masonry; the chief interest here is in the surface elaboration of the tunnel vault, all of carved Barnack freestone instead of the usual plaster. But the English staircases seldom rivalled the grandeur, sometimes the sheer *panache*, of many to be seen on the Continent, especially in Italy, although from the sixteenth century onwards they

★To refer to these as *spiral* staircases is a misnomer. That term relates to open spiral stairs made of cast-iron or steel.

gradually became more spacious. The broad stairway in the garden of Haddon Hall (**117**) dates from the Jacobean period. Each step incorporates a projecting rounded piece called a nosing. The treads, risers and nosings are all cut in one piece sectionally, although there are joints along the length. (The larger the slabs the better). The ratio of light is always a factor to be taken into account in the design of an external staircase in stone. Usually, as here, the treads are much lighter than the risers, which is satisfying aesthetically, for the surface of the treads is approximately two thirds of the whole. Both for comfort and for good appearance, a riser should not exceed 6 ins., and $4\frac{1}{2}$ or 5 ins. is more elegant and makes for an easier ascent. Treads should not be less than 11 ins. wide, and 12 or 13 ins. is, again, more dignified. The artistic success of a stone staircase will often largely depend upon getting these subtle relationships right. Incidentally, slightly worn surfaces are an asset, comparable to weathering. A brand new stone staircase may well appear unduly hard.

Internally the newel stair gave way in the Tudor period to the right-angled type, comprising a succession of short straight flights built round a central core, as for example at Montacute. This in turn was succeeded by the cantilever staircase, which is still the normal kind today, although most commonly in wood. Structurally the cantilever stair represented a great advance. Its obvious feature is that the support comes from one side only; the handrail side is free. Each step, therefore, has to be continued into the wall to a depth sufficient to provide the required support; how much will depend upon the width of the stair itself. A narrow stair will require about 9 ins., a wider one up to 18 ins. Landings are often cantilevered from the outer wall in exactly the same way.

Needless to say, cantilevers are much more easily constructed in wood than in stone, which is so much heavier. The stone selected has to be of the best quality. The earliest example of a cantilevered stone staircase in England is believed to be the modest one in the Queen's House at Greenwich, inserted about 1630 by Inigo Jones. With this type of staircase the balustrade is often of wrought or cast iron, as here; the repeating pattern, with a tulip-shaped top, accounts for the name: the Tulip Staircase. Much longer is Wren's famous Geometrical Staircase in the south-west tower of St. Paul's Cathedral, again with a wrought iron balustrade. The Georgian and Regency periods produced many examples of cantilevered staircases, often of the highest accomplishment, and when in the Victorian period the level of taste degenerated, there was certainly no decline in technical mastery.

117 Haddon Hall, Derbyshire: steps and balustrade in garden

118 Filkins, Oxfordshire: limestone slab fencing

FENCES AND BALUSTRADES

Fences are generally of wood: sometimes they are of cast iron: rarely now of stone, for stone is too valuable to be employed in this way. But they can still be found here and there. In Cotswold limestone there are several in the village of Filkins (**118**, **162**), much older than most of that village's houses.

It is, however, in the slate areas, North Cornwall, North Wales and especially the Lake District, that stone fences are chiefly seen today. There are still quite a number of them in the vicinity of Hawkshead (**119**) and Ambleside. These slab fences are not very high, seldom over 3 ft., for to obtain stability about a quarter of the total height of each stone has to be buried in the ground; but they are a delightful survival.

Balustrades are a very different matter. Each one demands skilful masoncraft. They are both functional and, at best, highly ornamental. Positions where they are seen to great advantage include roof parapets, balconies, staircases, garden terraces and bridges. Many different patterns were evolved. Some are continuous, but the great majority are divided into panels by solid piers, which are often emphasized by the addition of stone balls, vases, miniature obelisks or even statues. These intermittent piers serve not only aesthetically, as 'points of punctuation', but functionally, as strengtheners (**120**).

121 Lancaster, Lancashire: detail of aqueduct

The design of a good balustrade depends on a number of factors, of which the most important of all is to determine the right relationship of the solid parts to the voids. If the balusters are too widely spaced they will look weak. The shape of the balusters themselves is obviously of great importance, but the size and scale of the base and the hand-rail also have to be carefully considered. With a staircase balustrade the raking angle produces an additional design factor.

Stone balusters are either round-turned, 'square-turned' or flat-plated. Round-turned balusters of a familiar type are seen on the Lune aqueduct at Lancaster (**121**): some have had to be renewed. The essential tool here is the lathe. The mason begins by preparing the pieces of stone to the length and section required, and roughly shapes the barrel. It is then passed to the turner, whose task is by no means simple. Some stones are more easily turned than others; the presence of shells in the stone can be troublesome. The smoother, finer limestones and sandstones are better for turning than those which are harder but shellier. Thus Ketton stone is for this purpose preferable to Clipsham, and was in fact much used for balusters in the Stamford region and at Cambridge. Great care has to be taken in lathe-turning because undue vibration, together with the pressure of the chisel, may fracture the baluster at the neck. This can be as little as two

166

inches in diameter, so is always the vulnerable point. Often a turner will start by soaking the stone in water, in order to reduce the dust to a minimum.

The bulbous-shaped baluster seen on the Lune aqueduct is certainly the favourite round form, but lathe-turned balusters with a central waist are also not uncommon. This form was much favoured in England in the seventeenth century; it can also be seen, to excellent effect, at Montacute (153) and on the Palladian bridge at Wilton (130).

'Square-turning' is one of those expressions widely current in the stone trade which is nevertheless a misnomer, for balusters of this form are hand-wrought and not turned on a machine as are the round ones. The garden stairway at Haddon Hall (117) provides a good illustration. Every arch has its emphasized key-stone and the entire balustrade is rusticated. All had to be carved by the banker mason except the balls, which were lathe-turned. The high artistic value of these balls, occurring at carefully determined intervals, needs no emphasis.

Flat-plated balusters are also hand-carved. They can be seen on the small balcony of the terrace pavilion at Chipping Campden (99): another Jacobean survival. There was not much space here, so it was convenient to keep the balusters as flat as possible; these are probably no more than 2 ins. thick. In this situation they look exactly right.

Balusters of all types were usually held in place by means of dowels. Unfortunately these were usually of wrought-iron, which has given a great deal of trouble, as described earlier (cf. p. 78). An alternative method, excellent if the stone allowed it, was to cut tenons at either end of the baluster, to fit into mortices in the upper face of the base and the underside of the rail.

BRIDGES

Throughout history, and all over the world, one of the loveliest uses of stone has been for the construction of bridges: one of the loveliest and, let it be said, one of the most durable. The Pont du Gard is not the only Roman aqueduct to have survived for nearly two thousand years. And why? Because they were so well built. All the old bridges were of load-bearing masonry, entirely self-supporting, with every stone designed and made to suit its own special purpose. Many of the finest belong to the eighteenth century.

Stone bridges earlier than the fourteenth century were never common in Britain and are now very rare. The earliest type was the clapper bridge, which consisted simply of single slabs laid between rudely constructed piers. Much the best surviving example is at Postbridge in the middle of Dartmoor (**122**). Here the Dart is crossed by three immense slabs of granite, each about 15 ft. long and up to 6 ft. wide. In the centre of the stream are two piers of roughly shaped granite blocks, built up without mortar. At the two ends the abutments are of natural rock. Although the age of this bridge is not known, it seems likely to be at least two thousand years. Tarr Steps, just across the border into Somerset, may be still older; this clapper bridge, which now belongs to the National Trust, is five miles north-west of Dulverton, on the edge of Exmoor, and crosses the Barle, a tributary of the Exe, in a situation of great beauty. But unfortunately the supporting piers do not rise nearly so high above the water as at Postbridge, and the flag-stones, seventeen of them, extending over a distance of 180 ft., are smaller, so several times they have been carried downstream by floodwaters, and have had to be recovered.

Rivers in flood were the greatest hazard for the early bridge-builders. A stone bridge erected across the Tweed at Berwick in 1285 was carried away after only nine years. Since the two wooden bridges which preceded it had met a similar fate, it was over two centuries before any further attempt was made to bridge the Tweed here. Timber bridges were constantly foundering in the floodwaters, but they could usually be reconstructed much more easily, which is why the great majority of our bridges in the Middle Ages were of wood – as also, apparently, during the Roman occupation, for England has no stone bridge which is authentically Roman. However, there were a few other stone bridges before the fourteenth century: the Monnow Bridge at Monmouth, although later (as so often) widened, dates originally from 1272, and twenty years before that Bristol had one, spanning the Avon.

The typical stone bridge of the later Middle Ages had massive piers, big cutwaters facing upstream, carried up as roadside recesses, and arches of comparatively modest span, usually continuously curved but sometimes pointed. Horse Bridge (**123**), which crosses the Tamar at a remote spot west of Tavistock, to link Devon with the Cornish village of Stoke Climsland, is a fine example built of the local Culm Measures sandstone in 1437. There are seven arches, stretching over 200 ft., and the stonework is still in excellent condition, for, being on a minor road, it has not had to suffer buffeting by heavy traffic.

There would never seem to have been specialist bridge-builders in
mediaeval England, as there were in France. The Church, and especially the
monks, often regarded bridge-building as an act of piety to the
community, and as a result the same masons who worked on the cathedrals,
abbeys and churches would also be expected to design and build bridges. It
was the patronage of the Church which accounts for the little stone chapels
which were sometimes added at one end of the bridge or even over a pier in
mid-stream. Only four of these survive, all much restored: at Wakefield,
Rotherham, Derby and St. Ives in Huntingdonshire. At Bradford-on-
Avon the bridge chapel was rebuilt in the seventeenth century as a lock-up.

Most of the early bridges were erected on the sites of ancient fords. These
had been located at points where the watercourses were shallow, or,
alternatively, at places where the river bed was stony and therefore firm, as
at Stamford. Both above and below this town the river, the Welland, is
alluvial and marshy, but at this one point the valley contracts between
limestone hills: hence the original name, 'Stoneford'.

Obviously, solid rock provided the best foundation for a bridge and the
old practice, where the water was not too deep, was to make timber
caissons or cofferdams and pump out the water with hand-pumps, so that
the foundations could be laid on something really solid. But in many parts
of England there is no rock to be found. After bedrock it might be
supposed that the next best foundation would be hard gravel, but clay is in
fact preferable, provided that it can be kept continuously moist. Gravel
tends to be displaced by the continual vibrations produced by heavy traffic,
whereas clay will absorb them. Into the clay it was sometimes necessary to
drive huge wooden piles, which might be as long as 10 ft; elm was a
favourite wood for this purpose, and it might be treated with tar first, or
deliberately scorched in a bonfire. It is astonishing to learn how durable
wood can be when employed in this way.

Apart from the clapper bridge, all bridges before the Industrial
Revolution depended on the arch. The builders had no iron, steel or
concrete to help them, except perhaps for a few iron cramps at critical
points; what was therefore required was a complete understanding of poise
and counterpoise, of thrust and counterthrust. The masonry itself was thus
of paramount importance. There was a preference, wherever they were
obtainable, for large stones, very carefully cut so that the joints fitted as
closely as possible. The amount of mortar, which was made with lime and
contained no cement, was thereby reduced to a minimum. And wherever
the stone could be ashlared, it invariably was.

Every arch had of course to be constructed on a wooden scaffolding known as a centering; for a large bridge this had to be immensely strong, for, depending on the size of the span, it might have to support a weight of anything up to two thousand tons, until the final moment, with the insertion of the keystone. The centering could then be dismantled and, if the span were the same, reused for the next arch. The engraving of about 1812 (**44**) gives a good idea of the strength of the centering needed in the construction of Rennie's Waterloo Bridge in London, which was built of Pelastine granite from Cornwall.

As time went on the size of the spans gradually increased. The three arched bridge over the Swale at Richmond in Yorkshire, designed by John Carr of York to replace one carried away by a flood in 1771, is a model of quiet confidence and strength, with the minimum of adornment (**124**). The material is Carboniferous sandstone from the quarry on Gatherley Moor, a few miles to the north. The old angled cutwaters have here assumed a rounded form, but are still carried up to the full height of the parapet. Over the top surface of the arches but beneath the roadway, it was usual to add a layer of clay. This was found to be more satisfactory than loose stones, for it could be beaten down into a kind of solid, waterproof mass, which would stop the water on the carriageway from percolating down through the stonework of the piers and arches and perhaps damaging the lime mortar joints, as well as being a better counter than loose stones to traffic vibration.

Among many other beautiful river bridges built in the eighteenth
century there is only space to mention two. The most satisfying are nearly
always those which have not had to suffer later widening to accommodate
increased traffic. Very delightful is the three-arched bridge over the Nene
at Fotheringhay (**125**), which differs very little in design from the bridges of
three centuries earlier. It is built, again, with fairly large blocks of, in this
instance, oolitic limestone, probably from King's Cliffe, about five miles to
the north-west. Here the cutwaters were not carried up to road level.

Also of limestone and triple-arched, but totally different in character, is
Pulteney Bridge over the Avon in Bath (**126**), erected in 1770. The designer
was none other than Robert Adam, and this bridge was obviously of
classical inspiration, with his favourite Triumphal Arch motif at the centre
of the superstructure. But the classical vocabulary is employed with
Adam's characteristic delicacy. The notion of a bridge flanked on both
sides with shops is, since the disappearance of old London Bridge over two
hundred years ago, unique: it was, of course, a wholly urban concept. A
few such bridges survive on the continent, notably the Ponte Vecchio in
Florence. The cutwaters, though as large as at Fotheringhay, play only a
very modest role in the overall design. During the last century a number
of unfortunate changes were made to the superstructure; the careful

restoration of Pulteney bridge was the Georgian Group's contribution to European Architectural Heritage Year (1976).

Most of the stone bridges built since about 1600 have stood the test of time very well indeed, despite the ever-increasing weight of the loads which they are called upon to carry, far in excess of what was originally envisaged. Some years ago, at Berwick, it was necessary to transport an extremely heavy piece of machinery across the Tweed. The huge Royal Tweed Bridge, built in 1925–28 of concrete, could not cope with it, but it

was carried across the Old Bridge, finished in 1634 with fifteen arches of sandstone, without the slightest mishap. The fact is that with firm foundations and sound construction a stone bridge will take almost any load that is required of it, because masonry joints, normally under compression, will accept and compensate for a limited amount of tension and lateral movement provided that they are made with lime mortar.

Some of the most impressive, if also the last, of the great masonry bridges were designed by engineer–architects, working first for the canals and then for the railways. Among the former, none perhaps is finer than the aqueduct at Lancaster (**127**), completed in 1797, which carries the Preston to Kendal Canal over the Lune. The canal was Rennie's, but the designer of the bridge was the Scottish architect and civil engineer Alexander Stevens, who specialised in 'buildings in water'. This was his last, and also his grandest. There are five arches, each with a span of 75 ft. The rock-faced Millstone Grit of which it is constructed is still in excellent condition.

With the advent of the railways there was a need for many more bridges and a substantial number of viaducts, and visually some of these are among the finest achievements of the Victorian period. Not by any means all, of course, were of stone; the majority were of brick, and a good many, including the wonderful Forth Bridge and also some of the ugliest, were girder structures of iron and later steel. But most of one's favourites are of stone masonry, and some were prodigious structural achievements. Ballochmyle Viaduct, on the old Glasgow and South Western line near Cumnock in Ayrshire, designed by the Scots engineer, John Miller, has a central arch with a span of 181 ft. Although this is 19 ft. less than Thomas Harrison's Grosvenor Bridge over the Dee at Chester of 1832, which has the widest span of pure masonry ever achieved in Britain, the Ballochmyle arch, when completed in 1848, was the largest railway arch in the world, and remained so for fully fifty years. The centering was a masterpiece of

27 (left) Lancaster, Lancashire:
aqueduct over River Lune

128 and 129 Penistone, Yorkshire:
railway viaduct; and a section of
one of the piers

carpentry, and at the time of its erection this won almost equal fame.

In England most of the stone railway viaducts are in the north. The abundance of very tough sandstones, notably Millstone Grit and the products of the Coal Measures, and the almost insatiable demand for new railway construction in industrial Yorkshire and Lancashire, combined with the frequent hilliness of the terrain to yield a proliferation of bridges and viaducts. The one close to Penistone (**128**, **129**) is typical; it was built in 1885 for the Lancashire and Yorkshire Railway. These viaducts were essentially utilitarian, yet at best they have something of the grandeur and self-assurance of the aqueducts of Imperial Rome. The material here is Coal Measures sandstone. At the time the big blocks all had to be finished by hand, which accounts for the rock facing; this not only looks absolutely appropriate here but, as compared with ashlar, saved a good deal of labour.

Other bridges strike a very different note: so far from being objects of utility, their *raison d'être* was usually purely aesthetic. But in English landscape gardening the damming of a stream to create a stretch of ornamental water was regarded as almost essential, and that gave rich

amateurs and their architects the chance of designing bridges which in the
Georgian age vie with one another in grace and charm. Happily hundreds
survive, usually in stone, even if it had to be brought from a distance.
Sometimes they carry the drive leading up to the house. The most exquisite
of all these creations may well be felt to be the Palladian Bridge at Wilton
(**130**), designed in 1737 by the ninth Earl of Pembroke ('the architect earl')
with the professional assistance of Roger Morris, on the inspiration of a
drawing by Palladio, and carried out in the finest Chilmark limestone. This
is still splendidly preserved. Within a few years two of Lord Pembroke's
visitors had been so captivated by it that they had commissioned copies: at
Stowe in 1745 and at Prior Park, Bath, in 1750. And no wonder. All three
bridges survive: objects of enduring delight. Later copies, built before 1764
at Hagley and in 1777 at Amesbury are recorded by Mr. H. M. Colvin but
have vanished. However, one other even later copy, in grey-veined marble,
still stands, and that is, of all unlikely places, in the grounds of the former royal
palace at Tsarskoe Selo, now Pushkin, near Leningrad.

31 Waterloo Bridge, London,
.W.1

The present century has seen the construction, all over the world, of more bridges than ever before, especially since 1945. These include some, particularly on the Continent of Europe and in America, of breath-taking audacity. Unhappily, however, most of them carry roads perched aloft on concrete stilts, and they seldom have much to recommend them visually but their daring. Stone cladding on the express roads would be an economic impossibility, yet what is certain is that presently these huge bridges will not weather but just become shabby. For more localised structures, such as a river bridge in an old town, stone (or brick) cladding should in our opinion be a *sine qua non*. A generation or two ago many engineers, and some architects, regarded this as structurally dishonest, but fortunately not Sir Giles Gilbert Scott, whose new Waterloo Bridge in London (**131**) was built between 1939 and 1945. By purist standards this is a particularly 'dishonest' building, for structurally it consists of two continuous girders of reinforced concrete, embracing five spans of 240 ft. each; these spans are given the form of low arches, which they are not, and then faced with Portland stone. And why not? Without the appearance of having separate arches the bridge would have lost much of its visual appeal; and as for the stone facing, the coursing of the slabs is vertical, which leaves us in no doubt that this is not solid masonry. 'Dishonest' or not, this is considered in the opinion of many to be London's most beautiful bridge; and, having regard to what it replaced, it needed to be.

The arches of today's bridges are nearly always of ferro-concrete and it is perfectly right and proper that they should be. But always in old towns, and as often as possible elsewhere, some form of cladding is essential, as is usually recognised. When the Great North Road was reconstructed some twenty years ago with a by-pass for Stamford, a new bridge was needed for the crossing of the Welland. Since this bridge is in full view from the town, there could be no possible argument. It is faced throughout with Clipsham stone.

HARBOURS AND EMBANKMENTS

An unspectacular but very important use of stone, which has a long history, is for harbours, quays, jetties, piers, breakwaters and embankments. For these, needless to say, the stone has to be not only very hard but resistant to the action of the water, whether salt or fresh.

Pre-eminent is granite. With its compact, crystalline character and generally uniform structure, this stone is exceptionally impervious to water (as also to smoke pollution). That it was not much used outside the South-West before the Victorian age was due to the great difficulties attendant on quarrying it and shifting it. With the Industrial Revolution it came into its own, and vast quantities were sent away from Cornwall, South Devon, and even, for a short period in the eighteen-sixties, from Lundy Island, to supply the demands of the engineers. In London the Thames Embankment was largely built of it, and so were several of the bridges. Tower Bridge, like Rennie's Waterloo Bridge, was built of Pelastine granite from Penryn. At Shap in Westmorland (now Cumbria), however, the quarrying of granite did not begin until 1868.

There were at least two other water-resistant stones available before the heyday of granite. In the South many of the early harbours and jetties were constructed of Portland Roach, or Cocklebed as it was often called. This stone, as mentioned earlier (p. 107), was difficult to quarry because of its hardness and never much liked for buildings until quite recently, but the deposits were on the coast, which was very convenient, while its open, cellular texture, very fossiliferous and containing also the voids of numerous empty shells, yields a pitted surface which, even when wet, provides an exceptionally firm foothold. In Dorset itself the Cobb at Lyme Regis, a breakwater which was constructed to form an artificial harbour, has a history which goes back at least to the thirteenth century, but the part illustrated (**132**), which shows very clearly the character of the stone, is late-Georgian: it is described as 'new' in *Persuasion,* which was written in 1815–16. The steps on the right of the picture remind us of Louisa Musgrove's foolish and ill-fated jump: she landed on the Roach! And as readers who have seen the film *The French Lieutenant's Woman* will remember, it opens with a dramatic sequence in which Meryl Streep is standing at the end of the Cobb with a stormy sea in the background and waves breaking over the harbour wall. For her it might have been an even more perilous matter if the building material of the Cobb had *not* been Roach.

Later, this stone was used extensively in the naval Dockyard at Portsmouth. At Portland itself the Naval Anchorage also depends upon Roach, but here the blocks were just tipped into the sea at random, in great numbers. This enables the water, after the main impact of the waves has been countered, to flow through the barrier, thus reducing the stresses on the breakwater. Normally, however, the practice was to prise out and roughly dress blocks as large as could be handled, and to drop them down into the place required. At vital points iron cramps, leaded in, might be used to hold them together. But no mortar was used; reliance was placed on the great size and weight of the blocks themselves to keep them in position.

Between the Thames and the Humber there was no stone suitable for marine works, so men looked to the North. The Aislaby quarries, near Whitby in North Yorkshire, supplied the answer. Like Portland the stone here is Jurassic, but a sandstone, not a limestone. The quarries today are unworked and overgrown, but for centuries they yielded a close-textured sandstone of fine quality which had a considerable reputation; the loading jetties still remain. Large quantities were shipped to East coast ports, and it is known that some of it was used for the London docks.

In recent times, however, stone for structures bedded in water has been largely superseded by concrete, which is easier to handle and costs a lot less. Visually this is regrettable.

Mention should be made of the use of stone for the strengthening and consolidating of river banks in the hinterland of the Wash, which has been going on intermittently ever since Roman times. The stone employed was a very hard rubbly Jurassic limestone quarried at Wansford, near Peterborough. From there it was floated in barges down the Nene into the Wash and the main channels needed for navigation to King's Lynn, Wisbech and Boston. These channels had banks of mud and silt which tended to fill and choke them and even to change their courses. Into these banks the stone was packed, up to a height of two or three feet above high water level. There was no coursing, and no mortar, so, when the tide came in, the water passed beyond the limestone, to flood extensive areas of sand, silt and mudbanks. But on the ebb the water drained back between the stones, while the silt, which had formerly been carried into the beds of the waterways, was trapped. The effect was gradually to increase the height of these mud flats, which could in due course be reclaimed for farming and market gardening, in soil of the utmost fertility, once the salt had leached out. Although nowadays the stone is more likely to be transported from Wansford in lorries, this good work still continues.

7

DECORATIVE USES OF STONE

The decorative enrichment of architecture is a subject big enough to deserve a separate book. In this one it will only be possible to give a few broad indications of the scope of this absorbing theme.

In contemporary buildings there is often no place for decorative enrichment. The forms are left to speak for themselves. Some people delight in the clean lines and broad unencumbered surfaces of the best modern buildings. Others no doubt find them somewhat stark. But it is evident that there is no place for carved capitals on an aircraft hangar, nor for fan vaults laboriously executed in concrete.

If the new materials, steel, glass and concrete, pointed the way, the traditional materials have not remained unaffected by the new aesthetic. Big areas of unadorned brick and stonework are now acceptable, to an extent to which there are surprisingly few parallels in the architecture of the past.

It is true, of course, that the past can show us some very plain buildings. But usually there is this important difference. When an old church was left unadorned externally, it was not because the builders considered this plainness beautiful but because the clergy, their patrons, wanted to direct people's thoughts inside, where all the enrichment could be consecrated to the glory of God. Today, on the other hand, when an exterior is left unadorned, it is as often as not because the architect considers that the absence of decorative enrichment is a positive artistic gain. Thus can the formal significance of the building, and perhaps its colour and texture, be all the better apprehended.

Old stone buildings which were deliberately left unadorned with aesthetic intent are rare. The stark appearance of some of the mediaeval castles, much appreciated today, was the product of practical considerations unconnected with art. Among the best examples of the intentional avoidance of sculptural or ornamental enrichment are the

London churches of Nicholas Hawksmoor: 'essays in solid geometry', as Sir John Summerson has termed them. The tower of St. Anne, Limehouse, is specially striking for its boldly geometrical composition in abstract masses, handled in a most original way. The Portland stone with which it is entirely faced is an ideal material for achieving that precision on which, in a design of this kind, so much depends. But the churches of Hawksmoor are unlike any others.

Restraint in the application of ornament, externally at least, is characteristic of Classical architecture. The principles were enunciated in a famous dictum of Inigo Jones which is nevertheless so pertinent as to be worth recalling. 'For as outwardly every wise man', he declared, 'carrieth a gravity in public places, where there is nothing else looked for, yet inwardly has his imaginacy set on fire, and sometimes licentiously flying out as nature herself doth oftentimes extravagantly, to delight and amaze

133 Arundells, The Close,
Salisbury

134 and 135 Attingham Park, near
Shrewsbury, Shropshire, from the
south-west; and detail of portico

us, so in architecture the outward ornaments ought to be solid, proportionable according to the rules, masculine and unaffected'. This was at once a protest against the extravagance of many Elizabethan and Jacobean buildings and, as time was to show, a guiding light for the Georgians. Even so modest a façade as that of Arundells in the Close at Salisbury (**133**), dating from 1749, illustrates Jones's precepts to perfection. There are the beautifuly articulated frame of the central doorway and the modillions of the white–painted wooden cornice; otherwise all depends on the justness of the proportions and on the beauty of the Chilmark limestone and good red tiles.

Where the decorative features are used so sparingly, however, an architect who gets his proportions wrong is in trouble, as can be seen at Attingham Park in Shropshire (**134**). The big classical block seen in the picture (there are the remains of an earlier house behind) was built of Grinshill sandstone in 1783–85 from designs by George Steuart. The tall columns of the portico are devoid of entasis and the effect is undeniably spindly; still more uncomfortable are the paired pilasters at the side, each supporting a scrap of entablature, and apparently introduced to add interest to a plain elevation very prominent in the view. This they do not succeed in doing. The only really decorative note here is supplied by the somewhat unorthodox capitals (**135**), which are too small and too highly placed to make much impression.

A few years earlier, at Heaton Park near Manchester (**136**), James Wyatt
had displayed a much surer touch. Not only are the general proportions
very good but the relationship of plain to ornamented surfaces seems
exactly right. Here too there was an older house, of red brick, now faced
with white stucco. Wyatt provided a new front in the local Coal Measures
sandstone, so tough that the profiles of the pilasters and other decorative
features are as crisp as when they were first cut. It was indeed, almost
certainly, the hardness of the stone which prompted the architect to avail
himself, for the sculptured panels of the bow and for all the capitals of the
central block (**183**), of a recently introduced synthetic material, Coade
stone, of which there will be more to say in Chapter 9.

With classical buildings the front elevation is usually symmetrical, and
where there is decoration it is likely to be concentrated at the centre. Bath
stone – using the term generically to cover the products of a number of
quarries to the east and south-east of the city – is easy to carve while it is still
'green', and the Georgian houses of this area abound in decorative details. A
house in The Parade at Trowbridge, one of a number of fine examples in
that once rich clothing town, has a boldly framed door with a Baroque
pediment, and garlands above hanging in broad flat bands (**137**). In Bath
itself, Rosewell House in Kingsmead Square has, above the central door, a
still more exuberant display (**138**). The Palladian architect John Wood
dismissed this scornfully as being without taste, and it is certainly very
questionable whether either of these houses is improved by this carved
ornamentation. With classical architecture reticence is seldom out of place.

139 (overleaf) The Town Hall, Abingdon, Berkshire (now Oxfordshire)

136 (left) Heaton Park, Prestwich, Manchester

137 (above) The Parade, Trowbridge, Wiltshire

138 Rosewell House, Kingsmead Square, Bath

Nor is originality a quality on which much store used to be set, in the decorative parts of a classical building. Abingdon, in the reign of Charles II, erected the grandest small Town Hall in England (**139**), with a place for a market under the open arcades below. The builder was Christopher Kempster of Burford, who, as noted earlier (cf. p. 75), had worked for Wren and was to do so again. The architect is not known, but it is possible that the great man himself had a hand in it, as a consultant. He knew that Kempster could be trusted. Moreover, Kempster had an interest in the quarries at Burford, and for the more ornamental parts, the pilasters with their moulded bases raised upon exceptionally high plinths, the capitals and the entablature, it was from there that the excellent limestone was brought. (The rest of the stone came from Headington.) The tremendous impact of this building derives from the boldness of its scale and its admirable proportions. The only ornamental feature of any importance in stone is the capitals, of the Composite order, which are identical throughout and strong but not specially sensitive in their carving. The heads on the keystones of the arcades are too small to register. Much more is owed to other materials, wood, lead and glass, which all contribute handsomely.

If from the buildings of the Renaissance we now move back into the
Middle Ages, we find not less but more interest in ornamental forms. Here
and there, especially in the Norman period, it is possible to light upon
examples of reticence, as at Southwell Minster, a former collegiate church
elevated to cathedral rank in 1884. The west front (140) had a huge central
window inserted about 1450, while the two side-windows and the short
lead-covered spires belong to the restoration by Ewan Christian in 1880.
Otherwise this nearly but not quite symmetrical twelfth century façade,
divided, as so often, by string courses into a succession of relatively small
stages, employs ornament with, some may feel, excessive restraint. The
principal motif is the columned arcade, mostly applied to a blank wall
surface. At the sixth stage the arcades are interlaced, and flow over the angle
buttresses. At the seventh stage, immediately under the spires, there are
head corbels; otherwise, as was general in the Norman period, the
ornamentation is all geometrical, and mostly zigzag. The door is enriched
by a succession of concentric mouldings built into the thickness of the
walls: a device as simple as it is telling. The material is Permian sandstone
from Mansfield.

Not all English Romanesque buildings employ ornament with so much
economy nor with such a sense of order; at Ely, for example, the west tower,
admittedly a very late example, Transitional in style, has no fewer than nine
tiers of arcades. But, except in Durham, one characteristic is recurrent: the
decorative stonework comprises an aggregation of small effects. Relative to
each other, the scale varies, but in relation to the building as a whole every
element is small: by comparison with the Town Hall at Abingdon,
minuscule. It was this which was to change dramatically with the advent of
Gothic.

Until the very end of the Middle Ages, as can be seen on Abbot
Lichfield's free-standing belfry at Evesham (141), which was not begun
until 1529, small scale ornamental units might persist; but they are
contained now within much larger ones: here only three in all, below the
parapet. The outcome is a sense of far greater assurance. With its boldly
projecting buttresses, stepping out several times as they descend, this tower
would have made its mark without any enrichment, yet this finely
wrought decoration, culminating in the truly gorgeous openwork
battlements and pinnacles, clearly inspired by Gloucester, is surely a great
asset. A great extravagance too: Gothic church architecture could be
wonderfully lavish. But the ornament, however luxuriant, is always
subordinate to the structure.

189

The Gothic architects gave much thought to their skylines, for which the crocketed pinnacle was certainly a most felicitous invention. Nor was it confined to churches. At Higham Ferrers Archbishop Chichele, a native of the place, built, in the churchyard, a new schoolhouse (**142**). The base is plain, the windows large and sober, for in a school good light is a major consideration; but at roof level there is a rich display of pinnacles panelled and crocketed, and strongly moulded battlements with open tracery. This is the principal feature of the building, and wholly delightful.

Window tracery in the late Gothic period often bears a somewhat machine-made look; that of the middle Gothic, or Decorated, phase was far more inventive. The preparation of tracery could be an exacting task for the banker masons. Nearly all the designs were rooted in geometry; great skill was required in the setting out. The first phase of Decorated window tracery is known as Geometrical, the second as Flowing. Geometrical tracery can be very tight and mechanical. The Victorians turned out such windows by the thousand, and these hard, stereotyped productions remain a blot on many churches. In the Flowing phase the masons could be 'too clever by half', as at St. Michael, Linlithgow, where the window tracery is a prize example of ingenuity misplaced. But at best they are masterly. One of the greatest glories of Flowing Decorated is the east window of Selby Abbey. At the apex the seven tall straight lights dissolve into a kaleidoscope of flickering shapes, in which the ogee curve figures prominently.

A variant, which Francis Bond described as 'a glorification of the ogee arch', is the reticulated window, from the Latin word *reticulatus*, meaning

144 (right) St. Mary, Redcliffe,
Bristol: north door

145 (overleaf, left) The Chapter
House, Wells Cathedral: vault

146 (overleaf, right) St. Mary,
Redcliffe, Bristol: nave vault

net-like. To see some fine examples of this type, there is no need to leave
Higham Ferrers (**143**). In the window illustrated there are ogee curves even
at the apex, which is very unusual. But otherwise, as Bond explains in
detail★, a reticulated window could be set out without difficulty, which
was one of the reasons for the popularity of this form in the first half of the
fourteenth century. The basis of the design was diminishing tiers of circles,
the tops and bottoms of which were scrubbed out when the time came to
inscribe the lines of the tracery. Within each circle was inserted a quatrefoil,
the tops and bottoms of which were similarly treated.

Ogee curves also figure in the stone frame of the most exotic looking
doorway in England: the outer door of the hexagonal north porch at St.
Mary Redcliffe, Bristol (**144**). This seems to prefigure the Manueline
architecture of Portugal two centuries before its time. The profusion of
carved ornamentation is almost unbelievable. In addition to a great deal of
conventional bossy foliage there is also a generous array of little figures,
exquisitely rendered. Formally, the two broad outer mouldings were
developed in a quite unGothic direction, but to glorious effect. The
material throughout is Dundry limestone.

The supreme achievement of the banker masons was in Gothic vaulting.
Here the English record surpasses that of any other country, and includes
some vaults which, whether considered structurally or as decoration, are
little short of miraculous. There is perhaps no lovelier example than the
Chapter House vault at Wells (**145**) carried out in Doulting limestone, and
completed about 1310. The room is octagonal, with an internal diameter of
about 50 ft. The support of the tierceron vault depends upon the central
pier, from which radiate no fewer than thirty-two ribs, each of which
meets one or more ribs rising from between the windows. At every point
of junction is a carved boss.

This was certainly a difficult vault to set out: the geometry is decidedly
complicated. The ribs are of slightly different lengths, so are segments of
circles each with a different radius. Some indeed may be segments of ellipses
rather than of circles. Moreover, the ribs are required to merge and taper
towards the base of the 'umbrella'. The actual cutting was not so difficult,
although it will be seen that each rib is itself filleted, to achieve a play of
light and shade over its surface. Short lierne ribs link all the tiercerons at their
apex. The bosses figure prominently. They are comparatively naturalistic,

★Francis Bond, *English Church Architecture* (1913), Vol 2, p. 623. Bond's two great books on
Gothic architecture are still richly veined quarries for students of mediaeval churches.

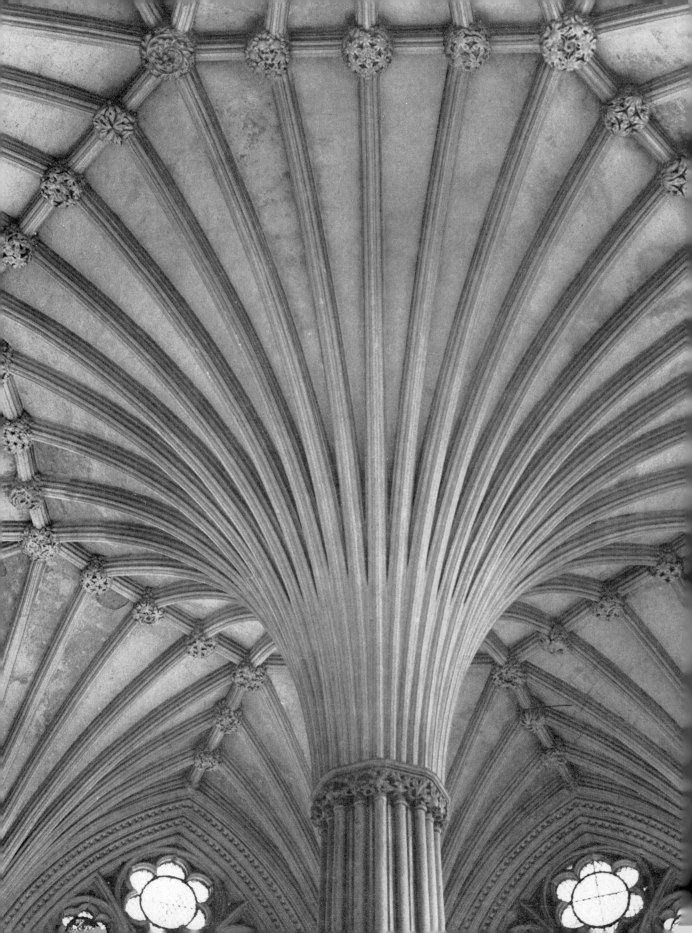

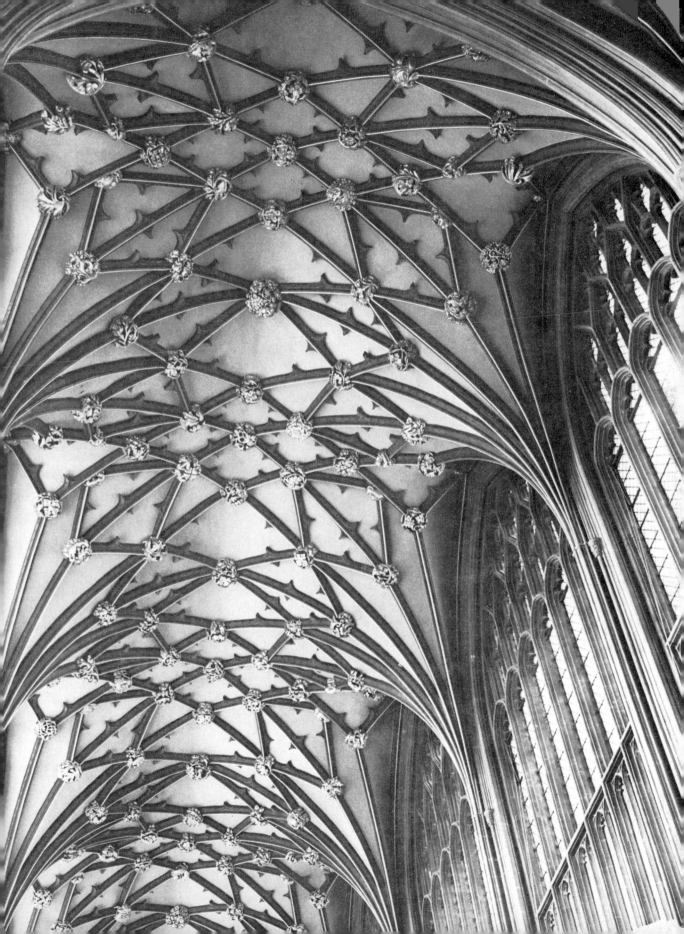

and some may weigh 3 cwts. or even more. Their purpose was not just to cover the joint, as in woodwork, where the boss can be applied when the structure is complete. Here the boss, or at least the stone block of which it is the ornamental face, is an integral part of the structure. Every block has short worked sections known as stoolings to receive the ends of each of the ribs converging on it.

But the bosses were not the responsibility of the banker masons, nor were the capitals, nor the profusion of ballflower ornamentation surrounding the windows. The banker mason would – and still will – cut the stone into almost any shape required, provided that it remains geometrical. This would include mouldings of every kind and section, with their stops, returns, sinkings and curvatures, and, as has been observed, the most intricate window tracery. But wherever carving was required, he would prepare a plain section or block and hand this over to the carver.

Carvers were usually trained in masons' yards. But they were men with a more creative urge which could not be satisfied by the cutting of mouldings and repetitive ornament. Sometimes, nevertheless, they executed designs prepared by others, and much of their work was done in relief and not in the round. But the carvers took over from the banker masons, often on the same job, as soon as the work ceased to be based on geometry.

A spectacular vault of the lierne type, belonging to the fifteenth century, surmounts the nave of St. Mary Redcliffe, Bristol (**146**). An English parish church that is wholly vaulted is a rarity, and there is no other on this scale. If stone is to be painted and gilded, which we do not usually recommend, a vault is certainly the best place for such treatment, because of its distance from the eye of the spectator. At Bristol the ribs are resplendent in chocolate and gold, for which the plain plaster covering the vault webs provides the perfect foil. 'Chocolate and gold' may sound over-succulent, but in fact the dark brown is very unassertive, while the gilding is confined to the bosses and the slender fillets on the surface of the ribs. The abundance of 'thorns', the one feature of this vault about which there could be reservations, are rightly left ungilded. The church contains nearly twelve hundred bosses in all. Although most of them have only foliage, some have shields of arms and others human and animal faces or figures, including a few of religious significance.

It has been said that Classical buildings are characterised above all by conformity, Romantic buildings by variety. In fact, of course, there is plenty of variety in Classical architecture too, but it is variation within a clearly ordered scheme. This is specially true of classical ornament, which is

147 Southwell Minster: carved
capitals of the Chapter House
doorway

mostly derived from ancient Greece. Egg and dart, bead and reel, leaf and
tongue, even the anthemion or stylised honeysuckle: all lack the freehand
quality. The repetitions are absolutely regular: once the pattern was fixed,
the process of repetition was mechanical. This is not to condemn it: such
chaste discipline is entirely appropriate to Classical architecture. But just
because the surface enrichment of Classical buildings is so restrained, so
precise, so often repetitive, it is, in the realm of the imagination, less
adventurous and less stimulating as a subject of detailed study.

In Romantic architecture a sense of order is important too; no
architecture can succeed which is lacking in order. But in this type of
building there are fewer rules, especially in the field of ornamentation. Here
variety counts for more than conformity; the carver is 'given his head' in a
way which just does not and cannot happen with Classical ornament.
Romantic ornament has an improvising quality which may not always
induce results that are completely successful, but which does contribute a
great deal to the interest and pleasure of visiting, say, the mediaeval
cathedrals and churches. Some of the corbel tables, especially of Norman
churches such as Kilpeck, are immensely entertaining, and in the Gothic
period the famous leaves of Southwell provide a perfect example.

Southwell Minster has a small but extremely beautiful Chapter House,
again octagonal, which is approached from the north choir aisle by a
passage and vestibule culminating in a masterly doorway. Round the walls
of the Chapter House itself are thirty-six gabled seats separated by shafts
crowned by foliated capitals. More of these enrich the wall arcades of the
passage and vestibule, and, above all, the doorway: it is the three capitals on
the right-hand splay of the door which are illustrated (147). We can picture
the carver sallying forth into the surrounding countryside to gather his
specimens: buttercup (on the left), vine and oak, with another vine running

197

148 St. Mary, Burwell,
Cambridgeshire

down the moulding. On other capitals are the leaves of many other trees
and plants: maple, hawthorn, ivy, hop, bryony, wild rose, potentilla, crab
apple, whitethorn. Most can be quite easily identified, yet – and this is of
vital importance – nowhere is Nature allowed to run riot. The decorative
aspect is paramount, so that, for example, large leaves are reduced and small
ones enlarged in the interests of artistic unity. The carvers, and there were at
least three of them, never forgot that their primary task was to produce a set
of capitals. Yet they were able to convey a far greater sense of life, and of
enjoyment, than those other carvers whose excursions into natural forms
were virtually confined to stylised renderings of the acanthus and the
honeysuckle.

Ruskin, in one of his lectures (Edinburgh, 1853), also praised the Gothic
builders for placing so much of their best and most delicate decoration at
eye level, where it can most easily be seen. Certainly, if carved decoration is
to be placed high up, it should be on a bold scale, as it is, for example, above
the chancel arch at Burwell (**148**). This, the best Perpendicular church in

149 St. Mary, Burwell: detail of
carving in clunch

Cambridgeshire, appears to be mainly built of flint, but the interior is
entirely clunch, which was still obtainable from the local pit here until its
closure about 1960 (cf. p. 28). This stone is not really weather-resistant,
which accounts for the recourse to flint externally. Because clunch is so
very easy to carve, delicate mouldings and panelling abound; above the
chancel arch, the nave being a good deal higher than the chancel, there is a
very rich display of decorative panelling, and above this a small wheel
window of unusual design, with eight *mouchettes* (curved daggers), a motif
from Flamboyant Gothic in France. Between the two runs an inscription
recording the name of the benefactor who paid for the rebuilding of the
church in 1464: John Benet.

Specially elaborate are the reredos below the five-light east window and
the niches with gorgeous canopies to either side of it. The carving is profuse
rather than sensitive (**149**); it would seem that, in such an easy material, the
masons could not resist showing off a little. The niches are unhappily
empty, but at their base are half length figures of somewhat earthy-looking
overweight angels bearing shields. This is work which would today be
done by a sculptor, trained not in a mason's yard but in an art school. But in
the Middle Ages there were no art schools, and sculpture did not even rank
as one of the liberal arts. The carver of these busts of angels was called an
imager (*imaginator*): one who specialised in figure carving. The imagers
were regarded as the most highly skilled of the masons (*caementarii*) and,
after the master-mason, who carried much greater responsibilities, they
were the best paid.

We know the names of a few of them, in particular those who worked
for the King. An important part of their work was the making of effigies,
which does not concern us here, since it had no architectural relationship;

150 **Exeter Cathedral, part of the west front**

151 **The Chapter House, Wells Cathedral: gargoyle**

but we may go further, and say that very little carving in the round, that is to say figure sculpture, is decorative, either in fact or in intention. Ranged across the front of a mediaeval cathedral, as at Wells or Exeter (**150**), the sculpture may be said to add richness to the architecture, especially when the figures are placed in orderly fashion under canopies; but this is no more than an adventitious benefit. The sculpture was there for its subject matter: it was intended to contribute to a theological scheme, worked out by the clergy. Each figure had a doctrinal or symbolic significance, grouped at both cathedrals round a centrepiece representing the Coronation of the Virgin. The other figures at Exeter include Apostles and Prophets, the four Evangelists, probably the four Doctors of the Church, and then a range of kings and warriors who would appear to represent the royal line of Judah, introduced as ancestors of the Virgin. All these figures were carved in the workshop, to the required size. When they were new, and all painted and gilded (as they always were), the effect must have been spectacular; but this screen of figures at Exeter is not well integrated with the rest of the architecture, and considered aesthetically, could be regarded as no asset at all to the front: in fact, a liability. Much the same is true of Salisbury and of Lichfield. At Wells the sculpture is much better integrated, but whether,

152 Wollaton Hall, Nottingham

even there, it enriches the front decoratively is open to question.

At all these cathedrals the external sculptures, after centuries of exposure to the weather, are a good deal decayed, and where renewals have taken place – and at Lichfield practically all the sculpture on the façade is Victorian – the quality of the work has usually been poor.

From the decorative aspect the most enjoyable church sculpture is to be found in small items such as corbel-heads and gargoyles, which, if not entirely in the round, are largely so. The gargoyle illustrated, on the Chapter House at Wells (**151**), must be purely decorative, for at this point there can be no concentration of rain-water requiring to be thrown clear. Church gargoyles can sometimes be a source of great delight.

After the Reformation building activity was transferred in large measure to the domestic sphere. Between 1540 and 1640 some enormous houses were built, none more ostentatious than Wollaton Hall (**152**). There was still plenty of work for the carvers, and since this client, Sir Francis Willoughby, was not only a landowner but the richest coal merchant in England, ample resources were available to pay for the best. The use of Ancaster oolite, a limestone of the highest quality, which had to be brought from Lincolnshire, would seem to have been a great extravagance, until we learn that on the return journey the Trent barges and the pack-horses could be used to carry his coal into Lincolnshire, which was badly in need of it. The ornamentation is profuse: an abundance of niches, pilasters and obelisks for the banker masons, and busts in roundels framed by elaborate

cartouches, innumerable masks in the friezes, big strapwork gables with nothing behind them, culminating in statues perched on small pediments every one of which had to be carved specially. The statues and busts are so accomplished that it is believed that they were either imported from Italy or carved by Italians working on the site. Despite the proximity of the formerly smoky city of Nottingham, which now owns the house, the stonework is still remarkably well preserved.

A few years later came Montacute House in Somerset (**153**), a property of the National Trust, which was built by Edward Phelips, M.P., a highly successful lawyer, who, not long after its completion in 1601, was knighted and elected Speaker of the House of Commons, and in 1611 became Master of the Rolls. So, needless to say, he also had a town house in London. For his country mansion a stone coarser in grain and not as compact as Ancaster but no less beautiful was readily at hand, on Hamdon Hill, little more than a mile away. Though also large, Montacute is not on the scale of Wollaton, and more restrained in its ornamentation, which is a reason why most people prefer it. But it is by no means devoid of decorative features, which

154 Sherborne Abbey, Dorset:
south-east corner

on the east front include shell-headed
niches, bowl-shaped roundels, gables
in the Dutch manner and a profusion
of obelisks with distinctive finials. The
balustrading of the 'waisted' form,
seen both at roof level and flanking the
forecourt, has already been comment-
ed on (see page 167). Specially delightful are the two six-columned *tempietti*
crowned with open spheres perched
on ogee-shaped tripods. The least
successful feature is the sculpture:
figures intended for the Nine Worth-
ies, from Joshua and David to Charle-
magne and Godfrey of Bouillon but
all in Roman attire, are somewhat naïve in execution and crowded
in between the upper windows
where there is insufficient room for them. The master mason at Montacute
was probably William Arnold, who was later responsible for Wadham
College, Oxford.

One of the most decorative uses of sculpture in relation to architecture is
in the carving of coats of arms. There is a prize example at Montacute itself,
in the centre of the opposite (west) front. This is in the same stone but
belonged to another house, Clifton Maybank, a few miles away, from
which it was brought in 1786, when the west front of Montacute was
ingeniously reconstructed. Also in Ham Hill stone is the coat of arms of
Edward VI, to be found, most unexpectedly, at the south-east corner of
Sherborne Abbey (154). This had been the fourteenth century chapel of St.
Mary le Bow. In 1560 it was walled off from the church and converted into
a two-storey house for the Headmaster of Sherborne School, a monastic
institution which had been refounded by Edward VI. This accounts both
for the domestic-looking aspect of the chapel, which is now used as a
baptistery, and for the rather swagger royal arms in a heavy but imposing
frame with twisted colonnettes.

An exquisite example of heraldic adornment is at Wroxton Abbey (**155**: see also p. 23 and **7**). At this originally Jacobean house all the carved enrichment is concentrated on the central bay, around and above the porch. The entrance itself is framed by a somewhat rustic but endearing version of the Roman triumphal arch motif, with shell-headed niches, an entablature, strapwork and tall finials. The coat of arms, with the earl's coronet (for the house was mainly built by Sir William Pope, who was created Earl of Downe) is decidedly more accomplished, and a delightful touch is added by the lettering of the motto. The gable is a specially pretty variant of the Dutch type, with a strong coping enriched with dentils and five typically Jacobean finials. On the other hand, the three strictly rectangular panels provide an accidental link with the gatehouse at Stanway (**156**). This building, dating from about 1630, is an odd stylistic amalgam. The bays derive from Gothic architecture and the gables from Holland, while the chimney-stacks and the frame of the gateway itself are fully Renaissance in character. Into the pediment, however, was introduced, nearly a hundred years later, a coat of arms within an eared architrave, nearly square, with, above, a classical pediment which can only be regarded as wholly inappropriate. The scallop shells also have a heraldic significance, being the badge of the Tracy family, who built it. Another distinctive feature is the design of the plinths below the columns: these have what is sometimes called Jacobean rustication. But whatever reservations may be felt about this gatehouse on grounds of design, as a piece of masoncraft it is superb. It is built of one of the most famous of the Cotswold oolites and one of the very few still to be quarried: the orange-yellow Guiting stone brought from over the hill to the south-east. (This stone can be too yellow for visual comfort, but here happily there is much grey lichen to tone it down). The ashlared stonework, as noted earlier, is masterly, and all the moulded and carved details show superlatively good craftsmanship. The state of preservation is also well nigh perfect.

Compared with the Continent, English Classical architecture is as sparing in the use of external sculpture as it is of ornament. The representation of the human figure, and certainly of the nude, seems to come much more easily to Mediterranean artists. Now and again on English buildings – the Clarendon Building at Oxford is a good example – figures are seen perched against the sky, usually well wrapped up (understandably so) yet still looking decidedly chilly. But anything like a display, as on some of the Gothic cathedrals and churches, is rare. Here and there figures are introduced to provide an accent above a window or

155 Wroxton Abbey, Oxfordshire: central bay, west front

156 The Gatehouse, Stanway House, Gloucestershire

doorway; a charming example is in the centre of the south front at Wilton House. Here, above an arched window which is a variant of the favourite Venetian type, Inigo Jones added, on either side of a cartouche with the arms of the Earls of Pembroke, sculptured figures believed to represent Mars and Venus, their poses inspired ultimately, one would think, by Michelangelo. They are not in the round but in bold relief, and, in the fine Chilmark oolite, extremely successful.

Half a century later an architect who has never been identified designed, as 'points of punctuation' at each end of the immensely long west front at Petworth House, a trio of recesses below the first floor windows, in which are an eagle and two graceful busts, One of the latter is illustrated (**157**); its delicacy is in marked contrast with the vigour of the base on which it is placed. From a little way off it must be said that the latter is the more telling. Excellent though the bust is, something bolder seems to be called for.

We will end this short chapter with two works nearly five centuries apart, for one dates from the 1290s and the other from the 1780s, which could not be more different yet which have one thing in common: both hover on the brink of the dividing line – if such exists – between architecture and sculpture. The Albert Memorial in London's Kensington Gardens, much larger than either, belongs to the same group. Architecture or sculpture? Surely, both.

157 Petworth House, Sussex: ornamental bust

The touching story of how, after the death of Queen Eleanor of Castile at Harby in Nottinghamshire in 1290, her grief-stricken husband, King Edward I, caused memorial crosses to be erected at all the halting-places of her funeral procession thence to Westminster Abbey is of course well known. Of the Eleanor Crosses, as they are called, only two survive, both in Northamptonshire. (Waltham Cross in Hertfordshire is a restoration.) Hardingstone, a mile south of Northampton, is the finer, but Geddington, three miles north-east of Kettering, a smaller cross than the others and not mentioned in the accounts, is the better preserved (**158**). Only the stepped base here has been renewed. The stone for this cross came from Weldon, a quarry which is known to have been worked for the Crown quite early on: for example at Rockingham Castle. The height is about 40 ft. The monument, which is mainly triangular, dissolves near the top into a star-shaped hexagon. There are pinnacles at two levels, and the lower surfaces are delightfully diapered, in a manner not very unlike that to be found in Westminster Abbey, on the inner face of the north transept. The three statues of the Queen (**159**), with faces now somewhat blackened, are about life size. In all three she wears a distinctive head-dress and is clad in a heavy woollen cloak hanging in ample folds, which convey a feeling of great dignity.

The Georgian monument (**160**) is in the churchyard at Burton Lazars in Leicestershire, two miles south-east of Melton Mowbray. It is about 20 ft. high, and commemorates William Squire, who died in 1781. Although as late as this, the spirit is decidedly Rococo, and delightfully inventive. On a high base with lobed ends reposes the sarcophagus, supported at each corner by a volute. Above this is an obelisk, the four sides concave and all delicately carved, and at its centre a pierced oval containing an urn. On the short sides there are two seated figures in copious draperies but unfortunately headless, two reliefs in ovals, and the conventional emblems of mortality: a skull, crossbones and the rest. The carving is of good quality, and so is the stone, which is thought to have come from Ketton in Rutland. But unluckily the obelisk was perched on four cast-iron cannon balls, which were held in position both above and below by cast iron dowels: yet one more instance of how mistaken the old builders were to introduce them. For, inevitably, the iron rusted and in the course of time expanded with corrosion until the day came when the stonework started splitting. In the nineteen-fifties the obelisk was for a while in imminent danger of collapse. It was saved by the action of the Georgian Group. As one of us has good reason to know, the obelisk had to be fitted with new feet in Ketton stone and the cannon balls had to be scaled and encased in lead sheeting to counter any further danger of corrosion. New dowels had to be fitted in the alloy known as Delta metal. The task was achieved without hoisting the obelisk out of position, and for a total cost, almost inconceivable today, of under £100. Thereby was preserved, for the interest and pleasure of posterity, an unusual and fascinating example of the decorative use of stone.

160 The Squire Monument, Burton Lazars, Leicestershire

8
STONE ROOFS

Slabs of stone, and especially of limestone and sandstone, can provide the most beautiful of all roofing materials. For stone buildings, no other roofing material can begin to rival them visually. On timber-framed buildings also, they are a feature of commanding authority (**161**). But because each stone has to be hand-fashioned, such roofs are costly. And a very robust framework, traditionally of wood and, in all the best examples, oak, was required to carry them. So limestone and sandstone roofs have unhappily become rare on new buildings. Fortunately there is still an immense legacy from the past; such roofs in the course of time require attention, so even with only very little new stone roofing the need for trained craftsmen and apprentices is certain to continue.

The distinction between slabs and slates is ill-defined; in general, slabs are thicker and heavier. But often the word slates is used to describe them all. The term has several variants. Stone slates are known in different parts of the country as slats, flags, flagstones, flatstones and thackstones, also, frequently, as stone tiles, a term that we do not favour, since a tile is a manufactured article whereas these are natural products. Tilestones might perhaps be better, but is not current. It is a pity that no other word has been invented, for 'stone slates' is geologically confusing, since they have nothing to do with the metamorphic rock known as slate, whose contribution to English roofing will be considered towards the end of this chapter. For the sake of clarity, true slate should always be referred to in the singular ('Welsh slate', 'roofed with slate', etc), and usually is.

The first English stone roofs date from the period of the Roman occupation. None, of course, survives, but stone slates have been found during the excavation of Chedworth villa in the heart of the Cotswolds and of Roman sites at Godmanchester and Great Casterton, near Stamford. From the Middle Ages until the present century they were quarried or mined in many localities. Here is a summary of the principal areas in which

they can be seen; the slate areas are also included:

Limestone slates: Dorset, S. and E. Somerset, N.W. Wiltshire, the E. half of Gloucestershire, S.E. Worcestershire, W. and N. Oxfordshire, Northamptonshire, Rutland and the Kesteven division of Lincolnshire.

Sandstone slates: Northumberland, Durham, Yorkshire, Lancashire, Derbyshire, the Welsh Border counties (Cheshire, Shropshire, Herefordshire, W. Gloucestershire), the West Midlands (Worcestershire, Staffordshire and Warwickshire), central Northamptonshire, S. Surrey and Sussex.

Slate: Cornwall, W. Devon, Leicestershire (Charnwood Forest area) and Cumbria (Cumberland, Westmorland and N. Lancashire).

In the nineteenth century slate from Wales percolated into most parts of the country.

LIMESTONE SLATES

To be suitable for roofing, the stone must be naturally fissile, but stone with this property occurs in many different geological formations. Limestone slates are mostly Jurassic: the best known are those of the Cotswolds and the adjoining part of Oxfordshire. In this region there was once a very extensive local industry; from one quarry alone, Naunton, the output in the year before the first World War was about 30,000 slates a week. 100 men were employed here, of whom 20 were skilled slaters, slatters or slate makers (all these terms were in current use). By 1958 there was just one slater left, aged 70. Many of the Cotswold slates, including those at Naunton, were 'presents': that is to say, pieces of stone which had already been split naturally while still in the ground. Except for holing and perhaps some shaping, they were ready for use, and were therefore presents to the slater. Many of the earliest stone slates are likely to have been of this kind; 'presents' – the term is only current in the Cotswolds – were always found near the surface, and were therefore the most accessible. Quarries yielding

162 Council Houses, Filkins, Oxfordshire

163 Church of the Holy Sepulchre, Cambridge

them were seldom deeper than 8 ft. Regrettably little use has been made of them in recent years, but it is good to be able to say that in 1981 two small quarries were reopened for the production of these slates: at Brockhill near Guiting Power in Gloucestershire and at Filkins in the south-west corner of Oxfordshire. A number of buildings in this village are roofed with these slates (118), including some unusually good council houses built a generation ago with the local hard rubblestone (162). This stone is Forest Marble, one of the coarser Jurassic limestones, which has yielded many excellent roofing slates. Small but fairly heavy, they can be seen again a few miles farther west, at Poulton Manor in Gloucestershire (60). They are very attractive to mosses and lichens, which in moderation can be a pleasure; in profusion, however, these are not welcome, as they encourage birds to search for insects and, where mortar is exposed, to peck at it for grit: moss also holds the damp. A much more unexpected place to find Cotswold and Oxfordshire 'presents' is on the Church of the Holy Sepulchre at Cambridge (163). This building was reroofed about thirty years ago, and, no doubt because they have been used a good deal in Cambridge, it is sometimes stated that these slates are Collywestons. This is an error: they are of smaller average size and thicker, and laid 'dry', without any mortar, in the traditional Cotswold way.

There were at one time a good many quarries in the Cotswolds, most of them quite small, which yielded stone that was fissile enough for roofing.

The typical Cotswold roof is rich in texture and delightfully varied in colour. The slates are small and fairly thick, and, as can be seen at Owlpen Manor (**164**), the edges were not always carefully squared. Other roofs, however, wrought from the oolite, are more urbane (**103**).

The great event in the history of limestone slates was the development of the frosting process. It is believed that the first frosting of stone slates was done by nature, at places where the stone outcropped on the hillsides and escarpments. Slates used by the Romans were probably split in this way. When and where frosting first became an industry is not precisely known. It was probably towards the end of the sixteenth century or shortly after 1600. And it was almost certainly either at Stonesfield, a village four miles west of Woodstock, and thus not far from the Cotswolds, or at Collyweston, a village three miles south-west of Stamford, but in Northamptonshire. These were the only two places to become famous for frosted slates. The earliest known reference to frosting dates only from 1676, but by this time it is clear that production at Stonesfield was well established.

At Stonesfield the stone was first obtained by means of adits, horizontal

164 Owlpen Manor, Gloucestershire

165 Abbey Barn, Enstone, Oxfordshire

passages driven into the hillside. But from about 1770 some of the stone, and from about 1850 all of it, as at Collyweston, was mined. The deepest shaft here was 69 ft.; at Collyweston about 40 ft. At Collyweston most of the mining was done by the slaters themselves, but the majority of the Stonesfield miners were farm labourers for most of the year; they were only wanted for digging out the stone between late October and February. This was not a pleasant job, as the galleries were only 5 to $5\frac{1}{2}$ feet high, so work had to be done in a crouching position or lying on one's side. But it was reasonably well paid, for to do it properly required both skill and experience. The stone came out in slabs of random sizes and shapes, from about $2\frac{1}{2}$ to 4 ins. thick; at Collyweston this was known as the log, at Stonesfield as the pendle. If there was enough room below it was stacked there and covered with wet sand until the weather became really cold and frosty. It was then hoisted to the surface, laid out on the ground and watered incessantly, but especially at dusk, because it was vital not to lose the natural dampness known as 'quarry sap' (cf. p. 26). Water seeping into the laminations of the slate expands after freezing, so what the men now waited for was a succession of frosty nights. If the frost failed temporarily, the stone would be covered, usually with a light covering of earth or straw, and kept watered. After frosting, a few taps with the cliving hammer would suffice to separate the slates along what are called the veins. All that then remained was the final shaping, dressing and holing. But this was the most skilful part of the whole operation; without long experience a great many of the slates would be broken and wasted. At Stonesfield these processes were entrusted to the cream of the work-force, the sole part to be employed full time. But at Collyweston, because the slaters also did most of the mining, the majority of the workers were in continuous employment. In the summer months all these men were up on the roofs

215

laying the slates which they had been so assiduously preparing.

A typical roof of Stonesfield slates can be seen on the Abbey Barn at Enstone (**165**). This is a barn built in 1382 by the monks of Winchcombe, and
the original roof would certainly not have been of the quality of the one to be
seen today. But most roofs of this type need to be stripped and reslated
after, say, two hundred years, even when, as is often the case, a high
proportion of the slates can be reused. Stonesfield slates can be seen on the
roofs of many Oxford college buildings, and over the whole of the western
part of Oxfordshire. They travelled into Berkshire and Gloucestershire and
sometimes farther afield, especially for buildings of quality. At Stanway
they grace both the House with its exquisitely masoned gatehouse (**156**)
and the adjoining church (**166**). Compared with Collyweston these slates
are small and thick ($\frac{1}{2}$ to 1 in.) and a roof of Stonesfields weighs nearly a ton
per 100 sq. ft. But 'presents' are considerably heavier than that.

The industry flourished throughout the eighteenth and most of the
nineteenth centuries, and then suddenly declined: the last mine closed in
1909. Today even the sites of the Stonesfield workings are difficult to
identify. At Collyweston the situation has been rather better. Although the
output became much reduced, three firms were still supplying these slates
in the nineteen-fifties, and three mines remain usable. The fact that no new
slates have been mined here since 1969 is largely due to a succession of
winters so mild that there could be no frosting. For the slaters this proved
extremely frustrating. There is also at present a big stock of second-hand

slates. But there is no intention of allowing this fine old craft to die out, and the recent establishment, through voluntary private enterprise, of the Collyweston Slaters' Trust bodes well for the future.

Collyweston slates, like Stonesfields, are a hard, fine-grained limestone from the oolitic belt. They are not quite so rich in texture nor so varied in colour as their rivals, but in some respects they have always had the advantage. Their average size is larger – slates measuring 3 ft. by 2 ft. are not rare – but they are thinner: their average thickness is only $\frac{3}{8}$ in. This makes them considerably lighter: a hundred square feet of this stone weighs only half a ton. Thus they did not demand such a robust, and therefore expensive, wooden framework to support them. The method of laying is different here. Collywestons have always been bedded in lime mortar, along the bottom and up the sides of each slate. In olden days the slaters burnt their own lime on the spot. In recent times manufactured hydrated lime has been used: this requires the addition of cement, the very idea of which would have seemed shocking at Stonesfield!

But how well these roofs can look is seen to excellent effect in the village of Collyweston itself (**167**). As in all the good examples, the mortar in which these slates are bedded is unobtrusive. Along the base of each stone it should always be kept well back, as here, for the little shadows under each slate are aesthetically important. The pointing of the visible joints prevents rain and snow from being blown into the roof. With a similar intention, it was at one time the practice in the Cotswolds and elsewhere to lay the slates on a bed of moss, or at least to drive moss down between the joints. There

was even a tool with which to do this: a mossing-iron. Introduced thus moss could no doubt be an asset; too much of it on the exposed surface (**177**), on the other hand, is, as already indicated, a decided liability.

Another way of making the stone slates more water and weatherproof was by using what was known as *torching*. This comprised a mixture of lime, sand and cowhair which was applied to the underside of the roof between the laths or battens: a most irksome task to perform. There is fortunately no longer any need for this, thanks to the invention of bituminous waterproof felting, which is now used as a matter of course whenever a roof is relaid.

Many other pits were able to produce limestone sufficiently fissile to be suitable for slates, but not by frosting. There were a number in the Cotswolds, of which the largest, Naunton, has already been mentioned. Eyford near Stow-on-the-Wold was well-known: Slaughter was another. There were others further south, towards Stroud. All these slates come from the Jurassic rocks: they are either oolitic or from the Forest Marble. They are much thicker and heavier than the frosted slates, Collywestons in particular; in fact, Purbeck slates, seen very well in the village of Corfe Castle (**168**), are the heaviest of any, among the limestones: they weigh about $1\frac{1}{4}$ tons to every 100 sq. ft. Even though some have clearly been mortared, and not too tactfully, the contribution of these roofs to the good appearance of the village is immense.

From the topmost beds of the Upper Lias came the beautiful slates

169 and 170 Great Chalfield Manor,
Wiltshire: finial figures

168 Corfe Castle, Dorset:
Purbeck stone roofs

formerly produced in great numbers on Hamdon Hill, a prominent feature
of Abbey Farm House and barn at Preston Plucknett, about 4 miles to the
east (6). A good many can be seen at Sherborne, where a few years ago a
local builder waxed eloquent about Ham Hill slates. 'You can almost feel
them bend!' he exclaimed, in praising their freedom from brittleness. They
are, he added, easy to cut and to drill, and extremely durable. On a roof at
Sherborne apparently renewed recently for the first time since c. 1550, it
was possible to reuse about 80 per cent of the old slates.

Reference has already been made to the Forest Marble as a source of good
slates in Gloucestershire, at Poulton and at Filkins (page 213). This

formation takes its somewhat unexpected name from the Forest of Wychwood in Oxfordshire and from the fact that some of its products can be polished for internal use, in the manner of Purbeck and other English so-called marbles. It yields hard, shelly flagstones which vary in the degree of their lamination; some can be split into quite thin slabs, others not. The thinnest, which are all 'presents', have been used for roofing slates at many places in the South. They are much in evidence in the Sherborne neighbourhood, cheek by jowl with the Ham Hill slates. St Cuthbert's Chapel at Oborne (**58**) is a good example, a roof which again illustrates the propensity of this stone to harbour mosses and lichens. The Forest Marble also provided the slates for many buildings in north-west Wiltshire, including the splendid roof, 168 ft. long, of Barton Farm Tithe Barn at Bradford-on-Avon, now a National Monument. The pitch here is unusually steep for stone slates. Other beautiful roofs of this stone in the same neighbourhood include Easton House near Corsham (**87**) and Great Chalfield Manor (**169, 170**), which goes back to about 1480.

Until the middle of the seventeenth century most stone houses were gabled, sometimes quite steeply. In order to afford some protection for the roof from winter gales, and in particular to counter the danger of slates being blown off by strong winds, it was good practice to build the gable walls so that they projected well above the slating, as at Great Chalfield and Great Weldon Manor House (**171**). The ridge of the gable was protected by coping stones stepped and lipped over each other at the joints to prevent water seepage. At the apex of each gable the better buildings were adorned with finials or small pinnacles, which also provided terminal points for the ridges of their roofs (**164**). At Great Chalfield six of these finials have vigorously carved figures, which include two armoured knights and two griffins brandishing the arms of Thomas Tropenell, the builder. Each figure, with the cusped and gabled apex stone which served as its base, is carved out of a single block of stone; that these are unrestored pieces of external sculpture that have occupied a most exposed position for over five hundred years says much for the quality and durability of this Corsham stone.

When an old stone roof requires attention, the primary reason is scarcely ever because the slates have decayed. It is almost always the framework and the fixing which fail first. These had, let us admit, a very testing task to perform, for the weight of a stone roof is, as we have seen, formidable. It was fortunate that England had such an abundance of stout oaks able to support such loads. Very often the rafters of an old stone-slated house will

be found to be sagging, and no wonder. The usual method of hanging the slates was by oak pegs, or sometimes the leg-bones of sheep, hung on riven oak laths. At a set distance from the base, varying with the size, every slate was holed; until recently this was done with a slate-maker's pick, but for this one process the slater now uses an electric drill. The holes were about $\frac{3}{8}$ in. in diameter. The oak pegs, made, like the laths, by the slaters themselves, were about $2\frac{1}{4}$ ins. long and also $\frac{3}{8}$ in. in diameter but square, which prevented them from dropping through the holes. The laths were riven from straight sapling oak, and were under an inch thick. They were normally attached to the rafters with hand wrought nails. These were the vulnerable points of every stone roof. In the course of time, perhaps a couple of centuries, the pegs would tend to shrink and drop out, the nails to rust and perish, and the laths to give way under the weight. Nowadays the laths have been replaced by sawn battens of the best red deal, probably imported from the Baltic, and treated with an insecticide-preservative. To these the slates are now attached with nails of galvanized steel, copper, or rustless alloy requiring of course only much smaller holes.★

★Better than nails are metal pins with angled tops, driven into the rafters just below the thin laths, thus avoiding the danger of splitting them. These have quite a long history in some areas, and are what the Department of the Environment uses today when re-roofing buildings in its care such as the Triangular Lodge at Rushton, Northamptonshire, and Lyddington Bedehouse in Rutland.

One of the particular pleasures of old stone roofs is that the courses were always graded, with the largest at the eaves. In order to throw the rain-water from the roof as far from the building as possible, the eaves slates often projected considerably: sometimes as much as 12 ins. For further support, as can be seen at Oborne Chapel (**58**), an additional course of strong slates known as undereaves or cussomes, bedded directly on to the top of the wall, was introduced. This also helped to deflect percolating rain-water.

Stone slates were made in many different sizes, each of which had its own name, which might vary slightly or considerably from one locality to another. Some of these names have great charm. At Collyweston there were mopes and mumfords, inbows and outbows, shortuns and longuns; at Stonesfield cocks, tants and becks; in the Cotswolds pricks. All had their ba(t)chelors. Wibbuts in the Cotswolds were Wibbets at Collyweston and at Stonesfield Wivet(t)s or W(h)ippets. Muffities were the same as muffers and movities. These are all limestone slates. In Wales, as we shall see, quite another range of names was used.

Dressing is on three sides only; the head of the slate, with the nail-hole, is of course concealed from view. Less than half of every slate is exposed: the part known as the 'skirt'. So every lath is covered wholly by two slates and partially by a third. Before work on a roof began the slates would always be sorted by length, this being measured from the peg or nail hole to the base. Width was no problem as the widths were always random, so that all that mattered was to select a slate of the right width to complete the row. Very few frosted slates – none at Stonesfield – were much more than 2 ft. long; from this they gradually diminished to 6 or even 4 ins.

The pitch of these roofs varied considerably, but was never as low as 45°, which Lutyens called the 'ugly angle' – and how right he was. A favourite pitch for Collywestons was 48°; in Oxfordshire and the Cotswolds it was usually about 50° or just above that. Where the pitch is considerably steeper, the buildings may well have been originally thatched. Steep pitches show off the slates to great advantage (**165, 171**) but place an additional strain on the oak pegs, and are also extravagant with the timber required for the framework. On the other hand they are more weatherproof. Wind and rain are much more likely to drive between the slates where the angle of pitch is gentle.

The ridge at the apex of the roof is nowadays often finished with fired clay or even concrete tiles of 'half-round', 'angular' or 'hogback' section, produced in various colours intended either to match the slates or to contrast with them. These tiles are all much inferior aesthetically to the special ridge pieces, which, from a solid section of stone, were cut into a V shape with pick and chisel (or, later, sawn) and bedded on to the ridge with mortar. Plenty of these ridges of worked freestone can still be seen in and around the Cotswolds (**155**, **156**, **169**), but elsewhere they are by no means as frequent as could be wished. Occasionally the ridge is of lead rolled round a pole of wood; this will only be found on buildings of quality.

Lead rolls can sometimes be seen on hipped roofs too, where the slanting junction of the two surfaces always posed a difficult problem. More often shaped tiles of fired clay or concrete have provided an inferior substitute. Almost always in the Collyweston area, and sometimes elsewhere, the practice was to mitre each course of slates together at the meeting point. To do this it was necessary that the sides of every slate should be specially tapered (**167**).

Most stone roofs present one or two problems that require special skill. One is the handling of dormers. These are often no ornament. From the aspect of appearance, the general rule is the smaller the better (**171**). But there can be exceptions. At Collyweston (**167**) the dormers, which are quite large, are brought forward flush with the front wall and carried down below the eaves. This is not common, but it is very successful, because thereby they have become better integrated with the rest of the structure.

Particular ingenuity was needed at the point of juncture between two inclined planes; where a projecting wing meets the main roof, for example, or where, as at Collyweston, a dormer breaks forward. The easiest way was first to cover the length of the join, called the valley, with a strip of lead, and then to taper the edges of the slates, as with a hip but in reverse. The lead might be left to show or be covered completely, in which case this is known as a secret valley. Provided, however, that the slates were not too thick, some slaters could be much more resourceful than that. The angle between one slope and the other could be negotiated by 'sweeping' the slates. To do this, specially prepared wedge-shaped slates were required. Using these, each course could be carried round horizontally, to achieve what was known as a swept valley, as can be seen at Collyweston (**167**). Another method was 'lacing'. With a laced valley each pair of horizontal courses turns upwards as it approaches the point of junction, to meet in a specially large tapered slate laid aslant on a wide board covering the valley floor. If the cutting and fitting are really skilful, nothing more was required to render the valley watertight. But 'sweeping' and 'lacing' are among the virtuoso practices of the craft.

SANDSTONE SLATES

Sandstone slates are usually much thicker and heavier than limestone. To this dictum there is, however, one exception: the geologically very ancient Ordovician slates, only seen in Shropshire. This shelly, calcareous sandstone, which was quarried at Hoar Edge, some four miles west of Much Wenlock, yielded small slates (only about 8 ins. long) rough in outline but, as can be seen at the Prior's Lodge at Much Wenlock or at Stokesay Castle (**172**), rich in texture. The roof problems are faced: the slates are mitred at the hip, and there are even attempts at swept valleys. But compared to the refinements of the Jurassic limestone areas this is a very unsophisticated roof, with somewhat irregular coursing and very little gradation.

Most of the other sandstone slates tend to be dismissed a little disdainfully in Cotswold and Collyweston circles as 'slabs'. The fact is that none of the sandstones is naturally laminated to the extent that some of the Jurassic limestones are; there are plenty of sandstones that can be split, but most of them only into rather thick pieces. Some sandstone slates are very large: a length of 3 ft. is not uncommon, and even 4 ft. is not unknown. Since they can also be as much as 3 ins. thick, the sheer difficulty of lifting them into position must have called for great physical strength, as well as a tremendously robust timber framework to carry them. It has been said, therefore, that they are hardly a natural roofing material.

172 (left) Stokesay Castle,
Shropshire: roof

173 (below) Burgoyne Hotel,
Reeth, Yorkshire; chimney and
part of roof

174 and 175 (right) St. James and St.
Paul, Marton, Cheshire; with detail
of sandstone flags

With this view we do not agree. The great majority of sandstone slates
come from the Millstone Grit and from the Coal Measures, and are
therefore much more characteristic of Northern England than of the
South. On the slopes of the Pennines from Derbyshire to the Border and in
such areas as the Yorkshire Dales, where they so obviously 'belong', they
can look magnificent (**173**, **47**). At Reeth the lower edge of each slate has
been chamfered, evidently to help the thickness to appear less obtrusive.
(This roof also has, at the base of the chimney, a slate of a type seldom seen.
Its purpose was to throw the rainwater running down the stack clear of the
topmost joints).

In Cheshire most of the sandstone is Triassic, but this is not fissile. The
roofing slates are therefore, again, gritstone. The principal quarries were at

Kerridge and at Tegg's Nose, both near Macclesfield. On the old timber-framed church at Marton (**174**) with its dainty shingled tower and spirelet, their presence is almost overwhelming. The close view of the south-west corner (**175**) shows well-mitred hips. Gritstone often weathers, as here, to a somewhat sombre hue, and in the industrial areas of the Northern counties air pollution has unfortunately tended to blacken all the sandstone slates. Pollution also prevents the growth of mosses and lichens, thus doubly marring the appearance of these slates. Stone of this type is too heavy to lend itself to such subtleties as swept and laced valleys, and the pitch tends to be rather less steep than with the limestones. No sandstone slates are obtainable by frosting. The pleasure here depends on the sheer size of the stones and on the fact that these too are always carefully graded from eaves to ridge.

A good way of ascertaining whether slates were ever made in a particular sandstone area is to examine the field walls. If these contain fragments of fissile stones, that is a sure sign. For, owing to its weight, it was not practicable to carry the waste material from the quarries very far. So it was in the construction of field walls that it was used up. The slates themselves might be carried up to about thirty miles for an important building such as a church or a manor house. But for more modest buildings they would seldom travel further than ten miles. So there are many more slated roofs in eastern Cheshire than farther west.

It is not always easy to distinguish slates from the upper fissile strata of the Millstone Grit and from the stone-slate bearing levels in the Coal Measures. But their distribution is very wide, ranging from Northumberland (**57**) to the area around Bristol. Very few survive here, but in mediaeval times many of Bristol's buildings were roofed with thick slabs of Pennant sandstone from the Coal Measures. A county very well provided with such slates was Derbyshire, though none is made there now. Some of the Derbyshire gritstone slates are not as heavy as elsewhere, as can be seen on the stable block at Haddon Hall (**176**).

Among the sandstones the Carboniferous slates greatly predominate, but, apart from the Trias, most types have made their contribution. Herefordshire is the county for Old Red sandstone, and a notable roof in this stone is at Staick House, Eardisland (**177**). The grading is somewhat rough and ready, but with these smaller, lighter slates it at least proved possible to produce a long swept valley between the main block and the projecting wing.

From the Jurassic rocks the slates are nearly all classified as limestones,

176 Haddon Hall, Derbyshire: part of stable roof

177 Staick House, Eardisland, Herefordshire: 'swept' sandstone roof

although some are very sandy. The dividing line between the limestones and the sandstones in this system is to some extent disputable. But from shallow mines at Duston near Northampton pleasant brown slates which were classified as calcareous sandstone used to be available.

Much better known are the so-called Horsham slates from the Weald of Sussex. These belong to the Cretaceous system, so are, geologically, the youngest slates of any . 'Horsham' is no more than a generic name, for they were produced at many places in the Weald, and not only in Sussex: in south Surrey too, and to some small extent in Kent. Until the eighteenth century, they provided the roof covering for every house of any consequence in this region, even though most of these houses, like Brook Farm at Maplehurst (161), were timber-framed. Their weight, which is about $1\frac{1}{2}$ tons to every 100 sq. ft., demanded a very robust oak framework, but in the South-East, where the oak tree was so abundant as to be known as 'the Sussex weed', this presented no problem. Horsham slates weather beautifully, and are a great embellishment to the Wealden country, where they were also much in demand for floors.

It is largely because most of them require such a strong structure to support them that sandstone slates have fallen out of use. But they are still required as replacements, and new ones (flags, as these heavy slates are called there) can still be obtained, admittedly at a high price, from a few quarries in Yorkshire. At Kerridge they are no longer produced, for purely economic reasons. The stone can be sold for fireplaces, rockeries and, alas, crazy paving at prices well above those obtainable for slates, and with less preparatory work. Fortunately there are, in some places, good supplies available of second-hand slates, retrieved from buildings that have been demolished.

The preparation and laying of limestone and sandstone slates are skilled operations calling for long apprenticeship and experience, and the number of men so trained is now relatively small. But so interesting is the work, and so worthwhile, that a steady trickle of young recruits continues, eager to carry on a great tradition. The modern practice of replacing the stone-slated roofs of houses and cottages, farmsteads and barns with inferior materials has in many places done great harm to the environment, depriving us of some of the greatest delights of English architecture. And let it never be forgotten that these stone slates give distinction not only to many large and well-known buildings but to numerous small market towns and villages, as well as isolated farms, scattered over a very broad area of the country. Such importance, indeed, is now attached to them by Planning Authorities and the Historic Buildings Council that in the Conservation Areas and on Listed buildings owners who are prepared to undertake the work of restoration and preservation will in approved cases qualify for grants that may amount to as much as half the total cost.

SLATE

Over most of England 'a slate roof' means Welsh slate. This is a pity, because Welsh slate as seen in England is essentially a utility product, with very little aesthetic appeal. From the practical standpoint it has proved invaluable. Although all too brittle, Welsh slate is hard and strong, completely impermeable (which all stone slates are not), resistant to frost and remarkably light. This is because of its extremely fine laminations. A skilled slater, using a broad, thin, triangular-shaped chisel, can, with one tap of the mallet, split off a piece of slate no more than $\frac{3}{16}$ or $\frac{1}{4}$ in. thick, and even $\frac{1}{8}$ in. is by no means unheard of.

Welsh slate is known to have been employed in Chester as early as the fourteenth century, and it reached Shropshire in the fifteenth century. But it was not until the reign of George III that its use in England began to grow rapidly. To the Georgian builders it was a great boon, because they often liked to conceal their roofs behind parapets and only with Welsh slate could this be done easily; being so thin, and provided that the lap was adequate, it could be laid at a very low pitch without letting the rain in, and concealed behind parapets its machine-made appearance and absence of gradation were not factors that mattered. So by 1800 London was largely roofed with Welsh slate, and even in Bath, whenever the original limestone slates needed replacement, Welsh slate was usually preferred.

In the early days of the industry there was a good range of sizes. Their names, surprisingly enough, were drawn from the female aristocracy: princesses, duchesses, marchionesses, countesses, viscountesses and ladies all refer to different sizes, and there were also small duchesses, narrow ladies and wide countesses! In the eighteenth century and until about 1840 they were sold not by the count but by weight. Supplied in this way they could be graded and laid in diminishing courses. But as the demand grew, and with the construction first of canals and then of the railways, transport became easier, production was standardized into a few sizes which were sorted at the slate works into separate stacks, all of one size (**31**). Although the old methods of quarrying by blasting, the use of sledge-hammers and wedges and the preparation of these completely rectangular slates together entailed an appalling degree of wastage – at least 75 per cent was normal – it did certainly make them much easier to order and to lay; but the standardization is a principal reason why roofs in this stone, when compared with graded limestone and sandstone, usually look so monotonous.

Nor is the colour a source of much pleasure, especially the purple, which consorts very ill with red brick. The majority are dark grey, which at least has the negative virtue of often harmonizing better with stone than do red tiles. But in Wales itself more attractive slate can sometimes be found, slate for which there was no export market. The best, aesthetically, is the green slate, obtained (if at all) from the lowest strata of the quarries; this is very hard and by no means as fissile as the commercial product.

The abolition of the tax on slates in 1831 gave a momentary fillip to the industry, but this was followed, three years later, by the removal of the tax on tiles. However, the rapid growth of industrial towns under Queen Victoria guaranteed a market for Welsh slate, which had an additional asset in being able to stand up better than any other stone to pollution of the atmosphere. Ultimately, however, between the two world wars, tiles captured the English market, and the advent of concrete tiles administered the final *coup de grâce*. The production of roofing slate in North Wales continues, but at a very much reduced level.

Of England the same is true. In the Lake District, which produces our most attractive slate, several quarries are active, but much more is now sold for cladding modern ferro-concrete structures than for roofing. Happily, however, a great many Lakeland slate roofs survive in this part of England, and indeed in the Lake District itself red tiled roofs are, very properly, not allowed. This metamorphic stone does not all have the same geological origin, and accordingly differs in texture – some is rough, some fairly smooth – and particularly in colour. Perhaps the most enjoyable is the greenish slate from Borrowdale and Buttermere. But those of the Langdale and Coniston areas and of the Kirkstone Pass, predominantly grey with hints of blue-green, are also very pleasing. Others are rather more sombre in tone (**56, 106**). As usual in the North, these Westmorland slate roofs (as they are usually called) are all rather low-pitched; but the grading which is such a delightful feature of the limestone and sandstone roofs is no less in evidence here. Westmorland slates are a good deal heavier than Welsh, which is visually all to the good.

Easily the largest slate quarry in England is at Delabole near Camelford in Cornwall. This is an immense hole nearly 500 ft. deep and about a mile in circumference, which reveals itself suddenly, without warning: quite a dramatic experience. Only in Snowdonia are one or two of the slate quarries comparable in size; at the lip the area is about 40 acres. This quarry was forced into liquidation in 1977, but it has been reopened, although on a very much smaller scale than during its Victorian heyday. Not by any

means all the slate being produced is for roofs: some goes for doorsteps, window-sills, fireplaces and crazy paving, and large quantities are crushed and converted into granules for surfacing roofing felt.

The products of the deepest beds are a pleasant grey-green. But most of this slate is grey with patches of brown, and inclined to be sombre. Until the nineteenth century the sizes were always graded, but then, in order to compete with the Welsh industry, here too they became standardized (**22**). Delabole roofs are to be seen all over Cornwall, and a good deal of the slate travelled farther afield.

Nowadays the processes are partly mechanized. There are a circular saw to do the preliminary shaping and a revolving cutter which works like a guillotine to assist the trimming. The cliving (or cleaving) has still to be done by hand in most places, but in North Wales a machine has recently been invented which can cope even with this intermediary process, thereby supplanting the skill of the most experienced slater.

There used to be many other much smaller quarries in Cornwall, and also in Devon, which produced roofing slate. Much of it did not prove durable; there have had to be many replacements. Devon slate is very pleasing, and large quantities were formerly shipped from Totnes as far afield as the South-East; but none has been quarried for more than a century.

It is not always possible to be sure of the source of roofing slate in the south-western counties. The roof at Winterbourne Monkton near Marlborough (**178**) is an example. This could be Delabole slate of the same date as the chimney-pots: ungraded and Victorian. What gives the roof its distinction is that the rafters are sprocketed: that is to say, there is a slight change of pitch close to the eaves, achieved by the addition of short lengths of timber dying into the face of the rafters near their base. There was a practical reason for sprocketing: to extend the rafters over the thick wall to the required projection, which was very important before the age of gutters. But its chief value here is certainly aesthetic.

England's only other slate-producing area was very small by comparison with the South-West and with Cumbria. The ancient, Pre-Cambrian rocks of Charnwood Forest constitute an unexpected outcrop in a Midland county such as Leicestershire, but roofing slate was quarried here even in Roman times. The quarries were along the east and south sides of the Forest, and mainly at Swithland, which, like Horsham, has become the generic name for all this slate. As elsewhere, it varies both in colour and in the degree of its lamination. The bluish-grey slate, which is usually between half and three-quarters of an inch thick but can be decidedly more than that, is the most pleasing. Another variety, tinged with purple, which could be up to 2 ins. thick, was much in demand in the eighteenth and nineteenth centuries for gravestones, for which outsize slabs might be obtained. We may not care much for the colour, but cannot fail to admire the lettering and often more elaborate engraving. Swithland slate roofs can be seen in most parts of Leicestershire and in the southern parts of Derbyshire and Nottinghamshire. They look specially good in their own area, that of Charnwood Forest, where the walls are sometimes of slate-stone too (**25**). But in the second half of the nineteenth century Leicestershire also found it impossible to stem the Welsh invasion. It is nearly a hundred years since the last of Swithland's seven big slate-pits was closed (1887). Half-filled with water, which in itself proves how impermeable is this stone, they are now secret, silent places, imbued with melancholy.

England is a country where, because of the climate, flat roofs invite trouble and are wisely avoided by almost everybody except a few modern architects. Roof coverings are therefore very much part of the English scene. In addition to stone, there are plain tiles and pantiles, some of very high quality, thatch, shingles and lead. How fortunate we are to be able to draw upon such a repertoire of colours and textures, varied still further according to whether or not they are congenial to lichens and mosses. Every region has its own architectural character, and to this the stone roofs have often made a memorable contribution.

9

SUBSTITUTES FOR STONE

STUCCO

Far and away the commonest substitute for stone has been stucco. To-day this is often not apparent, because stucco is now very properly regarded as a material in its own right, which when well maintained, can make a most valuable contribution to the visual aspect of a town, and especially of places away from the stone areas.

What, however, is not always realised is that when stucco was first used on a large scale, which was in the second half of the eighteenth century, it was invariably regarded as an economical substitute for stone. Thus, with the use of a special jointing tool, the surface of every stuccoed building was covered with a meticulous network of incised lines intended to suggest the mortar courses between stone blocks. With successive repaintings these lines have tended to become blurred, sometimes to the point of extinction; but frequently they can still be detected, particularly on façades of the Regency period, which was the great age of stucco. Not only in many London boroughs but in predominantly Regency towns such as Brighton and Hove, Leamington and Cheltenham, many examples still survive. At Cheltenham good limestone was near at hand at Leckhampton, and was used, and a great deal was also brought from quarries near Bath, but there is plenty of stucco too, no doubt because it cost less. Usually it was applied over brick, but occasionally the walling might be rubblestone, stuccoed in the hope that it would look, from a little way off, like ashlar. It was also used over timber-framing. On both the houses in the Close at Exeter (**179**) the joint lines are visible; on the right-hand house they are much deeper than usual. It will be noticed that the courses are all exactly the same distance apart, which normally they would not be with natural stone, so the deception is very obvious. The explanation, no doubt, is that the work was carried out by a plasterer ignorant of the nature of stone, and not by a stonemason.

Stucco may be defined as a hard, smooth, external finish; in England,

179 Cathedral Close, Exeter: stucco with trowelled lines

180 (right) York Gate, Regent's Park, London, N.W.I.

but not on the Continent, the term is usually restricted to external uses. Its basic ingredients are sand, lime and cement, blended so as to be able to provide a smooth, even texture, capable in some cases of taking a light polish. An early instance of its employment in England was over the main wall surface of the Earl of Burlington's brick villa at Chiswick, completed about 1730.

Large scale production of stucco renderings started in 1773 with a patent substance known as Liardet's cement. The exact formula was kept secret, but it was very soon being used in London by several architects, including Robert Adam and Thomas Leverton, for example in Bedford Square. A number of other stucco renderings were patented during the generation that followed, of which much the most important was Parker's Roman cement in 1796. This was mostly produced at Harwich, because near that town could be dug the nodules of argillaceous limestone known as septaria, which were its essential ingredient. The septaria underwent a firing process, which resulted in the production of a brownish-looking substance much superior to any previously known rendering both in strength and, what is always of special importance in England, in its resistance to damp. John Nash, who used stucco on a far greater scale than any previous English architect, relied tremendously on Parker's cement, to which a great deal of London's housing still bears witness (**180**).

From about 1830, however, although it is still obtainable in small quantities, 'Roman' was gradually displaced by Portland cement, which was manufactured to quite a different formula. This cement, though still

234

more durable, and easier to handle, has a less pleasing appearance, for its colour is a dead grey: it lacks the whiteness of Portland stone. But by the time that the use of Portland cement became widespread, the aesthetic basis of employing stucco rendering had changed; no longer was there the same desire to simulate stone, which indeed in the Victorian period was widely regarded as 'dishonest'.

It is safe to say that nobody would now go to the trouble of covering a stucco surface with incised lines intended to suggest blocks of stone. Stucco is a substance with a character of its own, which need not be painted. It is, however, much improved by painting, as well as becoming more costly to maintain, since it always requires repainting every few years. But when this is done, it is certainly much preferable to many varieties of brick, and even to some stonework.

ARTIFICIAL STONE

There are numerous modern alternatives to the use of natural stone for buildings where a stone-like appearance is desired and no supplies are available, or where costs and other factors predominate.

Variouslly known as cast stone, reconstructed stone, artificial or art stone, almost all of them consist of mixtures of sand, stone dust or other aggregate, with cement in various proportions, sometimes with the addition of powdered oxide colouring matter, and often with a concrete core.

It should not be too readily assumed or taken for granted that a manufactured stone is invariably cheaper than a natural one. This is not always so, and it can differ widely from one part of the country to another. There are several factors to be taken into account, and occasionally machine-worked natural stone has even proved less expensive. The cost is likely to depend on the amount of hand labour needed to prepare the natural stone for use, together with its availability reasonably near the site. With cast stone other considerations are the number and shape of sections of one size and pattern to be made from one mould, and the detail of the mould boxes necessary for the casting. For instance, if only two large shaped or patterned identical stones are wanted, a good bench mason will work them in about the same time that it will take a carpenter to make the wooden mould box required for the casting, when both are partly assisted by machines. Moreover, good sound walling stone, second-hand from demolished buildings, can cost less per ton than a similar manufactured variety, as also can undressed natural walling stone direct from the quarry.

Some specialist firms have taken infinite care to give their material the appearance, surface texture, colour and other characteristics of the real thing, even to the point of making impressions or moulds direct from the stone they aim to match. To have a wide range of random sizes is also essential. With other makers these refinements are unfortunately not always present; often their blocks are all the same size, with repetitive and unlifelike surface textures, and colours that do not look right. Reconstructed stones have proved to be sound and durable structurally, but some of them do not fit well aesthetically into the stone environments for which they appear to be intended. A particularly bad example is the High Street at Winchester, of all places, which not long ago was repaired with concrete replicas of York stone, which could deceive nobody of the smallest aesthetic sensibility. This is a disgrace.

Most manufacturers of pre-cast concrete products supply a range of artificial walling stone. There is a great variety in what is offered, so that a careful choice is essential if true harmony with the natural stone of the chosen locality is to be achieved. There is a method of making rock-faced walling from artificial stone, Large slabs of the material are cast, their thickness conforming to the course heights of the finished product. These are then cut to the required sizes under a machine known as a hydraulic splitter. Incidentally, this method can be used in the same way for the preparation of natural stone.

Besides the manufacturers of artificial walling stones, there are a number of firms which have reached a high standard in producing cast stonework. All the forms and sections of Gothic, Classic, and modern masonry are faithfully reproduced to architects' detailed drawings.

A most important aspect of artificial stone is the production of roofing slates. The best known, and the best, are of the Cotswold type and are made at Swindon. The rubber moulds, for which the manufacturers are themselves responsible, are all impressions of natural stone faces, so that the texture is rough. The correct weathered buff shade, which is suitable not only for the Cotswolds but also for parts of Dorset, Somerset, Wiltshire, Oxfordshire, Northamptonshire and the Kesteven division of Lincoln-shire, is achieved by the addition of oolitic dust to the cement and sand aggregate. Many different sizes are produced, including the wedge-shaped pieces required for swept valleys, and careful grading, in the proper manner, is no problem at all. Matching ridge and hip units are also available. Whether they will still look good in a hundred years' time it is as yet impossible to say, but so far they seem to have been remarkably successful; those introduced in 1970 (the earliest) have already begun to darken and attract lichen. These artificial slates are certainly a godsend to those who are faced with the need to restore their stone roofs and who find that natural stone slates to suit their purposes are not always obtainable. Second-hand natural stone slates, if not too weather-worn, would of course be preferable if all the requisite sizes were available in sufficient numbers, but unfortunately they may not be.

For the much heavier Coal Measures sandstone and gritstone slates of Yorkshire, Lancashire, Derbyshire and parts of Cheshire and Durham, an artificial product is also now available. When the great weight of the natural stone and the expense of providing a framework sufficiently robust to support it are taken into account, it is unhappily inevitable that the artificial slates should be somewhat thinner. They too are made in moulds: acceptable colours and textures are obtained in various ways. Some of them are given a hand-textured surface; some are faced with grains of a mineral such as crushed slate or granite which is of the shade required and reasonably permanent; some are just faced with sand, while a few are tinted with powdered oxides. With this Northern type of artificial roofing slate the range of sizes for gradation from eaves to ridge is more limited, but for the main slates three different lengths are produced.

Artificial stone must now be regarded as a development in the historical evolution of building materials. Like natural stone, it can be very indifferent, but it can also be good. Where the cost of natural stone has

become prohibitive, it provides a cheaper alternative which should not be despised. There is, however, one important proviso. The opinion is widely held that for restoration of the ancient stonework of historic buildings reconstructed stone should not be used. Their two natures are so diverse that it is not easy to get an exact match of colour and texture, and even if this is achieved the result will only be temporary, because they will age and weather in very different ways.

SCAGLIOLA

Scagliola was an Italian invention, much used in England in the grander buildings of the Georgian period. A mixture comprising sand, lime, gypsum, Roman cement and crushed stone or some other agent of the required colour was ground down, applied wet to a column or pilaster built up with rough stones or bricks, and then given a very hard polish until it resembled marble or one of the more dressy stones in vogue in the eighteenth century: a favourite was *verde antico*.

Its first use in England was by Vanbrugh, in the Great Hall at Castle Howard, completed in 1712. Its heyday was the reign of George III. The craftsmen were often Italians, and so skilful were they that it is sometimes quite difficult to be sure whether a column is of true marble or not. If in doubt, touch it: the genuine article will feel colder. Scagliola has proved extraordinarily durable, but as the retention of its high polish is an essential quality, it was only suitable for indoor use, Internally, however, as for example in the handsome range of rooms at Arlington Court in North Devon (**181**), designed by Thomas Lee, a pupil of Soane, in 1820–23, the Ionic scagliola columns, all reflecting light from their polished surfaces, are a great embellishment.

In the eighteen twenties and thirties some scagliola was made in the Coade factory at Lambeth by William Croggon, who by then had purchased the business. He got the commission to produce three scagliola doorcases for the picture gallery at Buckingham Palace. But the name Coade is chiefly famous for the manufacture of a particular kind of artificial stone.

COADE STONE*

While Coade stone was not the first artificial stone to be made in England, it is certainly the best known and most fully documented of any. It was invented by members of the Coade family and manufactured from 1769 until about 1840 in their factory in Narrow Wall, Lambeth (roughly where the Royal Festival Hall stands to-day) by Mrs Eleanor Coade (*née* Enchmarch or Enchmarsh, of Tiverton: d. 1796), her daughter Miss Eleanor Coade (d. 1821) and her distant relation William Croggon of Grampound in Cornwall (d. 1835).

It differs from modern artificial products in that it was not made with cement mixtures. Despite appearances it had in fact no physical relationship

*For much help with this section our gratitude to Miss Alison Kelly has already been acknowledged on page 6.

with stone, for it was a fired clay product similar to terracotta. The great skill was in making it look so stone-like. Most of the clays and sands used elsewhere in the manufacture of terracotta fire to shades of red, brown or yellow, but the Coade product was normally a pleasant pale cream. By adding various metallic oxides this could be made greyer, pinker, or nearly white. Light grey Coade is not unlike Portland stone.

For many years the secrets of its manufacture were lost. Now, chemically, these are known, but there is still some uncertainty about details such as the exact firing time. These could certainly be unravelled by a good ceramic chemist. But the sources of the clays are matters of some doubt. Some is believed to have come from Lyme Regis, where the family originated. Recourse was, however, also had to a much less plastic kind of clay, the white kaolin of (almost certainly) Cornwall. Grampound is quite close to St. Austell, which to this day is the principal supply point. The sand used in the manufacturing process came from near King's Lynn, where because of its purity (that is, freedom from particles of iron, which would discolour it) it is still dug for glass-making. These two materials, and the coal for stoking the kilns, could all have been brought by sea up the Thames.

But there was another constituent, of vital importance, which was known as grog. This was ground-up pottery which had already been fired before, and which was, as powder, kneaded into fresh clay of the Coade formula. Almost certainly this was the secret of the extraordinary stability of Coade stone in the kiln and of its exceptionally small rate of shrinkage. In the high temperature of a kiln, clay becomes extremely soft, but the grog, having already been fired, was immune from softening; the second time it went into the kiln it was inert, which made for stability. In the 1790s the Coades actually acknowledged by implication the use of grog when they referred to their product as *Lithodipyra*, a name so difficult to remember that few people did. But it is in fact a word made up from the Greek for stone (*litho*), twice (*di*) and fire (*pyra*). The *di* referred to the grog, which did indeed go twice into the fire, once as clay and the second time as powdered pottery.

The drying out and firing of terracotta are very difficult to control if distortion, shrinkage, discoloration and spoiled textures are to be avoided. It was in the grog (which is still used in the manufacture of some kinds of brick) that lay the secret of the Coades' success.

It is hardly too much to say that for about sixty years the Coade factory supplied most of the architectural ornamentation used in London, and a

182 Belmont, Lyme Regis, Dorset

183 Heaton Park, Prestwich, Manchester: Coade stone capital

good deal elsewhere besides. One of the reasons for this striking success was that the prices were so moderate. Once the moulds had been made, the cost of production was remarkably low.

In 1784 Mrs. Coade took over the lease of a house at Lyme Regis originally known, after its builder, as Bunter's Castle. It still stands. She had the front decorated with the products of her own factory in a manner not, to say the least, distinguished for its reticence (182). There are Gibbs surrounds with rock-faced blocks and portrait-heads on the keystones, rusticated quoins, a plat band, a broad frieze and urns on the parapet. At Exeter a terrace of houses, Southernhay West, each has a woman's head (the same one) on the keystone and, on all the other projecting blocks, vermiculation (184).

All the leading architects availed themselves of this remarkable new material for their decorative details. The greatest user was probably James Wyatt. The super-Ionic capitals at Heaton Park (136, 183) are so well preserved that they were formerly thought to be metal: bronze or iron. In reality they are Coade stone which was bronzed by being painted.

But much the largest Coade stone market was for sculptured figures and reliefs, and for complex and highly detailed work such as heraldry, including the Royal Arms. In the churches there are a great many monuments in Coade stone, and several fonts. For town and country houses they made chimney-pieces, chimney-pots (for example, for

241

185 County Hall, Lewes, Sussex:
Coade stone panel

Woburn Abbey), trophies, medallions and caryatides, torchères and lamp-holders, vases, urns and an occasional fountain. The factory also produced well-designed garden furniture: a good garden seat cost only three and a half guineas.

The Coades were careful only to commission sculptors and designers of repute. The Shire Hall at Chelmsford, a handsome building of 1790 by John Johnson, has on the second floor three panels in high relief representing Mercy, Wisdom and Justice, for which the designer was John Bacon the elder, one of the most successful sculptors of his day. More than twenty years later, when he was an old man, Johnson provided Lewes with a new County Hall that clearly derives from the earlier building, and which also has, at the top, the three Roman-inspired panels acquired at a combined cost of £94 10s. By this time Bacon was dead, and the Lewes panels are not identical with those at Chelmsford, although similar. It is evident from the illustration (**185**) how happily the Coade product marries with the Portland stone facing. Johnson was almost as dedicated a user of Coade stone as Wyatt himself, and the rather sumptuous corbels that replace the usual modillions here are also of this material.

William Croggon went bankrupt in 1833 and died in 1835. In that year his second son Thomas John re-established the Lambeth works, but on a much reduced scale and not for very long. The Coade moulds were sold in 1843. Some would seem to have been bought by Mark Blanchard, who, after serving his apprenticeship with the firm, had opened his own premises at Blackfriars in 1839. Various specimens of his work are known. The enterprise came to an end about 1870.

On J. M. Blashfield more research needs to be done. It is often stated that he too had worked in the Coade firm and bought some of the moulds when it closed down: but this is not so. What is certain is that, soon after the Great Exhibition of 1851, he opened a terracotta factoy in London which, in 1858, was moved to Stamford. Not long after that Blashfield retired, but the firm which he had founded continued until 1875.

It is known to have shipped its fine sand from King's Lynn. The clay used at Stamford fired to a somewhat creamier hue than in London, which suited the local limestones. So the Blashfield products are usually not difficult to distinguish from the original Coade pieces. Blashfields' had a valuable sponsor in the architect Sir Matthew Digby Wyatt, and a local patron in the second Marquess of Exeter, who to some extent financed them. It was this firm which was responsible for the imposing gatepiers installed in 1868 at Castle Ashby in Northamptonshire.

Although Coade stone is not stone at all, it looks so remarkably like it that, even to-day, it is constantly being mistaken for the real thing. The irony is that it is in fact more durable than most natural stone: like ceramic products generally, it is imperishable. The processes of manufacture were extremely efficient: too much so, perhaps, for complete aesthetic enjoyment. Because moulds were used, Coade stone ornamentation was endlessly repetitive. We pointed out earlier, to take only one example, how at Exeter (**184**) each vermiculated block of the same size is identical (cf. p. 116), whereas in natural stone, as at Fonthill Gifford (**69**), each is different. Nor, for all its powers of endurance, does Coade stone ever acquire much patina. What, in a word, it will never be is lovable. And that is exactly what a lot of stone is.

10

STONEWORK TO-DAY AND TO-MORROW

In the ten years preceding the Second World War a number of new buildings erected in Oxford, including Rhodes House, the front quadrangle of Somerville College and the New Bodleian Library, were faced not with the traditional ashlar but with rock-faced Bladon rubblestone. Freestone, which had to be brought from Clipsham in Rutland, was confined to the dressings. The reason cannot have been that the rubblestone was regarded as aesthetically preferable, for in the Oxford context it is uncouth and conspicuously deficient in urbanity, and the Georgian architects would not have countenanced for a moment such a rustic finish. No, the explanation was purely economic: the local Bladon rubblestone, a coarse oolite from the Forest Marble formation which cannot be ashlared, was considerably cheaper.

Since 1945 a great deal of new building has been undertaken at Oxford and Cambridge, as elsewhere, and, as all those who use their eyes cannot help observing, much of this new work fails conspicuously to measure up to the finest achievements of the past. The failures are less often those of design than of materials. Brick and concrete may be acceptable on virgin sites such as those of St. Catherine's, Oxford, and Churchill College, Cambridge. They consort uneasily with stone, at Oxford especially, where virtually every building was of stone or stone-faced until 1868–82, when Keble, in horrible machine-made brick, arose at a properly respectful distance from the rest, and again on a virgin site. Among the older colleges of Cambridge there is enough brick to justify the use to-day of this material: but not of exposed concrete. In the historic parts of Oxford a facing of limestone should, on aesthetic grounds, be obligatory.

But is this now a practical possibility? Happily it is, thanks to the remarkable progress made since the last war in the development of stone-cutting machinery. So efficient are these new machines that, if the stone is suitable, an ashlar finish is now the least expensive of any.

244

MACHINES FOR CUTTING STONE

Machines for stone-cutting, generally water-powered, existed on the Continent, both in Italy and in Germany, much earlier than in Britain, where they first appeared in the seventeenth century. A frame saw driven by water was in use at Aberdeen in 1730, no doubt for sawing granite. By 1748 there was another at Ashford in Derbyshire, also powered by water, while at Southsea in Hampshire there was a machine working in 1777 which was driven by a windmill.

But for the principal advances it was necessary to await the advent first of steam power and then of electricity. Apart from lifting gear such as cranes and gantries, one of the first machines to come into use for converting the large quarry blocks into finished masonry was the frame saw. When first invented, about the middle of the nineteenth century, these saws cut very slowly and laboriously, for they only had plain steel blades. Rarely were they toothed, and toothed blades could in any event only be used on the softer stones. They had to make their cuts in running water – all power stone saws have to do this, to prevent overheating of the carborundum or diamond segments and to reduce dust – and the cutting agent was abrasive grit, or sometimes for the harder materials steel shot, dropped into the water.

Through the years frame saws have been improved out of all measure. Some are now very large, with pillars at the four corners to support two heavy frames. One of these has vertical adjustment to suit the size of the block and to control the rate of the cut. The other carries the saw blades and moves horizontally backwards and forwards as the cuts are made. Nor is there only a single blade: far from it. In one of the workshops at Portland we saw a machine with no fewer than twenty-two parallel blades, which can all saw at once. The blades themselves are of steel, and nowadays have as the cutting medium either industrial diamond segments or inset tips of tungsten carbide. The cuts can be as much as 5 ft. deep, and be carried right through in a single operation.

The next invention was the circular saw (**186**). This had first been evolved for cutting timber; stone saws came later. They are much faster than frame saws. Moreover, with some of them the table on which the block is mounted can be swivelled round, so that all four sides can be cut without the block being shifted. Thus circular saws save a great deal of time. They are also economical of material, since they make very narrow cuts, so clean and accurate that little or no further finishing is required.

The usual circular saws, like the one at Weldon which is illustrated, will cut blocks of up to about two and half feet in thickness, but there are larger ones which will cut to a considerably greater depth. The cutting edge will either be of impregnated industrial diamond segments or of continuous rims of carborundum.

One of the early types of circular saw, still to be found in most yards, is the rack saw. This has, under the saw table, a rack, which is a continuous toothed steel rail, engaging with a pinion, which is a small toothed cog-wheel. The feed movement is controlled by the operator's handwheel. The saw seen on plate **186** is a larger, modernised version of a rack saw, which can make deeper cuts. In both, the block of stone is placed on a mobile table which moves along under the saw.

Another type of circular saw is the bridge or beam saw, which is made in many different sizes. This is used for cutting the remaining sides of a section of stone, following the deep cuts on the frame saw: an operation often known as 'dimension sawing'. The block is hoisted on to a table which can be adjusted hydraulically to suit the depth of cut required; the saw then travels across it on a bridge-beam. The table can be set for cuts at any angle. After the blocks have been accurately sawn to size on all six sides, many stoneworkers refer to them as 'scants'.

Other methods are also employed at some quarries for making deep cuts through large blocks. There are what are known as endless chain saws, and, mainly for slate and marble quarries, there is the continuous helicoidal wire saw. With this saw truly enormous blocks – which can be up to 5 ft. thick, 5 ft. wide and over 8 ft. long – can be cut free from the mass, perhaps a mountain, of which they form a part. This saw is also used on limestones and sandstones when there are exceptionally large, heavy blocks which need to be reduced in size before they can be moved or loaded. Originally invented about 1898 by a Belgian engineer, the idea was to run a continuous wire about $\frac{3}{8}$ in. diameter, kept in tension, over a system of pulleys to and from the sawing point. The cuts were made with abrasive sand and water. But the process was slow and the wires had constantly to be renewed, as in the quarries they still do, for there they may be as much as a hundred yards long, or even more. But in some of the workshops the last few years have brought great improvements. There it has been found possible to attach, to much shorter wires, diamond impregnated segments as the cutting agent. These not only wear much better but cut much more quickly.

A wide range of smaller power saws is also availabe today in the larger masonry yards. Many have been designed for specific purposes. All of them run in water, and have blades with a carborundum rim or diamond impregnated insets. It is on record that a certain Dean, on receiving an estimate for some new masonry which he considered to be much too expensive, exclaimed 'Goodness me! Your saws must be made of diamonds'. And of course as regards the cutting edge he was absolutely right.

For the cutting of moulded sections such as door and window jambs, mullions and cornices, provided that there are no internal angles, there is another invaluable mechanical aid: the planing machine. The operator has a zinc template shaped to the profile of the moulding, which is mounted rigidly at the end of the stone carriage. The motor is then turned on, and, passing under a static cutting tool which is now usually tipped with tungsten carbide, the carriage travels backwards and forwards and the worker makes the number of cuts necessary to bring the stone to the required section. To contemplate the immense amount of patient, devoted labour which went into the cutting of large mouldings in former times, and to realise that what used to occupy a man for a week can now be accomplished in an hour, is a moving experience.

More elaborate cutting than straightforward mouldings has still to be done by hand, but here too the stonemason now has a wonderful mechanical tool to help him: the pneumatic hammer, into which can be fitted a complete range of chisels, punches, claw tools and gouges. The power to operate these mechanical tools, which can be worked at high speed if required, is conveyed through a reinforced hose from an air compressor, driven by an electric motor or a small petrol engine.

Small power tools are also available for many other purposes. We have already noted (page 221) that the cutting of holes in roofing slates, essential for inserting the galvanized nails used for fixing, is now done rapidly and easily, and without wastage, with a small electric drill, held in the hand. Most monumental masons' yards now have lettering machines for cutting inscriptions. And in passing, perhaps it would be appropriate to mention here another machine which performs a very agreeable service for the banker masons: the fan or vacuum extraction plant which filters the air in the workshop and removes the dust.

For smoothing or polishing stone use has long been made of a machine known as the Jenny Lind. This is power-driven but entirely hand-controlled. It has a live shaft with a single head, to which a variety of grinding and polishing discs can be easily attached. The usual practice is to start with a grinding disc of coarse grain and gradually to substitute finer ones as the work proceeds. Since the machine is mounted on a radial arm that can move in almost any direction as required, and with the pressure carefully controlled, every part can be reached. Nowadays there are much more advanced machines that have multiple working heads and an entirely automatic action.

There is also a machine now which does the opposite of the Jenny Lind: producing not artificially smooth surfaces but artificially rough ones! The hydraulic splitter is an invention of the last twenty years or so. Its purpose is to produce rock-faced walling stone where ashlar might be felt to be inappropriate. It is used in quarries and in masonry works as well as on building sites. The block of stone is placed upon the working table of the machine between two rows of hardened steel cutters, which are in alignment: that is to say, the top one is exactly above the lower one. The upper one can be adjusted for height to suit the thickness of the stone; the lower one is operated by hydraulic pressure from beneath the table. As this is applied, the stone fractures along the line of the cut, leaving a rock face which needs very little further attention if this is the finish that is required.

At the quarries there have in the past few years been two advances in cutting technology of major significance. Both have been developed in the United States.

The problem of how to pierce and sever extremely hard substances, such as some metal objects, has exercised men's minds for a great many years, and as long ago as 1887 a process was evolved for cutting various metals by mixing certain gases with oxygen and using blow-pipes. But it was not until 1955 that a variant of the same process was applied, in America, to the quarrying of granite.

Quarrying this rock by traditional methods has always been very slow and laborious. The invention of what is known as the thermic lance, which was first used in Britain about 1965, has been an immense boon to the granite industry. Not only has it meant a great saving in man-power but a considerable reduction also in the amount of granite which was inevitably wasted when reliance had to be placed upon conventional explosives.

The lance consists of a long steel tube $\frac{3}{4}$ in. in diameter, to which additional sections can be attached, with couplings and control valves. These are connected by hoses with cylinders for gases, compressed air and water. Long and very deep channels up to 4 ins. wide can now be cut into the virgin granite by using a mixture of oxygen and paraffin in the lance. This mixture is ignited to burn at the cutting nozzle at a temperature of about 1300° C., causing heating and expansion of the granite. After this the application of jets of water brings instant cooling. This causes the rock to come away in quite small pieces, which are cleared away by the application of compressed air.

The granite thus released will have a pleasantly rippled texture; this is often left as the finished surface. The action is free from vibration and reasonably quiet, and throws up very little dust. It is often now referred to as the jet flame process.

An alternative method involves packing the steel tube with thin rods of iron or mild steel, in order to increase the quantity of iron available for combustion at the already pre-heated cutting tip. The oxygen is then forced through the tube and, when it reaches the cutting nozzle of the lance, ignited. The heat generated by the melting of the rods is sufficient to cause the granite to split and spall. At the crucial moment, again, a small quantity of cold water is injected to assist the process.

This second method was first developed in France after the end of the war in 1945. The French wanted to get rid of many massive concrete forts, gun emplacements and airfield runways which were an unwelcome legacy from the German occupation. With the thermic lance they were able to bore holes into these heavy concrete structures so that they could be demolished with explosives.

The other technical innovation is very recent indeed. This is known as the Vetter mini-bag pressure method of cutting and lifting stone, and bids fair to supersede the long established plug and feathers method described on pages 65–66.

This invention was first put into service in July 1981 at the well-known Tate quarry in Georgia. The essence of the system is the use of inflatable pressure bags of great strength and durability, made of vulcanized rubber reinforced with cotton cords and steel wires, in a manner not unlike that employed in the manufacture of motor tyres. The bags, which are produced in various sizes, are only one inch thick. Each has a safety valve.

For detaching a block of stone, slots no more than $1\frac{1}{4}$ ins. wide are made mechanically at intervals along the line of the desired cut; for a block 7 feet long only two slots are required. Into each a bag is inserted, linked by reinforced hoses to a compressor. Then, as pressure is applied, the bags inflate, until the block is severed. The process is remarkably quick and the fractures are very clean.

Another great advantage of the pressure bags is that they can be used for lifting heavy blocks of stone to enable hoisting chains to be placed underneath when required.

This new method is said to save a great deal of labour, to free the quarrymen from the vibration always associated with drilling holes for plugs and feathers, and to operate nearly twice as quickly. Blocks measuring up to 7 ft. × 5 ft. × 5 ft. have been cut with remarkable speed.

In sum, the debt of the stone industry to those who, mostly in quite recent years, have succeeded in inventing and perfecting all these new machines to make cutting so much easier is immeasurable. In this field it is the outstanding achievement of our time, and augurs well for the future.

THE CLEANING OF STONEWORK

It is difficult now to realise that as recently as 1950 nearly every stone building in a town of any size was more or less dirty, and that in the industrial cities of the North of England the normal colour of all of them was jet black. The first great city to clean its public buildings systematically and on a big scale was Paris, at the prompting of André Malraux, Minister of State for Cultural Affairs under General de Gaulle. The visual revivification – for it was nothing less than that – was greeted generally with delight, and it was not long before England, among other countries, started to follow suit. Today, although a great deal still remains to be done, the changed aspect of stone architecture in this country is already sensational. With St. Paul's Cathedral, Westminster Abbey (inside as well as out), the British Museum and many other stone buildings, great and small, now cleaner than they have ever been since the first years after their erection, the appearance of London has been transformed, and so, with the extensive cleaning of university and college buildings, have the cities of Oxford and Cambridge; Leeds Town Hall is no longer a kind of three-dimensional silhouette. Heaton Park (**136**), since the cleaning ten years ago, has recovered the gracious buff-coloured sandstone garden front that it had when it was first built. These are but a few examples among many.

Dissentient voices can still occasionally be heard. In Edinburgh cleaning is not on the whole encouraged, and there is a list of streets in which cleaning is not allowed. To this we shall recur. But in general it must be said that the cleaning of stonework is not just a matter of aesthetics; there is a very practical side to it too: to arrest decay. For a long period factories, not to mention countless domestic fires, used to discharge into the atmosphere every year tons of sulphur dioxide. Contact with rain transformed this into sulphuric acid, which is very harmful to stone. Nevertheless, the cleaning process is by no means free from risk. It is the harder stones which stand up to it best; the medium hard and softer stones can easily be defaced, particularly if the treatment is at all drastic. It is of the utmost importance not, by unskilful cleaning, to remove any part of the stone's surface skin nor to destroy the patina produced by the natural process of weathering.

Limestones and sandstones present very different problems where cleaning is concerned, and it will be well to consider them in turn.

For cleaning limestone, sprays of cold water and bristle brushes are often all that is required. As little water as possible should be used, and the stonework should not be saturated, for if this happens any wrought iron fixings – ties and cramps – will almost certainly corrode, and the ends of wooden beams – joists, rafters, and so on – embedded in the stone may begin to rot, both of which could in time become very serious. Applied in very large quantities water may also deprive the stone surface of some of its patina, and cause staining, which is due to any salts that may be present in the stone being brought to the surface by the washing process. These stains, it is true, usually fade away in time, but for a while can be very disfiguring. With the limestones no solvent chemicals should ever be added to the water. Nor should steel-wire brushes be used, for they will leave a fine residue of steel on the damp stone which is bound to stain it as it dries out.

In skilled hands clean water may suffice to remove all the dirt from plain, smooth surfaces, but there will probably also be hollows and crannies where incrustations of grime have accumulated. This may be very difficult to dislodge. Scrubbing brushes are available with a few knots of non-ferrous wire at their centre, and copper brushes may also be used. With the harder limestones only, which can be taken to include Portland stone as well as those of the Carboniferous series, dry or wet grit can be sprayed on to the surface through a high pressure spray gun; the grit should consist of a carefully selected, fine soft sand. And, as a last resort, if the accumulation of dirt is still recalcitrant, a high pressure low volume lance may be employed. But it cannot be too strongly emphasised that these last two methods, in particular, should only be entrusted to those possessing the requisite skill to handle them with circumspection. Chemicals, we repeat, should *never* be used on limestone.

The cleaning of sandstone presents more difficult problems, owing to the composition of the stone, which consists of particles of quartz, and in some cases mica and felspar, cemented together by a matrix which in the hard kinds is always siliceous but which in the softer varieties can be far less cohesive; it may consist of calcite, dolomite, oxide of iron, or perhaps just clay, which is very treacherous. The great danger, therefore, is that if much pressure is used, and for a long period, not only the dirt but also the matrix will be removed, leaving the surface much roughened, with the hard quartz grains standing out and the certainty that before long more dirt particles will lodge in the interstices. This danger occurs even if the pressure is only from too powerful a jet of water; if grit is used it becomes, of course, much greater still.

On the more friable sandstones nothing should ever be used except clean cold water. But the principal cleaning problems with sandstone have been in the industrial cities of the North, where in the later nineteenth and early twentieth centuries the pollution from coal dust and chemicals was very bad indeed. On parts of Leeds Town Hall, for instance, the dissolved dirt had penetrated the stonework to a depth of $\frac{5}{8}$ in. Almost all the sandstones in these Northern towns came either from the Coal Measures or the Millstone Grit, which are siliceous and usually very durable. At Leeds both were employed, the Coal Measures stone coming from the Bramley Fall quarry.

Various methods have been adopted for cleaning these types of stone. Dry grit blasting is the one which has been used most frequently. The nature of the abrasive, usually silica sand, has to be determined anew in each case, having regard to the stone of the building being treated, and to the degree of impregnation. The grit is sprayed upon the surface through a spray gun; the operator can and must control the pressure of the compressed air jet with great care; he should use no more than the lowest that will do the work effectively.

Sometimes the grit is mixed with water, hot or cold, or steam; a wet spray has the advantage of damping down the dust. But a wet abrasive requires just as much skill as a dry one; with a strong jet it is all too easy to damage a carved detail, or blur an arris, and it can be fatal to the preservation of the original tool marks. There is also the additional risk of water penetration.

Mechanical cleaning is carried out with rotary brushes, flexible silicon carbide discs and carborundum stones of various shapes and sizes, all attached to power tools. This has been the method generally adopted at Newcastle-upon-Tyne; it is much better suited to classical buildings than to Gothic. But in the hands of an operator who is less than highly skilled the risks of damage to the stonework are still greater than from grit blasting.

The third method of tackling these hard sandstones, and also granite, is by chemical cleaning. This is the most drastic of any, and indeed there is only one chemical whose use has won even partial acceptance: hydrofluoric acid.★ Added to water in a proportion of about one to ten (never more than ten per cent of the acid), it removes the grime without abrasion and leaves no injurious residue. The most elaborately carved decorative details survive undamaged. This chemical has proved invaluable in very bad cases, such as Leeds Town Hall in 1972–73. But in the handling of it even more care and skill is required from the operator, for mistakes can be disastrous. Before the chemical is applied the building has to be washed to remove grease. On no account must it be allowed to come into contact with glass, which it will damage irretrievably; every window must therefore be sprayed with a plastic film, which can be peeled off when the cleaning is finished. Lead pipes, telephone and aerial leads and all paintwork must also be protected. Great care has then to be taken with regard to the timing. After application, the acid should never be left on the stone for more than ten minutes: sometimes less. It should then be washed off with a high pressure water jet.

Diluted hydrofluoric acid is applied most safely to granite. In London a few years ago the granite piers of Westminster Bridge, which date from 1862, were cleaned with it very successfully.

All these methods can be dangerous to the operators if proper precautions are not taken. Those using hydrofluoric acid should wear

★There is now available a chemical bearing the trade name Neolith 625S, which is based on hydrofluoric acid but has the advantage of embodying a rust inhibitor to counteract the danger, during the washing off stage, of rust stains appearing on stones containing particles of iron.

rubber gloves and aprons and always goggles to protect the eyes, and for all the processes protective clothing and helmets are recommended. Nor must the importance of safeguarding the public ever be overlooked.

It is partly because of the risks involved that in some cities, notably Edinburgh, cleaning is not greatly encouraged. But pollution is of course not so serious in the Scottish capital as in more heavily industrialised places; indeed, the Maintenance Manual for the New Town of Edinburgh (1978) asserts that 'there is little evidence to suggest that the accumulation of surface dirt harms durable, siliceous sandstones sufficiently to justify cleaning.' Therefore the only justification for cleaning is aesthetic. And even here feelings are not, or used not to be, unanimous. A writer on Lancashire, in 1955,* delighted in 'the thick deposit of soot, of the even texture of black cloth,' looking 'even more beautiful when outlined by a sprinkling of freshly-fallen snow'. 'The effect upon stone buildings', he added, 'is one of sombre dignity'. Today, though, this would surely be very much a minority view.

Where we do have aesthetic reservations about the desirability of cleaning is in relation to terraces, squares, circuses, crescents and streets wearing an aspect of uniformity. There it should certainly be all or none. One dirty house-front in a terrace in which all the others have been cleaned stands out like a sore thumb. It so happens that Edinburgh New Town abounds in streets of this kind, which is probably another reason for this city's somewhat querulous attitude towards cleaning. But where an entire street can be treated as a single operation, as with Pulteney Street at Bath, the visual improvement is surely incontestable.

The cleaning of elaborately carved stonework, whether limestone or sandstone, presents particularly difficult problems, especially when it is hundreds of years old. A triumphant exemplar of the right way to do it was provided in 1977 by the work undertaken by the Department of the Environment, under the direction of Mr. John Ashurst, on the south porch of Malmesbury Abbey, which has one of the finest displays of Norman sculpture in the country. Its condition had deteriorated so badly that tourists had started to pick off details, and much of the limestone was also nearly black. Cleaning and some restoration was therefore essential. But even the mildest jet of water would have been too fierce for this perilously frail carving. So what was evolved was an abrasive of extreme delicacy, applied through a tube no thicker than an ordinary pencil. Every detail that

*Peter Fleetwood-Hesketh, *Murray's Lancashire Architectural Guide*, p. 159.

**187 Stamford, Lincolnshire:
two houses in St. Martin's**

had become detached, or nearly so, was put back and supported by a lime-based filler, consisting of lime putty with a little lime dust. Furthermore, each detail was photographed both before and after; thus everything that was done has been most scrupulously recorded. This is another aspect of stone cleaning, but one which may become increasingly important in the future.

The cleaning of stonework, then, is by no means as simple a matter as may at first appear. It should only be undertaken after consultation with experienced technical advisers, who will be found in the Department of the Environment and in the Building Research Station at Garston near Watford. Only reputable firms with experience of stone cleaning should be entrusted with this work and buildings listed under the Planning Acts should never be cleaned without the approval of the Area Planning Authority. Irremediable damage can be done to stonework if unsuitable methods are followed or inexperienced people employed.

But all over England the results of enlightened cleaning are now evident. Plate **187** shows two handsome houses in St. Martin's, Stamford; the stonework of one has been cleaned, of the other as yet not. The contrast is striking. For those who love stone, there is, in the current vogue for cleaning, much case for rejoicing.

THE PROSPECTS FOR THE FUTURE

What, then, are the future prospects for stone? In some circles an idea is prevalent that stonework is a thing of the past. There are a good many architects who have never had the opportunity of working with this most rewarding of all building materials.

After the last war there was something of a boom for the stone industry. Considerable damage had been committed by aerial bombardment, and the routine maintenance of historic buildings had for some years been allowed to lapse. So there was plenty to be done, and ample employment in the stone trade.

By about 1970, however, much of the work of restoration had been completed; costs were now rising fast and the state of the national economy was changing. As a result, quarries all over the country slowed down and often closed, and some firms regrettably went out of business. Others only kept going by turning to commercial advantage by-products which were formerly wasted.

This process is from every point of view desirable. At the slate quarries, in particular, the wastage was at one time immense; incredible as it may seem, 75 per cent was normal (as stated earlier) and in places it amounted to as much as 85 per cent of the total. Thus, as anyone who has ever visited a slate quarry will know, enormous waste dumps of broken slate have been accumulated, which are formidable eyesores. Now, in granulated form, there is a demand for this waste slate as a filler or aggregate in bituminous and similar products. Although as yet far too small to have much effect on the removal of the 'slate mountains', it is at least a step in the right direction. In the limestone quarries there are a number of possibilities. There is of course a steady need for roadstone, and stone which is too small or otherwise unsuitable for building can be broken and graded, and sold for this purpose. Where limestone and clay are both present, cement can be manufactured. Some quarries have an overburden of fireclay; this is a most useful mineral out of which are manufactured firebricks and fire-resistant parts for furnaces. The stone can also be burned and turned into hydrated lime for building mortar. Furthermore, particularly in regions like Fenland where the soil is acid, agricultural fertilizer is a permanent requirement, and small stones which would formerly have been wasted are now often ground up to produce carbonate of lime. A limited amount of finely ground limestone has even found an unusual outlet in the manufacture of cosmetics.

Yet these, it may be thought, are all the desperate remedies of a dying man, and can give no satisfaction to the would-be builder in stone. Are there no more positive grounds for hope? There are some.

There are good prospects in slate. Because of the fissile character of this stone, slabs can be sawn or riven down to thicknesses of no more than an inch or even, sometimes, $\frac{3}{4}$ in., yet it is just as strong and just as weatherproof as other kinds of stone : perhaps even more so. This renders it an ideal material for cladding modern buildings of structural steel or ferro-concrete which are so much improved by a facing of natural stone. Moreover, the sizes can quite easily be standardized. Slabs measuring 27 ins. × 9 ins. are popular because this is a convenient size for handling, but much larger panels (6 ft × 2 ft. 6 ins, for example) are often required, and can be supplied without difficulty. Such a thin material is particularly valuable for the cladding of very tall buildings, for a reduction in the weight of the facings means that the costs of the steel or ferro-concrete frame and of the foundations can also be proportionately reduced. It means, too, that the hoisting and fixing are easier, and therefore more speedily performed. The principal area for the production of these slate panels is the Lake District, where the slate is not only very durable but often most attractive in colour: generally grey-green or grey-blue. The Cumbrian quarries and masonry works are happily very active, and there is a demand for their slate not only in Britain but on the Continent of Europe and also across the Atlantic.

Except in a few specially favoured regions, there is, alas, not much prospect of there being many more houses or cottages faced with either limestone or sandstone. Stone cladding in these materials can seldom be less than two inches thick, so is inevitably expensive, even when it is obtainable at all. In areas such as the Cotswolds, north Northamptonshire and Rutland, and in parts of northern England, there is still some new building going on that makes use of stone for the facing : in specially regarded villages this is indeed compulsory. In the Cotswolds, in deference to the beauty of the local limestone, bricks have to be stone-coloured, and red roofs are rightly banned ; and the same applies in the conservation areas of Stamford.

On the other hand there is, and must always be, a continuing demand for stone, all over the country, for restoration work. For the good maintenance of the fabric of our cathedrals, churches, country houses and many other historic buildings constructed of stone, in which more interest is now being shown than ever before, more natural stone is the only answer; there is no viable alternative. Wherever possible, it need hardly be said that the best stone to employ for restoration is that used for the original building. Lincoln Cathedral is specially fortunate in owning a quarry – not the original one but with stone of identical character – only a mile away along the Cliff. (Unfortunately the exposed stone in this quarry is now very shallow on the bed: not more than 12 ins.). St. Mary Redcliffe at Bristol is also built of oolitic limestone, and although the quarry on Dundry hill a

few miles away to the south is no longer worked, this famous church fortunately has (or until lately had) access to reserves. The replacement of some of the pinnacles shows (**188**) that, in dexterity at least, modern stonecarvers can vie with their predecessors. York Minster is built of Magnesian limestone, largely brought from Huddleston near Sherburn-in-Elmet, and for the great restoration of the 1970s this quarry, long abandoned, was quite rightly reopened. Hardwick Hall was built of Coal Measures sandstone taken from a quarry less than half a mile down the hill to the west; this too was recently reopened by the National Trust when new stone was required for restoration. The upper part of the tower and spire of the church at Saffron Walden was rebuilt by Thomas Rickman in 1831, not in local stone because, except for flint, there is none in Essex, but of Monk's Park oolite brought by barge from Corsham near Bath; and recently for the restoration the same stone was used again, happily from a quarry that is still working. Ketton oolite, from Rutland, was extensively employed for university and college buildings at Cambridge, and, although the output of building stone from the Ketton quarry is now limited, it is, very properly, to Cambridge that most of it goes. For Oxford, Taynton stone is unfortunately no longer available, at least in the quantities needed, and Headington and Wheatley stone, even if they were, would never be used again there. Clipsham is farther from Oxford than Ketton is from Cambridge, but it is the best stone for colour and for durability, and has become the standard material for Oxford restorations, disdained only by some architects who think they know better and will probably be found out sooner rather than later.

For some restoration work, particularly but not only in the South-East, limestone is now imported from France. This is explained on the grounds that the English limestone quarries are running on such small numbers (even at Portland there are now only twenty quarrymen) that they are no longer able to meet the requirements, and that, even when available, the native limestone is not always of the right colour nor of the desired strength. That the French stones appear to be of excellent quality is not in question, but they too do not often seem to 'marry' very happily with the English limestones. Nor is it yet known how in the long term they will accommodate themselves to our more rigorous climate. Since there are still great reserves of fine limestone in this country, it is a misfortune that for economic reasons they are no longer fully exploited.

The sandstone quarries are on the whole in better fettle than the limestone. There is a steady output of New Red sandstone from Hollington in Staffordshire; and as for the gritstones and the sandstones from the Coal Measures, quite a number of these, in West Yorkshire, Co. Durham and Northumberland, are still actively quarried, and not only for walling: stone flags for roofing and steps, jambs, lintels and sills can still be obtained without difficulty. This is important, for parts of the North-East rival the Cotswolds and the Stamford area as a region where, for building, only stone 'belongs', and where even a corrugated iron roof is visually an offence which in the National Parks is not now allowed.

So the prospects for stone are better than some people seem to think. The industry is not short of manpower, for in every stone area there are young men who are attracted to it. And, as we hope that this chapter has made clear, a great deal of modernisation of equipment has been taking place in the last few years. This will surely continue, for an England unable properly to maintain her marvellous inheritance of stone buildings is unthinkable.

GLOSSARY

ABACUS   The flat slab on the top of a capital.

ABUTMENT   A solid stone 'springer' at the lowest point of an arch or vault.

ADIT   A quarry gallery driven into a hillside more or less horizontally.

ARCH   A curved span across an opening, usually constructed of voussoirs (shaped arch stones).

ARCHITRAVE   (1) The moulded frame surrounding a doorway or window. (2) The lowest of the three divisions of a classical entablature.

ARRIS   The sharp edge produced where two flat stone surfaces meet.

ASHLAR   Masonry in which the stones are large and worked to a fine surface with close joints.

BANKER   The stone or heavy timber bench on which a mason works his stones.

BATS   A term used in some districts to describe small coursed ashlar, not usually more than 6 ins. high; elsewhere this is called range work. Ashlar bats are often made from the smaller quarry blocks and from offcuts.

BATTED   An alternative term to boasted (*q.v*) where the tool marks have been left on the stone face.

BATTERED   Walls which are not vertical, as sometimes with retaining walls.

BED, BEDDING   Terms used in the stone trade in many different ways. In the quarries a *bed* is a plane of stratification in a sedimentary rock, as laid down by nature. The height of each stratum is the *bed height*. Its top surface is the *top bed* and its bottom surface the *bottom bed*. (These terms are also used by banker masons and machinists when preparing worked stone). Between the strata there are usually layers of loose material known as *free beds*. On buildings the *bed* is the horizontal layer of mortar, cement, sand, earth, etc., upon which the blocks of stone, whether rubble, ashlar or shaped dressings (*q.v.*), are laid. (For stonework other than walling this is also described as fixing). With sedimentary rocks, stones are *face bedded* when they are set up on end and at right angles to their natural bedding planes: a bad practice, which nearly always leads to trouble.

BEVEL   (1) A splayed angle on a worked stone. (2) A tool for marking out angles, sometimes called a shift-stock.

BLOCKING COURSE   A large course of plain ashlar on top of a cornice.

BLOCK STONE   Large stone blocks roughly squared at the quarries.

BOASTED   Dressed with a boaster (wide chisel) and left as a tooled finish.

BOASTER   A chisel with a cutting edge up to $2\frac{1}{2}$ ins. wide used in the final stage of preparing tooled dressings. (See illustration p. 89).

BONDER   Any stone which is so laid that it increases the strength of the wall, either in thickness or length.

BROACH   (1) An inclined piece of masonry filling the triangular space between the base of an octagonal spire and the top of a square tower. (2) A type of chisel used for working narrow surfaces.

BROUGHT TO COURSE   Where random walling is brought up to a level line, as at wall tops, window sills, doorheads, etc.

BUTTRESS   A strong stone pier built against a wall to give additional support, often where there are outward thrusts against the inner face of the wall. It must be bonded into the wall.

CAPITAL   The culminating stone at the top of a column or pilaster, often richly carved.

CARBORUNDUM SAW   A circular saw with a cutting rim of carborundum abrasive.

CARSTONE   Stone of a coarse, pebbly or gritty consistency occurring in the Greensands of the South-East, from Norfolk to Hampshire: always some shade of brown, owing to impregnation with iron.

CENTERING   Temporary framework, usually of wood, on which an arch or bridge is built.

CHAIN SAW   A power-driven saw with tungsten carbide tips to the endless cutting chain.

CHAIN TACKLE   Pulley blocks with chains for lifting.

CHAMFER   A flat splayed edge between two flat plain surfaces.

CHISEL   A generic term for cutting tools of various kinds. (See page 87 and illustrations pp. 87 and 88).

CLADDING   Non-load-bearing thin stone slabs used for facing buildings.

CLAW TOOL   A type of chisel with a serrated cutting edge used in the hand dressing process; now made with replaceable and reversible bits. (See page 88 and illustration).

CLUNCH   Building stone containing large parts of chalk combined with some harder minerals.

COCK'S COMB   A thin shaped steel plate with a serrated edge, used like a drag (*q.v.*) for finishing mouldings and other shapes.

COFFERING   Sunk square or polygonal moulded panels on the soffits (*q.v.*) of vaults or arches to enrich their appearance and lighten their weight.

COPING   (1) The capping of a wall to give weather protection; sometimes of a more impervious stone. (2) The act of cutting York and some other stone slabs without a machine, by cutting a shallow groove on both sides and then bumping up and down this groove with a wide blunt chisel.

CORBEL   A bracket of stone projecting beyond the wall face, usually to give support to some feature above.

CORBEL PLATES   Plates of non-ferrous metal fixed into a structure to support stone cladding at intervals and over openings, in such a way as not to be visible.

CORDUROY WORK   A surface finish for ashlar, having very narrow convex reeds, each not more than $\frac{1}{4}$ in. wide, and generally cut vertically. Used, mainly in the 19th century, to give texture to plain surfaces.

COURSE   A continuous layer of stones of uniform height in a wall.

CRAMP   A metal device used to hold stones together more securely or to prevent movement.

CROCKETS   The carved projecting blocks up the angles of a church spire or on gables, pinnacles, etc.

DAMP COURSE   A course of slate, impervious stone, blue bricks, bitumen, lead, copper or aluminium, or combinations of some of these, built into the walls below floor level to prevent rising damp. Sometimes put into parapets and chimneys to prevent dampness soaking down through porous material.

DENTILS   Small rectangular blocks under a classical cornice, resembling a row of teeth.

DETRITUS   The fine powdered material forming a composite part of some stones.

DIAMOND SAW   A saw with a cutting edge of industrial diamonds inset into soft metal blocks.

DIVIDER   The mason's term for a compass with two points.

DORMER   A window projecting vertically from a sloping roof.

DOWEL   A short piece of non-ferrous metal or slate fixed into a mortice or sinking in the joints of adjoining stones to prevent movement.

DRAFTED MARGIN   The tooled margin round the face edges of a roughly squared stone, usually about $\frac{3}{4}$ in. wide: part of the process of dressing stone by hand.

DRAG   A steel plate with a saw-like edge, used to obtain a smooth surface as part of the process of facing a stone by hand.

DRESSINGS   A general term used to describe the quoins, sills, heads, cornices, string courses, pediments, copings, chimneys, etc., on the elevation of a building, when made of freestone (q.v.).

DRIP   A small sunk throat (*q.v.*) under copings, sills, drip-moulds, etc., to throw rainwater clear of the wall-face.

DRIPSTONE   A projecting moulding over the heads of doorways, windows and archways, to throw off the rain. Also known as a 'hood-mould' and, when rectangular, as a 'label'.

DRUM   A separate circular stone in a shaft or column.

DRY-STONE WALLING   Stone walling built without mortar.

DUMMY   A small tool of mallet shape, made of lead alloy, usually with a cane handle. Used when working with wooden-handled chisels on soft stone of fine grain.

EAVES   The part of a roof or other structure which oversails the wall-face.

EDGE BEDDED   Stones cut with natural bedding planes running radially and at right angles to the wall face as in arch voussoirs.

ENTABLATURE   In Classical architecture, the upper part of an Order, comprising architrave, frieze and cornice.

FACE BEDDING   See BED, BEDDING.

FACING   A layer of stone, usually ashlar, or brick, applied to the face of an external wall.

FAULT   A major natural fissure in a bed or stratum of stone at the quarry, usually more or less vertical.

FEATHERS   Steel plates of half-round section used for splitting block stone in the quarries; a plug or wedge is also needed. (See illustration page 65).

FERRUGINOUS   Limestone or sandstone containing a high proportion of iron oxide.

FILLET   A small member between mouldings. Also known as a quirk.

FILLET SAW   A small handsaw for cutting out fillets, rebates or similar features.

FINIAL   The topmost feature, generally ornamental, of a gable, roof, pinnacle, canopy, spire, etc.,

FISHBELLY   A large two-handed stone saw with a downward curve on the cutting edge, for hand-sawing large quarry blocks. No longer in general use.

FIXING   The operation of building with ashlar and with worked or moulded stones. See also BED, BEDDING.

FIXING MORTAR   Fine bedding material for fixing ashlar with very close joints, composed of lime putty, fine stone dust, and a small quantity of white cement.

FLAGSTONE   Stone naturally stratified in slabs about 2 to 3 ins. thick, much used for pavings, copings, etc.

FLINT   Nodules of siliceous rock found in some chalk deposits; they can be knapped or fractured to expose their texture when used for building.

FLOAT   A rectangular hand trowel made of wood for smoothing and straightening rendering (q.v.).

FLUSHWORK   The decorative use of flint in conjunction with dressed stone to form patterns, monograms, inscriptions, etc.

FLUTED STONE   Stone worked with regular concave grooves as in columns.

FRAME SAW   A large power-driven machine-saw mainly used for making deep primary cuts in quarry blocks, now with blades of steel tipped with tungsten carbide or impregnated diamond blocks. Several cuts can be made at the same time (see page 245).

FREE BED   See BED.

FREESTONE   Block stone which can be freely cut in any direction with toothed saws and worked with chisels and drags.

FRENCH DRAG   A facing tool first used in France for finishing plain surfaces of soft, fine-grained stones. (See illustration p. 88).

FRIG-BOB SAW   A handsaw 5 or 6 feet long with a steel blade and handle at one end only: no longer in general use. Sometimes called a Frig-a-bob: the origin of this strange name is not known. (See illustration p. 65).

FROSTWORK   Decorative stonework in which the surface is carved to resemble frost, stalactites or icicles.

GALLETING   The practice of inserting small stones into broad mortar joints, the purpose of which was originally structural but later became largely decorative.

GANTRY   A large overhead travelling hoist, used in masonry works for unloading heavy blocks, servicing the stockyard, and moving blocks to the machines. (In some yards this is still done by jib-cranes).

GAUGE   A tool used for marking out parallel lines when setting out a piece of work.

GIBBS SURROUND   A term applied to an architrave of a doorway or window when alternate blocks project. (See plate 184, p. 242).

GOUGE   A chisel with curved cutting edge, made in a number of sizes and with various curvatures.

GRAIN   A term sometimes employed to describe the natural bedding planes in the stone when they are visible.

GROUT   Liquid mortar used for filling perpends (vertical joints) and back voids in masonry, usually assisted by joggles (*q.v.*).

HAMMER DRESSED   Walling stone which has been shaped with a stone axe or dressing hammer.

HAMMER-HEADED CHISEL   A chisel with a head prepared for use with a stone hammer or a pitching hammer (but not with a mallet).

HARDCORE   Broken stone used for dry filling, e.g. under concrete floors. Large sized hardcore is employed as a foundation for asphalt roads.

HAWK   A small hand-held mortar board, mainly for use when pointing, and sometimes for fixing ashlar. Also called a hand-hawk.

HEADER   A stone which has its longest dimension built into the thickness of the wall to improve bonding and strength.

HERRINGBONE WALLING   Walling in which the stones are not set flat but at an angle of 45°, with their ends lapped intermittently.

HIP   The inclined angle at which two sloping roofs meet. The converse of valley (*q.v.*).

HOD   A shaped device for carrying mortar or other materials on the shoulder when climbing ladders, etc.

HOLDFAST   A metal fixing, usually for holding back stone facing against a main structure of brick, concrete, steel framing, etc.

HOOD-MOULD   See DRIPSTONE.

HYDRATED LIME   Quicklime which has been processed into an inert powdered lime ready for use.

HYDRAULIC LIME   A hard-setting lime with some tensile strength; when processed it is called hydrolized hydraulic lime. Very suitable for building and pointing limestone, because no Portland cement is necessary.

INBOND   Scots term for header or bonder.

INDENTS   Recesses left or formed, usually during building, to provide for later work to be bonded in.

IN SITU   Done in position, or on the spot; not introduced later.

JACK HAMMER   A hand-held pneumatic dressing hammer.

JADD   A cross-paned stone axe with a long handle used for roughing out, and in the past for dressing. Also known as a jadd pick, a racer or a scappling axe, and at Portland it used to be called a twibill. ('Cross-paned' means that the cutting edge is across the tool and not in line with the handle.) (See illustration p. 65).

JADD PICK   See JADD.

JAMB   The vertical side of an archway, doorway or window. The stones, sometimes called jambstones, to distinguish them from jambs in other materials, e.g. wood, may be rebated and moulded.

JENNY LIND   An early type of machine for grinding, smoothing and polishing flat surfaces.

JIB CRANES   Large lifting machines used in quarries and some masonry works; the main jib or shaft can swing from side to side, thus enabling the crane to deposit blocks where required. Now usually machine-powered.

JOB CARD   A card with particulars of each type of masonry and of the size required, passed round a stone works. Sometimes called a Production Card.

JOGGLES   Grooves cut into the perpends (q.v.) to improve the flow of the liquid grout.

JUMPER   (1) A hand-held tool-bar formerly used for sinking the holes in quarry blocks needed to receive the plugs and feathers. (2) A large walling stone which rises through two or more courses, to obtain interesting surface variation; this is called snecking in the north of England.

KEYSTONE   The central stone or voussoir in an arch or vault rib.

KNAPPED   Flint is described as knapped when it is split open to reveal its dark silica core.

KNEELER   A stone with a level bed at the bottom of a gable coping, and shaped to receive the angle of the gable coping stones.

LABEL   See DRIPSTONE.

LACED VALLEY   A valley (q.v.) in which each pair of horizontal courses of stone slates turns upwards as it approaches the point of junction, to meet in a specially large slate laid aslant on a wide board in the valley.

LANTERN   A small circular or polygonal turret with windows all round, crowning a roof or dome.

LARRY   A tool formerly used for mixing mortar, resembling a large garden hoe. A similar tool with three large prongs or tines was used for making fibrous plastering mortar.

LEDGER   A large flat stone covering an altar tomb or grave, and often forming part of a church floor.

LEVEL   A tool for keeping horizontal surfaces true and level.

LEWIS   A device for lifting worked stone blocks from their top centre so that they can be set on to their mortar bed. (For illustration see p. 76).

LINTEL   The block of stone spanning the top of an opening such as a doorway or window; sometimes called a head.

MANSARD ROOF   A roof with two pitches on each side of the ridge, the lower one steeper than the upper: thus giving more space and a better shape to attics.

MARGINAL DRAFT   See DRAFTED MARGIN.

MASONS' MITRE   An angle mitre worked solid from one piece of stone and not joined across the angle as in woodwork.

MATRIX   The calcite or other mineral which binds the grains of stone together.

MODILLIONS   Large brackets or blocks placed in series under a cornice or the eaves of a roof, sometimes with ornamental carving.

MORTAR BOARDS   Boards placed near the work to hold the mortar, which can then easily be picked up with a trowel by the mason.

MORTICE   A sinking or recess in a block of stone cut to receive a lewis, dowel or tenon.

MOULDS   Shaped patterns used for setting out the work, called templates in other trades.

MOULDINGS   Bands, projecting or recessed, used to enrich and to give shadows to a wall, arch, capital or other surfaces.

MOULDING MACHINES   Power-driven machines of various kinds for producing continuous mouldings on blocks of stone, some with tungsten carbide cutting tools, others with abrasive grinding wheels.

MULLION   A vertical member, usually moulded, for subdividing a window.

NICHE   A shaped recess in a wall, screen, etc., prepared to receive, usually, a carved figure.

OOLITE   Limestone mainly composed of abundant small calcareous grains, more or less spherical. The term is also applied to stones with a similar geological and chemical structure but in which the ooliths are less prominent.

ORIEL WINDOW   A window projecting from an upper storey, often corbelled underneath.

PADSTONE   A block of some specially hard stone, built in to sustain concentrated loads such as the ends of beams or rolled steel joists.

PERPENDS   The vertical joints, especially in ashlar masonry.

PILASTER   A flat pier of shallow projection attached to a wall, with a base and a capital.

PITCHED WALLING   Rock-faced walling which has been made or dressed with a pitching tool.

PITCHER   A wide chisel ground to a steep angle and not sharp like a
normal chisel, used for straightening the edges of stone slab pavings, and
for pitching off surplus stone when preparing a finished surface. Also
called a pitching tool. (See illustration p. 87).

PITCHING HAMMER   A special mason's hammer for driving pitching tools
and punches.

PLINTH   The projecting base of a wall or column, generally moulded or
at least chamfered (*q.v.*) at the top.

PLUG AND FEATHERS   A device for splitting the virgin blocks in the
quarries. (See illustration on p. 65).

PLUMB RULE   A straightedge (*q.v.*) about 4 to 6 feet long with an integral
spirit level, used for ensuring verticality when building walls. (The plumb
rule, formerly equipped with a lead bob, and the level, both of very
ancient origin, are probably the mason's two most important tools.)

POINT   Similar to punch (*q.v.*) but with a sharp cutting point. Used by
sculptors and carvers. (See illustration p. 88).

POINTING   The filling of the mortar joints in masonry. (This may be done
in various ways, some of which are unsuitable.)

PRESENTS   Limestone slates which are naturally laminated and do not
have to be frosted.

PRODUCTION CARD   See JOB CARD.

PUNCH   A hammer-headed tool with a very narrow cutting edge, used
for spalling off surplus stone. (See illustration p. 87).

QUARRY   Usually an open-cast pit, but sometimes a mine, from which
stone can be extracted.

QUARRY SAP   The natural moisture in stone containing pre-crystallized
calcite. This moisture dries out, leaving the calcite in the grain of the stone
to harden and crystallize.

QUOIN   A dressed stone at the external angle of a building or opening.
Quoins are often alternately large and small.

RACER   See JADD.

RAG   (1) Hard stone found in some limestone quarries and used for dry
stone walling. (2) Sometimes applied to coarse-grained, rather hard
freestone which contains many shells and shell fragments.

RANDOM   Stone walling which is not coursed and which has undressed
stones of many different shapes and sizes.

RANGE WORK   See BATS.

REBATE   A recess or reveal in a jambstone, cut to receive a door or window frame or for some similar purpose.

REEDED STONE   A surface finish for ashlar, similar to CORDUROY WORK (*q.v.*), but the reeds are bigger: up to 3 ins. broad.

RENDERING   A coating, usually of cement and sand, applied over rough stone work or other materials.

RESPOND   The name given to a half-column or pilaster attached to a wall, as in the end half-columns of a church arcade.

RETURN   Change in direction of a wall, member or moulding.

REVEAL   The side-wall of an opening or recess which is at right angles to the face of the main wall; especially the vertical side of a window opening or doorway. Known as a splay (*q.v.*) if cut diagonally.

ROCK-FACED STONES   Stones that have a rock-like face which has been made with a pitching tool.

RUBBLESTONE   Hard hammer-dressed stone in a variety of course heights, but seldom over 5 inches.

RUBSTONE   (1) An abrasive stone used for producing a fine surface on finished stones, applied with water. (2) A slab of an abrasive stone employed for sharpening chisels, also with water.

RUSTICATION   Chamfers or square sinkings round the face edges of individual stones to create shadows and to give an appearance of greater weight to the lower part of a building. When only the horizontal joints are sunk, the device is known as banded rustication.

SADDLE   The name sometimes given to the apex stone on a gable when there is no finial.

SCANT   The name given to stones sawn to exact sizes on machines, and which may need further work on them if intended for mouldings, sinkings, rustications, carvings, etc.

SCAPPLING   Rough dressing of large quarry blocks with a jadd pick or other tool to give them an approximately rectangular shape.

SECRET VALLEY   In stone slate roofing, a method of carrying the slates round the angle where two adjacent roofs meet as in a roof valley. The slates are cut to an angle and fitted closely together; under them is placed a secret gutter of lead or some other material which cannot be seen in the finished work.

SET-OFF   Where a vertical face of masonry has been set either back from or forward of the main face line of the building.

SHAKES   Fine cracks or vents in a block of stone, which are an imperfection.

SHEER LEGS   A simple early type of lifting device, originally consisting of three strong wooden poles erected as a tripod over the heavy block of stone to be lifted; from the apex, and passing over pulley blocks, ropes were suspended and connected to a sling round the stone. (See illustration on p. 68). A limited use is still made of sheer legs, which are now usually made of steel, with steel chains to do the hoisting.

SHIFT-STOCK   The masons' name for an adjustable bevel tool used for setting out angles on stonework.

SILL   (1) The threshold stone under a doorway if flush, i.e. not a step. (2) The stone across the base of a window opening. (3) A term used in geology for intermissions in stone beds.

SINKING   A recess of any shape or size sunk into stonework, as for instance for panels, coffering, trefoils, quatrefoils, blind tracery, etc.

SKEWBACK   The splayed stone at the top of the jambs from which an arch springs.

SNECKING   The name given in the north of England to walling of any kind containing stones which rise through two or more courses; these are also called jumpers (q.v.).

SOFFIT   The underside of an arch, vault, cornice, lintel, etc.

SPALL   The flakes of stone which are either dressed off with a punch or pitcher, or which split off because of some natural process, such as frost.

SPANDREL   The space, approximately triangular, between the curve of an arch and the rectangle formed by the mouldings enclosing it; or the space between the shoulders of two contiguous arches and the moulding or string-course above them. Also the triangular space between a horizontal surface and a sloping plane, such as a stair-spandrel.

SPLAY   Any surface which recedes at an angle and not as a square return (cf. REVEAL).

SQUARE   A tool which has a fixed angle; used to set out work and to keep such angles truly square.

STOOLING   A small section of stone left on window heads and sills to receive the moulded jambs and mullions.

STRAIGHTEDGE   A perfectly straight wooden rule of any length, used in setting out and keeping the work straight.

STRAIGHT JOINT   Where two vertical joints (perpends) in masonry are directly above each other, thus giving no bond, which is undesirable.

STRING COURSE   A narrow projecting course of stone across the elevation of a building.

SWAG   An ornamental wreath or festoon of flowers, foliage or fruit fastened at both ends and hanging down in the centre.

SWEPT VALLEY   In stone roofing, a method of carrying the slates round the angle between two adjacent roof slopes by tapering and bonding them so that no lead or other gutter is necessary.

THERMIC LANCE   A device for cutting granite in the quarries, with heat produced at the nozzle of a blow torch by burning a mixture of oxygen and paraffin gas, brought up to a high temperature. Grooves or channels some 4 ins. wide can be cut up to a depth of 5 feet or more, without damage to the granite.

THROAT   The name sometimes given to the small groove under a window sill or dripstone, intended to deflect rainwater from the wall face.

THROUGHS   Long bonders passed through a dry-stone wall from side to side, to provide additional strength: sometimes left projecting on one or both sides of the wall. Known also as through-stones.

TORCHING   Haired lime mortar applied between the rafters and laths of a roof to the underside of stone slates to prevent the entry of drifting powdered snow. This is when the slates are not bedded in mortar as at Collyweston and where there is no underfelt or boarding.

TRAMMEL   A device for setting out or 'striking' circles or parts thereof which are too large for a compass or divider. There is also an elliptical trammel for setting out 'four-centred' shapes.

TRANSOM   A structural member dividing a window horizontally.

TREADMILL   A large circular wheel-like cage inside which two men, walking round, could provide the power necessary for lifting heavy stones with winches and cranes. Much used for high buildings before mechanical lifting gear was invented.

TUNGSTEN CARBIDE   A very hard alloy which will keep its sharpness much longer than steel when used for the cutting tips of chisels, saw-teeth, etc.

VALLEY   The line at which two sloping roofs meet. It must have either swept or laced slating, a secret gutter underneath which cannot be seen, or an open gutter of lead, copper or aluminium.

VEINS   Coloured markings in limestone, marble, alabaster, etc.

VENETIAN WINDOW   A window with three openings, the middle one arched and wider than the others.

VENTS   The name given to small cracks or 'shakes' in block stone: an imperfection.

VERMICULATION   Dressing the surface of a block of stone so that it appears to be covered with worm-tracks, random ridges between irregularly shaped sinkings.

WASTER   A narrow chisel used by masons for roughing out.

WEATHERED   Stones that have been exposed in a building for many years may be described as weathered, either well or badly.

WEATHERING   The inclined top surface of a stone such as a coping, cornice, or window sill is called a weathering.

WEB   A large area of stonework recessed behind other members, especially if it is thin on plan and has no backing of solid masonry, as with the infilling of a vault.

WINCH   Usually a hand-powered device for lifting heavy stones, having reduction gears, a brake and a safety ratchet.

WINDLASS   A simple hand-powered barrel of wood, with handles, and on a frame, usually without a brake or ratchet, around which a rope or chain could be wound. Earlier than the winch, and not so safe in use.

PLACE INDEX

In this index notice has been taken of the county changes made in 1965, when the Soke of Peterborough was detached from Northamptonshire and united with Huntingdonshire, and Middlesex was gobbled up, mainly by Greater London; also in 1970, when after more than four centuries Monmouthshire was returned to Wales. But on April 1 1974 far more sweeping changes were introduced, based on administrative convenience and without regard for deeply felt loyalties or for history. Since there is a vast corpus of topographical and other books based on the old county boundaries, most of which will certainly continue to be used for many years to come, it has seemed best to retain the traditional classification, and to take no cognizance of the latest redrawing of the map of England.

Illustrations are in *italic type*, and indexed under pages: not plate numbers.

GENERAL INDEX

The most important references are indicated in **heavy type**.
Illustrations are in *italic type*, and indexed under pages: not plate numbers.

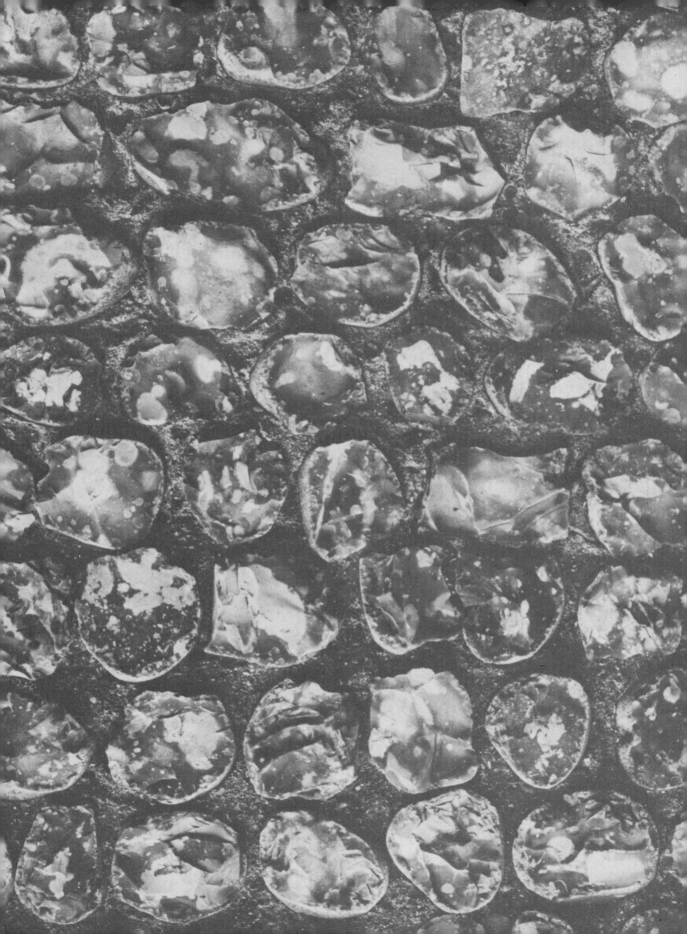